Britain's oligarchy. They also dramatized historical parallels of their Revolution, and located immorality largely in foreign lands. As a result of domestic political alignment with foreign powers, however, American dramatists tended to view foreigners from the time of the French Revolution until approximately the turn of the century, as means to present arguments concerning comparative politics, manners, or customs which agreed with the Federalist or Jacobin-Democrat persuasion of the playwright. So effective was the American System that it could change for the better the stereotyped comic Irish and foppish foreigners when they realized the beneficence of democracy.

When the romantic proclivities already inherent in drama that turned to foreign settings in an attempt to engender interest, were intensified through the increasing popularity of melodrama around 1800, didacticism relinquished its preeminence to romanticism and to a curiosity in the foreigner for his peculiar qualities. After the War of 1812, prior to the Jacksonian revolution, American drama continued a patriotic attitude which remained sensitive to American differences, yet did not respond to censure with the puerile antagonism apparent in late eighteenth-century Republican drama. By the year of Jackson's inauguration, Indian drama carried to maturity the conception of America as a paradise where even aboriginal inhabitants and later white citizens enjoyed natural liberty, democracy, and equality

STUDIES IN AMERICAN LITERATURE

Volume III

THE FOREIGNER
IN
EARLY AMERICAN DRAMA

A Study in Attitudes

by

KENT G. GALLAGHER

1966
MOUTON & CO.
THE HAGUE · PARIS

ACKNOWLEDGMENTS

I wish to express my especial thanks to Professor Hubert C. Heffner, without whose patient guidance this volume would never have been. I also would like to acknowledge the valuable assistance provided by the members of the documents department of the Indiana University Library. The administration at Ball State University has been particularly generous in allocating funds to aid with the publication of this study. I can find no words to voice my appreciation of both the tangible and intangible support furnished by Sandi Gallagher – *sans qui, rien.*

KENT G. GALLAGHER

CONTENTS

Acknowledgments   5

Introduction   9

  I. To Find a Foreigner 15

 II. Anti-Foreign Sentiments 37
    A. Revolution, propaganda, and chauvinism . . 37
    B. Historical parallels: political and moral 47
    C. Fops, dandies, and travellers 60
    D. Romantic motives and political villains 69

III. The Sympathetic Foreigner 74
    A. The period of the Revolution 74
    B. Enemies of the Republic 84
    C. Foreigners with American ideals 96
    D. Weakened American ideals 102
    E. The Irish 107

 IV. Comic Foreigners 115
    A. The Irish 115
    B. The English 134
    C. The French 143
    D. Other foreigners 151

  V. From Romantic Foreigner to Aboriginal Adam . . 157

 VI. Conclusions 178

8 CONTENTS

Appendix 193

Bibliography 200

Index 202

INTRODUCTION

The history of drama may be told in many ways. One can list plays from a given period; compile biographies of dramatists; approach plays as representative of the literature written in a specific era; examine drama aesthetically; study it formally; consider comedies, tragedies, farces, or melodramas as entertainment alone; investigate the cultural attitudes expressed by dramatists; and so on. Many writers choose to treat only the "important" eras or dramatists, consigning the remainder to some dusty file cabinet reserved for minor work which could not quite qualify as major literature. Even if the minor material does receive a modicum of recognition as having engaged the interests of its age, the critic passes hurriedly through it in order to spend time in a more fruitful epoch. The early period of American drama has been rather summarily handled by most writers on American literary history. A typical statement appears in Spiller's *Literary History of the United States,* employed by Alexander Cowie to conclude his chapter, "The Beginnings of Fiction and Drama" (note the conjoining of kinds, neither one warranting or meriting investigation by itself): "During this period the novel fared better than the drama: Brackenridge's *Modern Chivalry* and Brown's *Wieland* probably reached a higher level of achievement than any of the plays that appeared. Yet for a long time the harvest is singularly meagre in both forms." [1] The historian of American drama, were he to apply Cowie's evaluation of productivity, would surely reap a scant crop. But when the drama of the early Republican era of

[1] *Literary History of the United States*, ed. Spiller, et. al., vol. I (New York, 1948), pp. 190-191.

the United States is studied as substance revelatory of cultural attitudes, then the yield in relation to the amount of material covered increases markedly. The possibility for more than a meagre harvest presents itself, particularly when an investigation embraces all work in dramatic or dialogue form, including graduation exercises, farces, tragedies, comedies, melodramas, and operatic pieces, as well as material of foreign authorship either translated or adapted for the American stage. And what could offer greater reward than to study how a people, young in sovereignty and adolescent in attitude toward the countries where their cultural conceptions originated, conceived of those foreigners against whom they fought and with whom they dealt for the first fifty years of independence? If the drama of the early Republic is examined for attitudes which reflect the variety of ways Americans thought of aliens, it reveals not only the obvious conclusions relative to antipathetic enemies in wartime plays, but also unfolds the mutating attitudes Americans held about themselves and their own accomplishments in relation to foreign institutions and systems.

One way to summarize the gross changes in early American cultural attitudes would be to consider the major revolutions in politico-cultural thought. Since Americans in the first half century of their political independence were largely engaged in arguing the various attributes and aspects of democracy, a study of their culture must take into account the major changes in governmental theory and practice. The first of these, obviously, occurred in 1776. The Revolution had its immediate sources in colonial unrest over Crown measures to resettle colonists in the upper Ohio area, and in Parliamentary jurisdictional matters of 1763. By 1765 British taxation of colonial citizens had aroused a storm of ire. The situation worsened, the schism between colonial and Crown interests widened, and a desire for economic justice and political sovereignty resulted in civil war.

The Revolutionary period may be considered to close in 1788, when the Constitution was ratified and thoughts of Americans turned into other, but tributary, channels. From 1788 to 1800 Federalist oligarchical theory dominated American politics. Yet within the very construction of the Bill of Rights and the Constitution lay the outline of another revolution, effected in 1801 by the man largely instrumental in writing the Constitution. But before Thomas Jefferson became President, factions arose, uniting under Federalist and Democrat banners. The Federalist favored a close alliance to Britain, and a plutocratic government controlled by the propertied classes. Jefferson and the Democrats (to give them their later appellation) perceived danger in retying the lines of colonial dependence, and advocated a reciprocation of French overtures to coalition based on the recent Gallic Revolution. The inhabitants of these opposed political camps feuded until Jefferson won the election in 1800. His victory signaled the rise to supremacy of an ideal form of democratic theory based upon agrarian foundations.

Under Jefferson, democracy and isolationism became political watchwords, the latter to be substantially modified by none other than the third President as he found himself forced to react to the pressures of foreign intrigue and pragmatic politics. During the administrations of Madison and Monroe, foreign policy continued to command the attention of the American body politic until the War of 1812 and the Monroe Doctrine strengthened the idea of fortress America. The third revolution in politico-cultural attitudes occurred in 1828 with the election of Andrew Jackson to the Presidency.

Under Jackson the conception of democracy received a broader interpretation than ever before. Domestic policy climbed into ascendency on a nationwide basis as Jackson and his government struggled with nullification, the troublesome question of land distribution, Biddle's Bank of the United States, and the sovereignty of the common man. With the western frontier regions politically victorious over eastern urban areas, America's thoughts turned to internal problems. The importance of foreign relations to American culture, economics, and government faded noticeably. For that reason, the date of 1830 serves as an organic terminus when handling material which deals with American cultural attitudes – especially when the inquiry concerns those attitudes specifically related to foreigners.[2]

[2] See particularly Charles A. and Mary R. Beard, *The Rise of American*

Ever since the War for Independence the subject of American cultural inheritance and attitudes has been treated in considerable detail. Early Americans, conscious of a difference between themselves and their British colonial and insular forebears, had their ideas of peculiarity reassured by British commentaries and travelogues, commencing with Mathews' *Historical Review of North America,* published at Dublin in 1789. The European popularity of travelers' skeptical views concerning America – a popularity heightened by violent American counterattacks – continued after 1830, reaching a pinnacle in the furor aroused over Frances Trollope's *Domestic Manners of the Americans* (1832). On the other side of the ledger, Washington Irving, James K. Paulding, Thoreau, and Emerson – to name but a few – lauded American uniqueness in customs, manners, and mores. Recently, many studies have covered both early and late conceptions of America as a virgin paradise which worked a metamorphosis in attitude and outlook on its inhabitants.³ In the specific area devoted to study of America's acceptance, rejection, or recognition of foreign influences upon itself, Howard M. Jones has explored the subject of Gallic effect on American culture, and Jane L. Mesick has dealt with the impressions British travellers garnered for their travelogues and commentaries.⁴

Yet, despite all the interest in American thought, early American drama has received little consideration as a possible medium of expression for cultural attitudes. Arthur H. Quinn and Richard Moody treat the larger segments of American dramatic and theat-

---

Civilization (New York, 1930); Carl R. Fish, *The Rise of the Common Man* (New York, 1950); Vernon L. Parrington, *Main Currents in American Thought,* 3 vols. (New York, 1930); Arthur M. Schlesinger, Jr., *The Age of Jackson* (Boston, 1945).

³ See R. W. B. Lewis, *The American Adam* (Chicago, 1955); Henry N. Smith, *Virgin Land* (Cambridge, Mass., 1950); Parrington; Frederic I. Carpenter, *American Literature and the Dream* (New York, 1955), and "The American Myth: Paradise (To Be) Regained", *PMLA*, LXXIV (December, 1959), pp. 599-606; F. O. Matthiessen, "The Need for Mythology", in *American Renaissance* (New York, 1941).

⁴ Howard M. Jones, *America and French Culture, 1750-1848* (Chapel Hill, N.C., 1927); Jane L. Mesick, *The English Traveller in America* (New York, 1922).

rical history; however, their primary interests do not lie in pursuing the dramatic utterances of cultural ideas.[5] An investigation of characterization in drama from the early period to 1870 has been attempted by Reed, whose study offers inadequate preparation and presentation of its professed object: "determining to what extent, in what manner, and with what fidelity these playwrights have drawn their characters from distinctive American life, just as it actually was, during the different historical periods prior to 1870." [6] An unpublished doctoral dissertation by Stanley L. Glenn offers pertinent and perceptive commentary on the many ludicrous characterizations in American drama prior to 1860, but its author spends little time exploring the ramifications of foreign caricatures in reference to cultural attitudes.[7] William Dunlap approached a consideration of the drama as revelatory of American cultural attitudes when he reiterated time after time a plea requesting support for an indigenous drama and theatre as means for expounding the message of American virtue, democracy, and natural goodness.[8] The wealth of American dramatic material awaiting an investigation of its contents as communicative of cultural attitudes requires a systematic approach. A critical study of early American attitudes toward the foreigner fills in one section; to attempt more would mean that a careful scrutiny and assessment of attitudes concerning foreign-American interrelationships would be lost in a welter of generalization.

In order to facilitate both treatment and comprehension, the early American dramatic output containing material pertinent to this study has been organically broken down into five areas: the growth of American ideas of politico-economic separateness; the

---

[5] Arthur H. Quinn, *A History of the American Drama from the Beginning to the Civil War*, 2d ed. (New York, 1951); Richard Moody, *America Takes the Stage* (Bloomington, Ind., 1955).

[6] Perley I. Reed, *The Realistic Presentation of American Characters in Native American Plays Prior to Eighteen Seventy* (Columbus, O., 1918), p. 5.

[7] Stanley L. Glenn, "Ludicrous Characterization in American Comedy from the Beginning until the Civil War" (Unpubl. disser., Stanford U., 1955).

[8] William Dunlap, *A History of the American Theatre* (New York, 1832).

assertion and varieties of anti-foreign sentiments; attitudes evincing a sympathetic outlook toward foreigners; comic stereotypes of foreign nationalities; and romantic influences upon foreign depictions. Each area has, in its turn, been subdivided into groupings which contain discussions, first by nationality then by chronology and type, of the various attitudes and characterizations presented by the plays, dialogues, and operas. For instance, the chapter entitled Comic Foreigners has been quartered into sections dealing with Irish, British, French, and miscellaneous characterizations. Within each section the material again splits chronologically and generically; the Irish yielding servants, soldiers, immigrants, and protagonists. The final chapter gathers together and considers chronologically the trends and ideas shown in the characterizations and attitudes discussed in the text. The Appendix includes an alphabetized list of American plays, dialogues, and operas from the beginning until 1830 containing matter germane to the topic. The list does not pretend to exhaustiveness, especially in the category of romantic tragedies, melodramas, and comedies, because of the repetitious nature of much in that emulative drama.

I. TO FIND A FOREIGNER

In the search to ascertain not only the moment when, but the way in which the foreigner appeared in colonial drama, the Revolution serves as an obvious point of departure. Yet the conceptual foreigner antedates the despicably villainous Red Coat in Revolutionary American drama. In order that the insular British could be depicted as foreign to colonial soil, it was necessary for the colonists, at a series of loci along the plotted curve of pre-Revolutionary history, gradually to cease viewing themselves as transplanted Europeans and to commence thinking of one-another as sovereign inhabitants of the eastern North American littoral. The attainment of that outlook did not transpire in a thunderclap of self-realization for, as Tyler puts it:

Before the year 1765, we find in this country, not one American people, but many American peoples. . . . In 1765, on the assembling in New York of the first continental congress, the delegates from the several colonies, like ambassadors from remote nations, could at first only stare at one another as utter strangers in face, in character, even in name.[1]

The search grows more complicated when, based upon figures from the 1790 census, a reverse extrapolation into the colonial period would estimate a majority of English stock, more inclined to regard the colonies as distant buddings of the homeland.[2] The consanguinity between Britons and colonists ran especially close

[1] Moses C. Tyler, *A History of American Literature* (Ithaca, 1949), p. 522.
[2] The *Encyclopedia of American History*, ed. Richard B. Morris (New York, 1953), p. 445, shows 60% of the continental population English; 33% Scotch, Irish, German, Dutch, French; and about 7% unassigned.

in the New England and South Tidewater colonies, where the
Englishman predominated.

The French and Indian War, victoriously fought largely by
troops and officers from the homeland, renewed the colonial debt
to royal protection and pulled tighter the knot binding Britain and
her colonies. Colonists greeted the British Regulars as any endangered people would welcome the army arriving to defend them.
Enhanced by colonial troops and reserve officers (among whom
fought a colonel by the name of Washington), the red-coated
Regulars managed to overcome the French and Indians who prey-
ed upon British colonial holdings. On September 29, 1762, English
victories were celebrated at a commencement exercise in Nassau
Hall on the campus of the College of New Jersey. Entitled *The
Military Glory of Great Britain*,[3] this exercise commends and lauds
Great Britain; in other words, the empire as it then existed. Scores
for musical parts appear in it, with a narrative for four speakers
which glorifies battles, heroes, and victories of the war. The piece
ends on a "wish, for the continued prosperity of the British Nation". Its author, obviously, still thought of himself and his colony
as one with the mother country.

Yet another and earlier dialogue by Thomas Hopkinson entitled *A Dialogue and Ode, Sacred to the Memory . . . of George
II* – this one performed at the commencement exercises of 1761
at the College of Philadelphia – commemorates the death of
George II. Eugenio and Amyntor bucolically elegize the late monarch. Among the encomiums, the following few lines spoken by
Eugenio indicate the tenor of feeling that received approbation
from the early faculty of the College:

> ILLUSTRIOUS MONARCH! not the ROMAN boast,
> The generous TITUS, joy of human kind;
> Nor names of later date, WILLIAM and HENRY
> Or ALFRED's self, shall fill a brighter page
> In FAME's eternal roll, than shall the name
> Of gracious GEORGE! beneath his equal sway,
> Oppression WAS NOT; JUSTICE poiz'd her scale;
> No LAW was trampled, and no RIGHT deny'd;
> The PEASANT flourish'd, and the MERCHANT smil'd

[3] Complete title may be found in the Appendix (p. 185).

> And Oh! my friend, to what amazing height
> Of sudden grandeur, did his nursing care
> Up-raise these COLONIES; beyond whate'er
> Of ancient or of modern times is told.
> Prepare we, then, due ELEGIES to frame,
> Such as may well accord to heart of woe.

The bald statement that George II governed equitably applied not only to England, but also to the colonies. The British in North America polish some of Britain's splendor, which they acquire because of their inclusion among the ranks of Britons who rule an empire.

Admittedly the numbers of exercises and dialogues remaining from the period under scrutiny are sparse, yet their existence and sentiments mark a climate of thought which refuses denial. One can not forget that such commencements were publicly attended, and if they did not repeat a popular upper-class sentiment, the dialogues and exercises at least helped mold it.

The British colonies, prior to the Letters of Correspondence and the Stamp Act Congress, felt palpably their unity with insular Britain. Jacob Duché, graduating from the same college in 1762, a year after Thomas Hopkinson, speaks through one of his persona:

> Shout then, ye favour'd Race, ye Sons of Freedom!
> Bound every Heart with Joy, and every Breast
> Pour the warm Tribute of a grateful Praise!
> For o'er the Realms of BRITAIN reigns supreme,
> The Darling of his People, George the Good.[4]

A decade later, that identical phrase, "Sons of Freedom", would take on another meaning; in 1762 it expressed the loyalty of its author. In the year following Duché's *Exercise*, Nathaniel Evans, on the faculty of the College of Philadelphia, wrote for commencement a dialogue extolling George III, blessing England, and lauding the peace that had recently been declared between Britain and France.[5] Fourteen years later Philadelphia would receive the British as occupation troops while Congress would be forced to flee from the city.

---

[4] *An Exercise ... on the Accession ... of George III* (1762).
[5] Nathaniel Evans, *An Exercise ... on Occasion of the Peace* (Philadelphia, 1763, 1772).

Even as late as 1770, around which date Colonel Robert Munford wrote *The Candidates*,[6] local issues of the type shortly to be fought over crop up in the drama, but without any rancor towards Britain intended. Munford satirizes the methods of conducting elections for the Virginia House of Burgesses. Nothing in the play imputes any derogative comparison between foreign and native electoral systems. Munford holds in contempt unscrupulous techniques of campaigning, but these occur because of the foibles of man as a political animal, not because the Crown sanctions the system. In the play, Sir John Toddy, Mr. Wou'dbe, Mr. Strutabout, and Mr. Smallhopes are candidates for a seat in the House. Sir John is a sot, Strutabout a windy coward, Smallhopes a conniver, and Wou'dbe an honest and upright candidate who eventually wins. The most provocative scene occurs at a racetrack where the candidates gather to electioneer. The candidates who liberally dispense rum seem to be able to buy the most votes, while those iterating wild promise attain almost as much popularity. Wou'dbe's good sense operates to his advantage, as this caution to Sir John indicates:

Wou'dbe: You had better be more sparing of your honour at present, Sir John; for if you are a candidate, whenever you make promises to the people that you can't comply with, you must say upon honour, otherwise they won't believe you.

Munford treats Sir John, despite his nationality and vice, as one of the folks. Sir John's besottedness disqualifies him for office, but does not remove him from the community. In spite of the politicking (in the pejorative twentieth-century sense of the word) the best man wins, literally, and governance under royal charter withstands all gaff.

The foreigner in the thoughts of the lettered colonist of British extraction prior to the decade of the 1770's thus could not be considered British. A colonist would be more inclined to agree with an insular Briton, that the French, Germans, Dutch, Spanish – even though they might inhabit the same continent with him – con-

---

[6] Quinn, pp. 54-55, dates the piece by an allusion to the demise of Virginia's Governor Botetourt, who died October 15, 1770.

stituted the foreign element in the colonies. Similarly, the large and culturally isolated group of non-British colonials populating the middle-Atlantic colonies (e.g. the Germans and Scotch in Pennsylvania and Virginia) would tend to treat the British colonist as a stranger and foreigner. In brief, the European origin of the group making a judgment would, to a large extent, decide just which other nationality became the foreign element. The native Americans were savages, and they, too, seemed foreign to the emigrant.

The infrequency with which the colonist expressed himself in dramatic form is surpassed only by the incompleteness of the present day records and paucity of extant plays. Hill lists only twenty-seven plays by colonists prior to the Revolution and the onset of propaganda pieces.[7] A perusal of Dunlap's and Odell's histories of American drama yields long lists of plays imported from Britain and staged after the mid-eighteenth century by the first troupe of actors to remain in the colonies.[8] Relatively few men could spare the leisure hours to devote to the creation of drama. Moreover, religious groups such as the Puritans and the Quakers argued and legislated vehemently against the evils of dramatic entertainment – or entertainment of any sort, for that matter. Following Darby's *Ye Bare and Ye Cubb* (1665), the first recorded drama in English, plays written on this side of the Atlantic did not exactly abound. Governor Hunter wrote *Androboros* in 1714, after which an hiatus of plays ensues until the commencement exercises mentioned in previous paragraphs. In 1763 *The Paxton Boys* was printed. This play details the furor caused by a group of frontiersmen who attacked some Indians, then marched on the Pennsylvania legislature when it issued an order for their arrest. As with *Androboros*, the events which spurred the drama were strictly local; the consequences of an Indian uprising supply the material for each dramatist.

In 1766 Major Robert Rogers' *Ponteach* appeared in print.

---

[7] Frank P. Hill, *Bibliography of American Drama* (Stanford University, 1934).

[8] James C. Odell, *Annals of the New York Stage*, vol. I (New York, 1927).

Rogers had spent a parti-colored career in the colonies. Born and reared in New Hampshire, he had led Rogers' Rangers against the French and Indians, married a parson's daughter, to be later divorced, governed Mackinac Island so ineptly that he found himself sentenced to jail for a period of time, and finally fought against the colonials in the Revolution. One legacy, though, for which posterity must remain forever grateful to the redoubtable adventurer, is the existence of the first Indian play. A tragedy, this piece stands as the first by a colonist of British ancestry to ennoble the American savage – Pontiac in particular – and to derogate the British and French. From the Crown's officers who cheat the Indians, to the traders who ambush them and the French priest who attempts to rape a princess and misguide Pontiac, the white man earns all the calumny and condemnation heaped upon him by Rogers. McDole, an experienced Indian trader, tells the neophyte Murphey how to carry out their business.

> *McDole:* ... Our fundamental Maxim then is this,
> That it's no crime to cheat and gull an Indian.
> *Murphey:* How! Not a Sin to cheat an Indian,
> say you?
> Are they not Men? Havn't they a Right to Justice
> As well as we, though savage in their Manners?
> *McDole:* Ah! If you boggle here, I say no more;
> This is the very Quintessence of Trade,
> And ev'ry hope of Gain depends upon it ...

McDole continues in the vein, damning himself more completely with each line. If the residence of virtue and nobility in the breast of the protagonist, and the exploitation by outsiders of the native Indian can aid in deciding the identity of a foreigner, then the British and French in the play belong to other soil while the Indian fights for his usurped land.

Although Rogers did not remain all his life in the colonies, he nevertheless spent the majority of his allotted years in them; enough to have known not only the existence of the colonist, but that of the soldier and frontier administrator. These qualifications support his judgments as those of someone who experiences events at first hand. If *Ponteach* represents Rogers' opinion about foreigners and natives, his conclusions must have been that the people who crossed the Atlantic to take up residence on the land – particularly those who dealt with the Indian – formed the nonnative element. European nationality made no difference; French and British characters acted in a equally despicable manner.

It would be presumptuous to state that a clearcut conclusion can be drawn from the few extant plays, dialogues, and exercises dating from the beginnings of colonization to the mid-eighteenth century. What evidence there is, however, hardly asserts a general and pervasive spirit of political, ethnic, and cultural cohesiveness along the Atlantic seaboard prior to the middle of the 1760's. And without the spirit of nationality, there can be nothing foreign. The one engenders the other.

To find a foreigner in early American drama and thought, then, the spirit of nationalism must be sought out. What events, what acts, what drama contain the first traces of a unifying factor? The hunt must commence with some event of magnitude sufficient to engage the attention of a large segment of the population. The event should pose some sort of threat to, or call for some kind of an opinion from that segment. The decade commencing with 1754 supplies precisely the impetus required.

In the French and Indian War, which apparently glued the upperclass and intellectual British colonial more tightly to his transatlantic relative, lurked the seeds of nationalism. The entire British colonial settlement in America could not help but respond in some manner to the revivified perennial quarrel between the two thrones. Especially in the northernmost colonies were the depredations of the Indians under the aegis of the Frenchmen annoying. The Albany Convention in 1754 gathered delegates from New England, New York, Pennsylvania, and Maryland. The representatives from distant colonies found themselves forced to work out some ground for accord in reaction to the problem they confronted. A union of all colonies but Georgia and Nova Scotia to treat the Indian situation was called for, but rejected by the colonies and Parliament. The ground for a complete unification had been cleared, but the seeds were broadcast at the wrong season.

Until the cessation of hostilities in 1761, the continued attention of the British colonists remained focused upon the conflict which raged on two continents. The necessity of concerted action of a sort (characterized by the Albany Convention), the employment of Colonials with Regulars in the battles against the French, and above all the existence of a common enemy, served to unite the British colonists not only with their homeland which supplied protection, but with one-another in defense of their own lands. The realization that their holdings were precious engendered in the colonists the awakening knowledge that the word "colonial" might no longer apply to them, since it denoted a person who temporarily lived without the territorial confines of the mother country. In brief, the war gave them, in the argot of present political journalists, a national image; blurred, incompletely defined, yet definitely present.[9]

To return to dramatic expression of the urge to unite, it appears in a graduation dialogue already mentioned, *The Military Glory of Great Britain*. The passages laudatory of battles, heroes, and victories not only indicate that the author was sensible of the colonial debt to Britain, but that he appreciated the teleological existence of the colonies – be it political, cultural, or ideal – in relation to the colonizing country. This entity would not have existed prior to the French and Indian War, or before the popularization of mildly nationalistic sentiments by authors preparing their work for public attendance.

Another play, written in Boston and published in England in 1766, celebrates the posthumous victory won by Wolfe over the French forces at Quebec. *The Conquest of Canada*, composed by George Cockings, a minor functionary in the colonial governmental hierarchy, is an heroic-dramatic paean to the might and glory of Britain and her incomparable general, Wolfe. As much allegory as drama, the play renders the history of the battle into iambic hyperbole.

> *Wolfe:*   Say they thus?
> They shall e'er long, hear *Britain's* Thunder roll!
> And feel the *Bolt*! Our Troops and Tars shall roar
> Them such a Concert, as shall shake the strong

[9] See Tyler, p. 525, who sums the matter up with clarity.

And lofty Base of their *Quebec*!

* * *

I cannot boast twelve thousand Regulars,
With many savage scalping Bands; my Troops
Will scarcely to eight Thousand rise; but these
Are gallant Fellows; and I have seen them
Try'd: They're Britain's Troops, and from *Old
England,*
Caledonia and *Hibernia* drawn.

The devotion of an entire piece to an aspect of the campaign against the Indians speaks for the intensity of interest at the time of composition. The *Conquest of Canada* did not find a producer until it was played at the Southwark Theatre in Philadelphia, February 16, 1773.[10] The future seat of the rebel government, a short year and a half before the convening of the First Continental Congress, found an evening of strong pro-British sentiment not unpalatable. The pleasure that audiences sympathizing with the Loyalists found in the play is borne out by its production in occupied New York on October 4, 1783, a little over a month before the evacuation. Indeed, for the Philadelphia production, ten years earlier, soldiers and sailors of the British armed forces had been used to add realism in the battle scenes.[11] There have come down to the present no records of action or protestation against the inclusion of this play in the repertory of the company then at the Southwark. Lack of reaction generally implies at least several degrees of acceptance.

About 1765 Lewis Hallam's troupe of actors that had left the continent of North America for Jamaica in 1754 – there to lose and gain many members, then to return under David Douglass' leadership in 1758 and wage a campaign against injunctions and anti-theatrical acts – changed its name from The London Company to The American Company. In 1766 the Reverend Doctor William Smith, first Provost of Philadelphia College, wrote an exercise in dialogue for the commencement that year. The bulk of the exercise lauds Pitt and other Parliamentary "patriots" who espouse and carry to fulfillment the colonists' cause against

[10] Quinn, p. 30.
[11] Odell, vol. I, pp. 107, 229.

taxation. Smith also liberally lards his dialogue with statements about "liberty" and "freedom", likening the Indians' love of freedom and and lack of fetters to the same innate yearning possessed by the colonists. These two pieces, Smith's exercise and Cocking's play, mark a phase of an outburst of united reaction occasioned by the results of the French and Indian War.

Forced to find a means to replenish a depleted treasury, Parliament sought to lay imposts and taxes upon the colonies. In 1765 a colonial Stamp Act Congress convened in New York, at which all but four of the colonies were represented. Desiring to take concerted action, the delegates objected to Parliamentary taxation in a Declaration of Grievances sent to the House of Commons. At the same time the Congress asked the colonists to bring economic sanctions to bear against British imports, and with the loss of export income from the colonies, British merchants pressured Parliament to repeal the Stamp Tax.

Doubtless colonial response to these events caused Douglass' decision to change the name of The London Company. After all, since America seemed to be reacting in a unified manner to the British, the least he could do in order to aid the popularity of his company would be to remove the stigma of a British connection implied in the name of his troupe. Similarly, Smith's paean to liberty and Pitt sprang from a feeling which recognized that the freedom won was a freedom from too much interference on the part of that governing body of fraternal strangers across the Atlantic. The image of an aggrieved people had begun to take shape; nationalistic spirits had begun to make themselves known; the British foreigner had begun vaguely to appear.

The anonymous *Trial of Atticus before Justice Beau for a Rape*, which followed William Smith's exercise by five years, constitutes the next extant dramatic outburst against the colonial officers of the Crown. The author rather acerbically dedicated his play "To the most honourable, most worshipful, and most worthy Josia Beau, esq; Colonel of a Regiment of Foot, Justice of the Peace, and of the Quorum, for the County of - - - - -". The play does not contain any foreigners, *per se*, yet presents manifestations of an attitude toward the British as a people apart. The events employed obviously occurred at some locale in New England, but so pointed and topical are they that without knowing the people satirized there can be little specific meaning gained from the play. As in Mrs. Warren's *The Group*, however, a key to the characters is not necessary to understand the piece as a polemic against injustice. The author inveighs against the justice, a doctor, a lawyer a publican, a deacon, the farmer, and the wife who can not clearly recollect anything but that Atticus sat on a bed with her "some time between the middle of July, and the last of August, 1768"; two years before the trial. The evidence against Atticus, witnessed by the doctor, the deacon, and the publican, consists of past actions which have nothing to do with the case at hand. The deacon wishes Atticus condemned as an Arminian, while the doctor testifies that the accused once called him a quack. Atticus, whoever he was, remains the only character depicted without any rancor. The attitude of censure and satire contained in the piece resembles that which the acts of Parliament caused to spring up against the British. The Stamp Acts, the Quartering Act, the Townshend Acts, and the Boston Massacre all served to unite the colonists more completely against a power which, in their estimation, threatened the pursuit of capital gains.[12]

A similar sort of patriotism bursts from the lines of Freneau's commencement exercise, *On the Rising Glory of America*, spoken at Nassau Hall, the College of New Jersey, on September 25, 1771. The entire dialogue quite literally glorifies North America historically, as a refuge from oppression, as the ground for glorious battles, as superior to South America, commercially, scientifically, and as a future paradise. Within the same stanza, Freneau describes the British "heroes who fell in it [North America]; Wolfe, Braddock, &c." and decries British oppression.

> *Leander:* And here fair freedom shall forever reign.
> I see a train, a glorious train appear,
> Of patriots plac'd in equal fame with those who

[12] Beard, p. 220: "As soon as the Townshend program took the form of reality in America in the shape of an army of customs officers supported by British regulars and a fleet of revenue cutters, the war of American independence opened, not, of course, with all the panoply of the state, but in the guise of unashamed, flagrant, and determined resistance to law."

Nobly fell for Athens or for Rome.
The Sons of Boston resolute and brave,
The firm supporters of our injur'd rights
Shall lose their splendours in the brighter beams
Of patriots fam'd and heroes yet unborn.

Philip Freneau, sometimes called the voice of the Revolution, in this dialogue speaks out strongly against the motherland and its actions in the colonies without implying by statement or allusion that there should be a general rebellion. Although the premise for Freneau's dramatic poem predicates an intercolonial nationality that would take supersedence over an allegiance to Britain, colonial complaints had not yet assumed a magnitude requiring the assuagement of rebellion.

Thoughts of America as a country apart from Britain, by the second or third year of the 1770's, had achieved acceptance among many of the injured and "liberty loving" colonials. The more articulate of these men, self-avowedly patriots, spoke out against the evils of British tyranny and mis-government. Otis cried that taxation without representation could not be supported. Sam Adams formulated the Committees of Correspondence, to which belonged such men as Thomas Jefferson and Patrick Henry. Mercy Otis Warren – wife of Joseph Warren, who was to fall in the command of part of the rebel troops (or patriot – depending upon where one's sympathy lay) at the Battle of Bunker Hill, and sister of James Otis – became the dramatic spokeswoman for the American revolutionists in Boston. She wrote *The Adulateur* in 1773, inveighing against, as Knight puts it, "a majority of wealthy and aristocratic Americans, proud of the name of Englishmen and of the noble traditions back of their nationality, allied, too, by conscious ties of family and interest with the upholders of the United Kingdom, [who] refused to be carried along by the sentiments which led to warfare." [13]

Mrs. Warren's sympathies would be apparent from a mere perusal of the character names she uses in the dramatis personae. Rapatio, Governor of Servia; Dupe, Secretary of State; and Bag-

[13] Grant C. Knight, *American Literature and Culture* (New York, 1932), p. 71.

shot, Aga of the Janizaries (Governor Hutchinson and his cabinet) are set off against Brutus, Chief of the Patriots; Junius; Cassius; and Portius (Otis, Sam Adams, John Adams, John Hancock). Quinn states that Hutchinson was a native of Massachusetts who once had enjoyed simultaneously three governmental offices. Letters from him to members of Parliament suggesting that martial law be declared in the colonies, that the charter of Rhode Island be abrogated, and that other measures odious to the colonists be taken so order might be maintained, were secured by Franklin in England and sent to Massachusetts. The publication of these served as the material cause for *The Adulateur*.[14]

In the play, Hutchinson conspires with Bagshot to fire upon the people gathered on the Commons to protest some action of the British troops. The Boston Massacre ensues, which gives rise to American patriotic bombast. Brutus asks if Cassius saw the event which led up to the Massacre. Cassius replies:

> I saw it – and could paint a scene of woe,
> Would make the sun collect his scatter'd rays
> And shroud himself in night – While numbers
>   crouded,
> Thoughtless of harm to see the pageantry,
> And sportive youths play'd gamesome in the street.
> That wretch, that cursed E----r,
> Whom long this country blush'd to own her son –
> Urg'd on by hell and malice, unprovok'd –
> Hurl'd thro' the croud promiscuous death and
>   slaughter –
> One youth, unhappy victim fell – he lies
> Reeking in gore, and bites the hated ground.

The man who fired into the crowd, Adams insists, does not belong to "this country". The growing ease with which incensed colonials employed phrases such as "our country", "my country", "these patriots", and "those men whose crimes", marks a further stage in the development of the foreigner. *The Adulateur* indicates the intensity of feeling which British actions aroused in patriots' breasts. Even Rapatio groans after the massacre, "The cause is lost! the Patriot's up in arms, / Pant for revenge . . ." At last the

[14] Quinn, pp. 34-38.

British colonists commenced to differentiate between those whose interests they thought more closely aligned with Britain, and the men who believed in the American cause. The distinction between outlander and native, heretofore confined to nationalities other than British – nationalities against whom the British colonists felt anger or fought – caused the stigma of foreigner to be applied against the insular British.

The Group, another play by Mercy Warren, published two years after *The Adulateur*, contains an even more violent expression of dislike for colonists who sympathized with the British government. Crusty Crowbar (Josiah Edson, according to the key in Quinn, p. 40) speaks of the colonies as a country which can be betrayed; which has been betrayed by Governor Hutchinson:

> It is too plain he has betrayed his country,
> And we're the wretched tools by him marked out
> To seal its ruins – tear up the ancient forms,
> And every vestige treacherously destroy,
> Nor leave a trait of freedom in the land,

The occurrences of the two years between publication dates of *The Adulateur* and *The Group* had changed the aspect of the colonial situation. In this second play, probably written during 1774 – there is no mention of Lexington or Concord – the same men who had been previously depicted by Mrs. Warren as tools of Britain appear as outright traitors to their country. The Loyalists in *The Group* – Beau Trumps, Judge Meagre, Hum Humbug, Simple Sapling, Dupe, and others – to a man bemoan their defection and sedition, or boast of all the pillage and rapine for which they will be responsible. According to the authoress, the Loyalists of Boston comprehend completely the extent of their own despicability. Anomolously, Mercy Warren causes her satirized characters (to use a euphemism for bitterly antipathetic depictions) to utter sentiments which would seem to belong more to the patriots.

> *Beau Trump.* Not all the millions that she
>   [America] vainly boasts
> Can cope with veteran barbarian hosts;
> But the brave sons of Albion's warlike race,

> Their arms, and honours, never can disgrace,
> Or draw their swords in such a hated cause,
> In blood to seal a N[orth]'s oppressive laws,
> They'll spurn the service; Britains must recoil,
> And show themselves the native of an isle
> Who fought for freedom in the worst of times,
> Produced her Hampdens, Fairfaxes and Pyms.

The later edition of William Smith's exercise – first published in 1766 then reissued in 1775 – completes the tally of dramatic pieces expressing the anti-British solidarity of the colonies prior to the Revolution. Smith left large sections of his first dialogue intact when he revised the piece, since Pitt and the others mentioned in 1766 still belabored Parliament on behalf of the colonists in 1775. But the tone has changed completely. In 1766 the general impression an audience would have gained from the exercise was the conviction that the colonies were happy in their new-found freedom following the repeal of the Stamp Tax. An audience member or reader of 1775 would have received another idea entirely. Smith exhorts the down-trodden, self-sacrificing patriots to continue striving for liberty and freedom as they have in the field at Lexington and on the heights at Bunker Hill. His redefinition of liberty predicates rebellion.

Even the pro-British, anti-colonial dialogues of this period could not help but express some differentiation between Britain and America. The person who styled herself Mary V. V. and wrote *A Dialogue between a Southern Delegate and His Spouse* (1774) [15] ridicules the efforts of the First Continental Congress in instituting such procedures as the Courts of Inspection and the embargo on export and import with the British Isles – all of which, she claims, work untold hardship on the colonies as well as incur the wrath of Parliament. Despite the position of the authoress, though, a tacit acceptance of a difference between "those" British and "we" continentals permeates the piece. While Mary V. V. does not concur with the course pursued by Congress, she nevertheless does not consider that Congress should dissolve itself. The

---

[15] Paranthetical dates following plays refer to the first appearance – in print or on stage.

notion arises that Congress could have selected more suitable means to achieve its aims, but she suggests nothing further.

It did not take long for the attitude incipient in Mercy Warren's closet drama to intensify into outright antipathy toward all things British. The mortal strife was engaged and carried forth by both musket and quill. The creation of the United States of America as a sovereign nation served as the political origin of the literary British foreigner; the differences between British and colonial national interests were utilized to emphasize differences between British and colonial stereotypes. For the purposes of patriotic propaganda, it would have been far from astute to have recalled the British origins of the majority of the colonial population. The rabid patriotism expressed by such playwrights as Hugh Brackenridge,[16] John Leacock,[17] and many who chose not to sign their names,[18] turned the native Britisher either into a monster of no virtues whatsoever or a ridiculous oaf. The Whigs could not stomach the Tories, nor could the Tories abide the Whigs. The general strength and unanimity of sentiment against the British usually assumed by schoolbooks probably did not exist. Or if it did, it issued from a tendency to protect threatened interests. If those interests were not endangered by Parliament and the British colonial government, the colonist more than likely reacted in a lukewarm manner towards his "enemies", until whipped into some semblance of fervor by propaganda.[19] Americans, if they already did not believe it, were forced to admit their sovereign identities. That admission broke the final tie with the mother country and made total foreigners of the British.

Even the Tories, while certainly sympathizing with the British, tacitly recognized a difference between Britain and the American colonies. Although he did not agree with schism or revolution, a

---

[16] *The Battle of Bunkers-Hill* (1776), *The Death of General Montgomery* (1777).

[17] *The Fall of British Tyranny* (1776).

[18] *The Blockheads, or the Affrighted Officers* (1776), *The Motley Assembly* (1779).

[19] Colonel Munford's *The Patriots* (ca. 1785) emphasizes the advisability of maintaining a sense of balance among fervid partisans of both persuasions.

Tory such as Jonathan Sewall, who wrote *A Cure for the Spleen* (1775), also did not desire a return to the *status quo ante bellum*. The line of argument followed by the Tory characters in the playlet reasons against the bases for revolution put forth by Whigs: the King drove out the French, and the rebels now turn on the throne that protected them. It would not take a great degree of forensic ability to answer that argument as well as the others promulgated, but the Whigs, Fillpot and Puff, lack the requisite mental heft to find adequate response. The Tories speak of Lord North, Governor Hutchinson, and other men of British nationality or sympathy as friends. Sewall's characters, Tory or Whig, make no mention of themselves as native to Britain. Even the Tory accepted himself as different from his insular counterpart, and recognized colonial grievances, although he believed they should not be redressed through rebellion.

Issuing battle- and propaganda-stained from the seven-year civil struggle, came the prototypes of the Yankee and the American conception of John Bull. The Yankee in "Yankee Doodle", supposedly invented by the British in derision of the rebels, but actually in existence prior to the publication of Barton's *The Disappointment* in 1767,[20] struggled with his British counterpart through innumerable verses. It took but five years after the cessation of war for the progeny of these early personifications of national types to find a dramatic vehicle. Royall Tyler's *The Contrast*, first played in 1787, contains the original stage Jonathan and his opposite, Jessamy.[21] Tyler also compares the typification of quiet, patriotic, virtuous American manhood in Colonel Manly, to the Chesterfieldan insolence of the "British-ized" fop, Dimple. Already the violent antipathy of the Revolutionary polemicists had mellowed sufficiently to permit an American to be criticized as British in dress and manner without being suspected of seditious intent.

Through the creation and popularization of growing numbers of

[20] An air in that piece carries the instructions that it must be set to "Yankee Doodle".

[21] And that first Jonathan, curiously enough, arrived on stage from the area of the new Republic designated New England.

characters providing cultural comparisons – characters like Jonathan and Jessamy, Manly and Dimple – playwrights emphasized
the establishment of two realms; one containing things American, and another holding things foreign. The demarcation line
between these realms became clearly defined when the last official
link with Britain as a colonizing country snapped under the Treaty
of 1787, which declared the onetime colonial merchants as non-
privileged when it came to the importation of American goods into
Britain and her other colonies. Americans, despite plays such as
The Blockheads (1782), which bespoke a desire to rely again upon
the protection of England, finally awakened to the realization that
they were no longer part of the British empire.

The early republicans also reminded themselves that they had
fought their battles, won them, and were launched upon the greatest venture in self-government since the fifth century, B.C. The
type of person who could successfully promulgate and carry out
such a revolution in political thought must be of a unique nature,
so the sentiments went. Thus arose the idea of the American Way
of Life, encompassing mores (better and more virtuous than those
of other countries), government (the best of all possible), liberty
(the most permissible), opportunity (infinite). No sooner was the
peace treaty signed than dramatists began to thumb the dried
leaves of historical tomes in search of parallels.

Peter Markoe, in 1784, found one of the first. His play, *The
Patriot Chief*, takes place in ancient Sardis. The point Markoe
attempts to make appears in the preface to his piece.

The subject of the following Tragedy, which has never been acted or
published, is purely fabulous. It has human nature, but no particular
nation, or individual, for its object. The author thinks this declaration
necessary, as it may prevent malignant criticism from imputing sentiments to him, which he abhors. He wishes to be thought, however
obscure, an advocate for liberty, on the most enlarged and liberal
plan; but he is warranted, by history in affirming, that true liberty
may as effectually be destroyed by the machinations of a party, as
by the ambitions of a single person. An aristocracy appears to him
to be the most odious and oppressive of all modes of government. . . .

In the play, the old and righteous king wins out over the factions
that would usurp his throne. Yet the meaning Markoe apparently

intended seems to be that monarchy, by its inherently oppressive nature, encourages rebellion.

The Contrast, as an example of the play which contrasts the foreign and the American manners and mores, has been mentioned as a step toward tempering bitter characterizations of the British. Tyler's comedy of manners also serves to mark the birth of one of the most significant natives in American literature, at that time so young. Jonathan, as the years passed, became the sign, symbol, and purveyor of the unique traits which set Americans off from their fellow men.

Despite the Jonathans and the Dimples, the historical parallels and the foreign aristocrats, Americans in the waning years of the eighteenth century still gauged much of their daily existence by European standards. Socialites of the early republic could not finally decide that they stood apart from their former compatriots. Gallic aid during the Revolution went a long way toward convincing many Americans that the French rather than the British could be considered their real brothers, and after the French Revolution the idea became even more popular. It took the excesses of the Jacobins to convince a segment of the American populace that in the French there existed no true twin. At the same time, the Federalists cried that America's real allies were the British. The country became riddled with vindictive political strife between Democrat and Federalist, each finding the source for his attitudes toward domestic politics in the events occurring across the Atlantic. It required precisely this battle – including all the maliciousness of such mistakes as the Alien and Sedition Acts – to help convince Americans that the place to look for strength, politics, and identity was not in some "entangling alliance", as Jefferson put it, but in their own land of promise.

The heightened interest in European events and the application of the lessons in those events to this country may be studied in such plays as the anonymous *The French Revolution* (1790). In the preface to the 1793 edition, the author, mainly interested in the political message of his piece, states,

The revolution which our allies are struggling to obtain, and the late decapitation of Louis, are subjects which appear to interest every

American – every circumstance that we conceive to throw light upon the subject, or clear up any mystery in the course of events, we gladly acquaint ourselves with, and eagerly attach ourselves to. – The following pages are recommended as a means whereby the mind may be readily initiated into the knowledge of the events which lead to so complete an overthrow of French monarchy: –

The aristocracy plan and carry out nefarious deeds against the common people, then erroneously counsel Louis so that he acts against the excellent advice of Necker and LaFayette. Quite contrary to historical verisimilitude, Louis finally decides to establish a constitution according to LaFayette's suggestion. The play ends happily with Louis, still in possession of his head, granting rights to the people. The author disliked the excesses of the aristocracy as much as he did the revolutionary fervor of the Jacobins. His Federalist bias shows itself through the ideal settlement of French political problems, which surves to enlighten the reader or playgoer. The author obviously intended his American audience to believe that the French monarch fell prey to evil councillors, followed their admonitions, and thus lost his head. Constitutional monarchy (such as that found in Britain), one must assume, appeared to the playwright an admirable form of government.

Another foreign disturbance which furnished the material for numerous afterpieces, melodramas, and romantically patriotic plays, was the Barbary pirate trouble in the Mediterranean. Susanna H. Rowson's *Slaves in Algiers* (1794) stands at the top of the ledger as the first recorded American play on the subject. The author states in her preface,

My chief aim has been to offer the public a Dramatic Entertainment, which, while it might excite a smile, or call forth the tear of sensibility, might contain no one sentiment, in the least prejudicial, to the moral or political principles of the government under which I live.

She lives up to her intention, for Muley Moloc, Dey of Algiers, overcome by Christian remorse because he has heard so many American captives praising the virtues of democracy, frees the slaves and declares his country a republic. The morality of the play is as simple as that found in *The French Revolution*. If a man holds anti-democratic, un-Christian sentiments – if he keeps

slaves – his only salvation lies in espousing virtues the lack of
which makes him evil. The play, with others like it, aided the in-
culcation of an appreciation in Americans for virtues which they
grew to believe were particularly effective in their new nation.
They began to revel in the belief of a sort of Rousseau-like primitive and therefore good and highly moral state of democratic
society.[22]

By the time that Jefferson settled into office in the new capital
at Washington, D.C., the enmity between pro-French and pro-
British factions had neutralized itself sufficiently for an American
to take stock of himself. Jefferson's inaugural, including the now
famous misquotation about "entangling alliances", helped turn
the sight of the American people inward. The increased interest in
strictly domestic political matters, the successful campaign against
the Tripolitan Pasha, the Louisiana Purchase, the opened western
reaches, and the excesses of both French and British governments,
all caused an American trend to deny any political, social, or moral link between Europe and the new democracy.

Prefaces and prologues to plays, even as early as 1789, show the
birth of a movement to continue to make American letters distinct
from European – particularly British – efforts. Dunlap, in the
prologue to *The Father* (1789), finds a difference in moral tonality
between European and American plays. He personifies Thalia,
the comic muse:

> In Europe, long applauded and caress'd,
> She saucy grew, and modesty opprest,
> Descended for a laugh, to tricks too mean
> And stained the stage with many a jest obscene:
>
> * * *
>
> But since she visited this western clime,
> She well in study has improv'd her time.

From just such comparisons, the cry went out for a native American drama, as the demand in other fields grew for native American literature, mores, art, and outlook on life and politics. Amer-

[22] See Carpenter ("The American Myth"), who discerns a dual-natured
American Adam, premorally innocent and civilized in a modern world,
seeking idealism.

icans busied themselves finding out how wonderfully they differed from other people in the world, at the same time wondering why it was that more people were not inclined to try the democratic experiment so successfully completed in this country.

In this era, the dramatic depiction of the foreigner began to stabilize. No longer needed he be, as in Brackenridge's *The Death of General Montgomery*, Leacock's *The Fall of British Tyranny, The French Revolution*, or Rowson's *Slaves in Algiers*, merely an alien possessing some sort of rudimentary anti-American sentiments in order for his villainy to be patently obvious. Now, shaded foreigners appeared in the drama: foreigners whose character traits were more important than their nationalities in deciding sympathy or antipathy. Dunlap's *André* (1798) early exemplifies, in Major André, the nobility that can reside in a foreign breast even though that breast be covered by a red coat. Dunlap, however, was forced to change parts of the play to meet public disapprobation of an American character's dislike of the sentence meted out to André. *Liberty in Louisiana* (1803), by James Workman, shows the Spanish judge in New Orleans villainous not merely because he opposes America, but because he takes bribes, metes out lefthanded justice, and tries to carry off his young and beautiful ward. Yet he is amusing on top of it all – a characteristic not found in any of the British of the Revolutionary polemical plays.

In brief, early in the nineteenth century Americans had found an image of themselves, and in so doing had begun to look out at the rest of the world with vision which compared what it perceived to an unique set of American values. The foreigner seen by American eyes, who was judged to be different by American standards, commenced to become interesting because of his differentiating traits.

II. ANTI-FOREIGN SENTIMENTS

A. REVOLUTION, PROPAGANDA, AND CHAUVINISM

Of "the shot heard round the world", historians state that time
has eradicated the identity of the man who fired it. History,
however, has not treated the battlefield of Revolutionary
drama with such cavalier disregard. The engagement on the
green that set off the Revolution also fired the imaginations
of such dramatists as Hugh Henry Brackenridge, John [Joseph?]
Leacock, and many authors who chose to keep their identities
from the title pages of posterity. While the Continental Congress
of 1774 cautioned the states to " 'discountenance and discourage
all horse racing, and all kinds of gaming, cock fighting, exhibitions
of shows, plays and other expensive diversions and entertainments' ",[1] the output of writers utilizing the dramatic form to
contain their thoughts increased.[2] Although the truth of Beard's
statement that throughout the Revolution, the theatre "had suf-
fered a serious setback", may be debated, the appearance of the
first concerted effort to depict dramatically the foreigner can not
be denied.[3]

On the smoke of gunpowder blew the spirit of sovereignty; with
nationalism burgeoned propaganda; with the emergence of the
American propaganda play came the British villain. After the
dead Americans had been counted at Lexington, Concord, Bunker
Hill, and Quebec, the patriotic drama raised paeans to the heroism

---

[1] Beard, p. 465.
[2] Hill, pp. 136-138, lists seven plays for 1770-75, and twelve for 1775-80.
[3] Beard, p. 465.

of those martyred in the face of overwhelming odds and by despicable acts on the part of the enemy. A red coat crossed with white gaiters or a sentiment in the slightest anti-American sufficed to herald the arrival of the villain. Hugh Brackenridge, in 1776, wrote of the conflict near Boston in *The Battle of Bunkers-Hill*. The British officers in this play not only offer their troops plunder, land, and titles if they win, but hide during the battle, and then have recriminations of guilt about the whole affair once it is over. The Americans speak in lofty periods:

> *Gardiner:* But since we combat in the cause of God
> I draw my sword, nor shall the sheath again,
> Receive the shining blade, till on the heights,
> Of CHARLES-TOWN, and BUNKER's pleasant HILL,
> It drinks the blood of many a warrior slain.

While the British complain:

> *Burgoyne:* How long brave gen'rals, shall the
> rebel foe,
> In vain arrangements, and mock siege, display
> Their haughty insolence?

Not content to let the matter rest there, Brackenridge, in a stroke similar to the one used by Mercy Warren in *The Group*, has an English general characterize the Americans so as to make a comparison unfavorable to the British.

> *Howe:*   ... A people brave,
> Who never yet, of luxury, or soft
> Delights, effeminate, and false, have tasted.
> But, through hate of chains, and slav'ry, suppos'd,
> Forsake their mountain tops, and rush to arms.

Howe describes an early example of an American Adam. Issuing from the simple and bucolic setting, strong and virtuous, willing to fight trammelling tyranny, veritably Rousseauistic, the innate valor of the American soldier spurs Howe to regret his assignment:

> Would to Almighty God,
> The task unnatural, had been assigned,
> Elsewhere.

The description acquires dramatic power through Brackenridge's device of placing it in Howe's speech. What could denigrate more than to have a ranking Briton aware of the incomparable valor of his enemy, especially when that enemy has been emphasizing the utter evil of the usurpers? The extreme depravity of an already unsympathetic national group is enhanced by causing one of the important officers to decry the perfidy of his own cause, no matter how slight the dramatic probability of such an occurrence.

Were one to search assiduously through the corpus of dramatic literature, it would be difficult to find characters who could sink as low as these British. Brackenridge, spurred to heights of emotion by the impetus of civil war, a cause to further, and the bitter sense of injustice, manages to pluck some comfort from the defeat at Bunker Hill. Burgoyne complains that the battle did not go as well as it should have.

> Who could have thought it, in the womb of time,
> That British soldiers, in this latter age,
> Beat back by peasants, and in flight disgrac'd,
> Could tamely brook the base discomfiture;
> Nor sallying out, with spirit reassum'd,
> Exact due tribute of their victory?
> Drive back the foe, to Alleghany hills,
> In woody vallies, or on mountain tops,
> To mix with wolves and kindred savages.

Brackenridge's point is, of course, that no one reared in a land ruled by a monarch could ever imagine valor among the peasantry. But in America, the natural benefits of inhabiting those selfsame mountain tops and valleys where Burgoyne would have driven the rebels, inculcates in the Sons of Liberty a love for the cause of freedom and an inspiration to accomplish heroic deeds. Howe replies to Burgoyne in the quotation that commences, "A people brave . . ." (p. 38), and lauds the indomitable spirit springing from contact with the simple life of the soil. The only alleviating circumstance Brackenridge affords the enemy officers occurs when they experience the pangs of guilt. Apparently the author conceived of the British generals as possessing sufficient sensibility to realize the error of their ways, even though they could behave in no other manner. Gage, weighing the cause of George and Empire against the evidence of chained and starved peoples held captive by the English, has prickings of conscience, "Oh guilt, thy blackness, hovers on the mind, / Nor can the morning dissipate thy shades."

In explicit comparison to the American officers, the Britishers rank poorly. Prior to the battle, Howe offers the Red Coats plunder, land, and titles in the new world if they win the battle and the war. Warren, however, speaks to his troops of liberty and freedom, while Gardiner holds out the precepts of honor, justness, and the virtuous character of the continent as the bases for the American cause. During the battle, Gage creeps off to hide behind his troops, while Warren dies nobly in the vanguard, calling upon his men to fight valiantly. The Americans struggle well and long against impossible odds (Howe, to encourage his soldiers, assures them that they outnumber the Americans ten thousand to seven hundred). In the epilogue to the play, Brackenridge recounts the horrors of the battle's aftermath, closing with the statement that the English refused Christian funerals to the fallen Americans.

Brackenridge sets up a series of comparisons in the play, each one unfavorable to the British. First, he opposes both factions' reasons for fighting the war. To the Briton the war represents the effort to retain part of an empire, to hold a naturally free people in bondage. The American views it as the precise opposite, answering the call to arms willingly since he needs to defend not only his land and freedom, but his family from the rapine and plunder of the Red Coats. On the one hand, Brackenridge perceives a scurrilous cause, and on the other a noble one. Next he compares the natures of the commanders. Howe, Gage, Burgoyne, and Clinton all bluster before the battle, promise their troops plunder and the chance to work their will on the conquered people, cower rather than face danger, and in moments of self-introspection question the very motives of their cause. Warren, Putnam, and Gardiner refer to the noble cause of protecting the homeland, offer the troops nothing but freedom and glory if they win the battle, and fight hardily in the van where two of them fall. The American soldiers need no spur to battle but the knowledge that they move in defense of a just cause, while the British troops must be urged on by promises of riches, titles, and odds greatly in their favor. The characterization for the British as represented by Brackenridge during the first year of the Revolution remained in force in his plays and in the dramatic pieces of other American patriots until the peace was ratified. The ways in which the enemy perpetrated his nefarious purposes differed in degree but not in nature. Outright ridicule, the only method for further calumniating the British not employed by Brackenridge in either of his plays, occurs in the next drama, written during the same year as *The Battle of Bunkers-Hill*.

The violence of dramatic reaction to the war increased apace with the initial progress of the Revolution. In 1776 appeared *The Blockheads, or the Affrighted Officers* – its author choosing to submit to historical obscurity rather than to sign his name. *The Blockheads*, a propaganda play, caricatured the British blockaded in Boston. Quinn states that General Burgoyne's farce, *The Blockade,* first performed in Boston, 1776, inspired *The Blockheads* to be written in reply.[4] The plight of the besieged British was parlous, according to our anonymous patriot, for supplies and foodstuffs stood at a decided ebb. In the fourth scene of Act II, the British troops prepare for inspection:

Here is exhibited a prospect of the light horse, being so weak, are supported by ropes to keep them on their legs; the groom busy in giving them glisters – also, a review of their troops: – the whole looking like French cooks, in a hot day's entertainment; each company favor'd with a close stool pan.

Officers: Gentlemen soldiers, we are now agoing to fight against these *rebel dogs*; be not discouraged, but let us play the man.

Soldiers: We had much rather fight for a *good pudding*.

Ridicule serves as an excellent ingredient of effective propaganda. Burgoyne is satirized as Lord Dapper, spindly and tottering, engaged in an *affaire du coeur* with one of the less savory female members of the Bostonian Loyalists. In the end the British retreat

[4] Quinn, p. 46. See also Chapter IV for further comment on both the British and American plays. This play has been erroneously attributed to Mercy Warren.

from Boston, taking with them the Tories who pilfer as they depart.

At no point in the patriotic drama of the Revolution did British characters behave in as unconscionably evil a manner as in Brackenridge's second play, *The Death of General Montgomery* (1777). More a dramatic poem than poetic drama, the work details the events of Montgomery's abortive campaign against Quebec in 1775. Brackenridge spends as much energy relating the vileness of the British garrison in general and its commander in particular, as he does lauding the selfless and gloriously patriotic fervor of the American officers and troops. In the first act, Montgomery recounts how Carleton, the British commandant at Quebec, slew an ox and encouraged the Indians under his command to drink its blood as the symbol of Bostonian blood.

> *Montgomery:* [Carleton] Did call, the Savages,
>   to taste of blood,
> Lifewarm, and streaming, from the bullock slain,
> And with fell language, told it was the blood,
> Of a Bostonian, made the sacrement.
> At this, the Hell-hounds, with infernal gust,
> To the snuff'd wind, held up, their blood-stain'd
>   mouths,
> And fill'd, with howlings, the adjacent hills.

Brackenridge footnotes the passage with "What indeed could serve, to give us a more horrible idea, of the diabolical spirit of tyranny, than to have presented to our view, General Carleton, or his officers, by his derection, convening the Indians, at Montreal; roasting an ox, and inviting them, under that symbol, to partake of a Bostonian?" Later, when a group of American troops surrender to Carleton after he has promised honorable treatment, he reviles them, selecting three to be furnished his Indians as sacrifices. He relents only when he reflects that the siege has not lifted, and he might receive the same meed if the battle turns. Brackenridge footnotes his dramatic poem with quotations from correspondence between Congress and Carleton, soldiers' accounts, and allusions to the assumption that virtue succumbs to evil when tyrannical motives grip men's minds. Carleton stands as prime example of a man rendered despotic by living under monarchical rule.

Equally as polemic and just as vindictive against enemies of the Revolutionary government were the plays which dealt more specifically with American Loyalists or Tories. Prior to the Revolution, Mercy Warren had excoriated the British sympathizers of Boston. During the Revolution, feeling ran even more heavily agianst countrymen who turned from the colonial cause. If anything, Whig playwrights treated the Loyalists to dramatic scorn and vilification equal to that accorded the British foreigners. In *The Blockheads,* mentioned in a previous paragraph, the Tories are represented as hogs, litters of pigs, and broods of spaniels, "spewing in one another's mouths" aboard the ships that take them from Boston. *The Motley Assembly* (1779), attributed to Mercy Warren, satirizes that group of Bostonians who thought it *de rigueur* to scoff at the aims of the Revolution. A final example, *The Double Conspiracy,* was published in 1783, after the peace had been ratified. The author (thought by some to be Hartford wit John Trumbull) deals specifically with the actions of Tories who traded with the British from behind American lines. Patriots discover a conspiracy to invade and lay waste to the mainland from Long Island. They are thwarted by popular sentiment in their attempts to seize the known Tories, but declare that posterity will judge them correct. The Tories are depicted as despicable creatures who would sell their souls for a title and their daughters for pleasure. The British show moral turpitude equal to that of the Tories since they willingly employ such immoral types in their efforts to win the war.

With the establishment of the thirteen colonies as the United States of America, the need for immediately apprehensible British villains passed. The war and its drama had established the Briton – formerly a compatriot – as an antagonist and a foreigner who pillaged, plundered, raped, and murdered; or as a soldier hopelessly and ludicrously incompetent. Peacetime brought other problems to the fore, domestic ones. Yet the character of the foreigner who behaved villainously because he stood against Americans and democracy remained in the minds of the people. As late as the

1820's, a few playwrights handling Revolutionary material opposed the automatically recognizable British villain established fifty years previous to their historical American heroes.[5]

To return to a temporal sequence, the next appearance of the foreigner unsympathetic because of his antipathy towards democracy occurred after reaction to the French Revolution of 1789 had set in. At first Americans were taken with the obvious parallel between the French attempt and their own successful Revolution of a few years past. But after the establishment of the French Republic of 1792 and the French declaration of war on the British, Federalists tended to favor the British in the measure that they regretted the bellicose excesses of the French extremetists. At the same time, Jeffersonian Republicans (who took the name of Democrats) could only envision the neutral United States as having refused to honor the debt owed to the French for aid during the American Revolution.[6] Depending upon the political affiliations of the playwright, despicable or admirable Frenchmen appeared in drama in the late 1790's. Of the anti-French plays, the anonymous *The French Revolution* (1790) stands out among Federalist works. The dramatist announces that his play has been acted twice – first at Dartmouth in 1790.[7] He obviously did not rewrite the play after Louis XVI lost his head in 1792, for the 1793 edition of the play ends with Louis, advised by LaFayette, establishing a constitutional monarchy.[8] The noblemen falsely counsel Louis,

[5] Samuel Woodworth's *King's Bridge Cottage* (1826) and Mordecai M. Noah's *Marion* (1822), to name two.

[6] Dunlap, on p. 111 of his *History of the American Theatre*, refers to events of 1794 that indicate the situation. "As marking the state of the public mind at this time, we notice a circumstance, otherwise insignificant: Hodgkinson, when he came on the stage for Captain Flash, in *Miss in Her Teens*, dressed, as the part always is, in an English uniform, was hissed and called upon by the French party, who could not look at an English officer's coat without being in a rage, to 'take it off.' He came forward, and to the satisfaction of the French partisans, said, he represented a coward and a bully. Unfortunately, this was running on Charybdis to avoid Scylla, and the English partisans threatened vengeance on the actor."

[7] Quinn, p. 448.

[8] "The author, from his most extensive knowledge of history, had acquainted himself with many of the particular motives which stimulated Louis to action. – We have here a confirmation for our belief, that when Louis acted free, and unbiassed by bad counsel, he was nobly humane."

immorally prey upon the peasantry, and act villainously as they denounce equality and democracy. Says one of them:

> Far sooner shall the gates of hell prevail
> Against the Church, built on th'eternal rock,
> Than French nobility be brought to treat,
> In common with a beggar'd race of peasantry.

The climate of opinion which estimated the Republic of 1792 as a regrettable result of the Revolution permitted the Frenchman to find his way into plays as antagonist for reasons connected to, but other than anti-democratic sentiments. J. Robinson's *The Yorker's Stratagem* (1792) is a comedy which takes place in the West Indies, where Robinson had acted in the Old American Company. In it appears a somewhat humorous Frenchman who attempts to run off with the miser's wife. ("No, I assures you I love you vid a passion si vive, que je ne puis pas vivre that I can not live vidout you. A comme vous etez joli Venus meme est moins belle qui vous . . ." says the Frenchman.) Despite his comic characteristics, the Frenchman receives far from a comic comeuppance. He turns out to be a deserter and is hanged. Robinson must have felt secure enough about a favorable public reaction to create a French serio-comic character whose neck is summarily stretched for acts no worse than those of the miser-villain of the piece. Public sentiment would not have supported similar treatment of a Frenchman a brief five years earlier.

In 1798 John Murdoch had *The Politicians, or a State of Things* published. Monsieur Aristocrat, a French character in the play who vacillates with every change of French policy, asks American O'Callaghan Sarcastic what he thinks of the new Gallic government. Sarcastic replies that "your countymen [sic] are behaving damn'd uncivil to us". Monsieur Aristocrat grows angry, saying of America, "She ave done us wrong, and we will make you smoke for it." In Act II, Sawney Biscuit of Scotland takes to task Adz, an American ingrate, for not appreciating his government. The Irish immigrants also receive their share of verbal abuse for objecting vehemently to an unfamiliar yet benevolent government as soon as they arrive from the old sod. Appearing in the same year as the

Alien and Sedition Acts, Murdoch's play formed a dramatic argument for the desirability of Adams' government. It represented the viewpoint of those Americans who, alarmed at the strength of domestic opinion sympathetic to the French then beginning to prey upon American ocean commerce, attempted to silence Democratic reaction to Federalist politics. Mere possession of an anti-American sentiment sufficed to create without further characterization – as in Revolutionary patriotic drama – a villain.

Continuing into the early nineteenth century, the antipathetic treatment of foreign characters expressing rudimentary anti-democratic sentiments may be discerned in Samuel Elliot's (authorship doubtful) *Fayette in Prison* (1802) and James Workman's *Liberty in Louisiana* (1804). The first of the pair contains antagonistic Austrians who imprison LaFayette at Olmutz. Since LaFayette actually held firm position next to Washington as Hero of the Revolution, and since, in the play, he lauds the Americans and their fight for freedom;

> *LaFay:* When the brave yeomen of Columbia's
> fields,
> Impell'd by ALBION'S insolence arose,
> And led by WASHINGTON, their shackles broke,
> Twas there I found and serv'd a gallant people,
> Of manners unaffected, souls sincere. –

any character who treats LaFayette without deference and respect becomes a villain. The Major at Olmutz, a monarchist, fulfills the requirements for villainy: he separates LaFayette from his family and sends him to a deep dungeon for attempting to overthrow, as the charges read, a monarchy. In the second play, Don Bertoldo de la Plata, one of the Spanish grandees inhabiting New Orleans just before the Louisiana Purchase, unjustly adjudicates cases in his court room. After the Americans arrive and the Don receives his due, a long speech by the governing general on the attributes of American government and justice clarifies the moral of the play. Despite his comicality, Don Bertoldo serves as the warped character whose actions show American audiences what can happen when a people do not enjoy the felicities of the democratic system.

B. HISTORICAL PARALLELS: POLITICAL AND MORAL

As soon as the smoke had blown from the battlefields of the Revolution, American dramatists commenced digging about in history in order to dredge up parallels that, when polished, would reflect a favorable glow on the new Republic. While many of these plays, since their action occurs in remote locales and eras, could hardly be considered to contain realistic notions of contemporary foreigners, they nevertheless present pro-democratic, anti-foreign political sentiments through either message or characterization. In each of the representative plays chosen to illustrate this type, a tyrant or tyrannical form of government falls or is intended to fall beneath the efforts of some libertarian and patriot. Commencing with Peter Markoe's *The Patriot Chief* (1784) (in which the righteous monarch triumphs over a tyrannical upstart), and continuing into the nineteenth century to include Frances Wright's *Altorf* (1819) (a romantic love story set against the Swiss rebellion), each one of these plays sings the merits of democracy while it cries death to other more tyrannous forms of government. The sentiment contained in these plays, although they would not seem to comment on contemporary affairs at first glance, definitely may be deemed anti-foreign. Americans, enamored of their own governmental system, sought time and again to reassure themselves of its excellence.

Following Markoe's play[9] by more than a decade, William Dunlap's opera (in the eighteenth-century sense of the term – today it would be called an operetta) *The Archers* (1796) takes place in thirteenth-century Switzerland. Dunlap follows the broad outlines of the legend of William Tell, utilizing the apple incident, the meeting of the leaders of the three rebelling cantons, and the battle against the Austrians. While all the characters in the play are nominally foreigners, Dunlap intends the American audience to identify itself with the Swiss. Gesler, as in the legend, rules as tyrant over the Swiss, commanding obeisance to his hat hanging in the market at Altdorf. When Gesler has been killed, the Austrians beaten off, and a momentary truce declared, Tell speaks to the

[9] *The Patriot Chief* was discussed in Chapter I.

Austrian, Duke Leopold, in a strain that sounds as if it could have been written by Brackenridge or Leacock and placed in the mouth of an American leader of the Revolution:

> *Tell:* In nature's scale, I'm noble as the noblest:
> She made me man, and vice has ne'er debased me.
> Republicans no other nobles know.

Tell possesses natural virtue, valor, and a sense of equality: three concomitants of the true republican.[10] Naturally, all who oppose Tell and his Swiss compatriots must be viewed as anti-democratic; through their failure teaching a lesson to those unsympathetic to the American system.

The Joan of Arc story appears in American dramatic literature two years after Dunlap's retelling of the Swiss fight for independence. John D. Burk's *Female Patriotism* (1798) presents the precepts of democracy and freedom in mortal struggle with those of tyranny and oppression. Not only do the French led by Joan fight against the usurping British (a situation which would strike a responsive note in an early American mind), but the Dauphin, an avowed constitutional monarchist prior to his coronation, turns despot once the crown covers his brow. Monarchs, possessing absolute power, corrupt quickly. Chastel and the Dauphin converse in the first act, before Joan appears to turn the French fortune. Chastel, honest and forthright Gallic commander, propounds a democratic heritage for man's dignity.

> *Chastel:* My lord, I pray your pardon, if I use
> The privilege your goodness has allowed
> Of speaking truth; the fault is not in France,
> But in the species; man is not the same,
> The reasoning, brave, and proudly generous being,
> That in Rome's republic aw'd the world,
> Or in the Grecian states exalted *man*
> As high in greatness as our mortal state
> Could well admit. In commonwealths alone,
> We find this soaring dignity of mind,
> That loves the vast and aims at the sublime:
> Where now in all this land to save his country,

---

[10] An example of an American Adam, several centuries and several thousand miles removed.

> Could we a Scaevola or a Curtius find?
> *Dauphin:* Thou'rt right my friend;
> In monarchies the king is paramount,
> And man is nothing; holding life itself,
> (Tenure precarious) on another's will:
> The reasoning being sunk into a slave,
> He drops his spirit's agency and moves
> A mere machine. . . .[11]

Joan arrives, a latter-day Scaevola, to answer Chastel's question concerning saviors. As soon as she gets to know Chastel, she recognizes him as a defender of virtue in an immoral court. To this point in the play, the only animus is aimed at the British, whom Chastel describes to their faces in terms that would have pleased a patriot writing during the American Revolution:

> My name is Chastel, and my country France
> Which I do love as dearly as my soul,
> And much as I detest you, British wolves,
> Who with insatiate fury prey upon it,
> My principles are, love of liberty,
> And hatred and contempt of foul oppression;
> War's my possession, and my object, glory;
> What wouldst thou more?
>
>   * * *
>
> I am no rebel!
> 'Tis not the man who strikes at lawless power,
> But the proud tyrant, who doth tread on laws,
> On honor, wisdom, liberty, and faith,
> Who should possess the stain of such a name.

Joan solicits a promise from the Dauphin to form a constitutional monarchy once he has been crowned at Reims. Her position is all the stronger since, in response to the Dauphin's query about divine guidance, she answers,

> . . . my story was a pious fraud

[11] This patently didactic passage contains an argument that recurs constantly in early American patriotic drama. Ignoring the British and Swiss-French heritage of their ideas, the polemic playwrights maintained as self-evident truth that only in a republic or commonwealth could mind and body, both unfettered, develop their fullest potential. The argument totters on weak foundations, but fortunately, few Americans were of a mind to contest it.

> To raise the fainting courage of the land:
> If there be fault in it, O God forgive me;
> I thought it not a crime, and hope it none.

Burk thus easily separates Church and State in the ideal monarchy Joan battles to found. Of couse, the British, by enlisting the false aid of religion in the person of the traitorous Bishop of Beauvais, deepen the tincture of their own guilt in oppressing the French. Burk carefully opposes to the many admirable and libertarian aims of Chastel and Joan the scurrilous and despotic desires of the Bishop and the British. After his coronation the Dauphin reneges on his royal word, refuses to free the French peasants from bondage, and refrains from ransoming Joan, who had been captured through a nefarious British trick. Chastel dares to upbraid the King, who immediately orders that Chastel be put to the sword. The troops refuse to obey the King, since they respect and love their honorable and equitable commander. As she languishes in her dungeon, Joan writes a prophetic letter to Chastel. It closes on the prognostication that:

A virtuous band of English colonists, whose love of freedom forc'd them to imigrate to a vast unknown land beyond the great waters, shall first throw down the gauntlet to kings, and overturn the throne of their tyrant. – France will follow her example; shall overturn all thrones, and exterminate all tyrants. The nations of the earth will forget their former antipathies: Even England shall stretch out the arm of friendship to France. – This letter is the substance of a vision, and I almost pronounce it prophecy.

Once again those who uphold and attempt to establish democracy and equality maintain the protagonist's position, while all opposers to democracy's champion become ignoble antagonists. There exists no shadings between the extremes. One either stands for democracy or against it. The degree of villainy perpetrated by the antagonists functions in direct ratio to the strength of the democratic reforms proposed by the protagonist. For that reason the antagonists, although appearing but briefly in the drama, acquire a great share of opprobrium.

Another play by John D. Burk, *Bunker Hill,* was produced at the Haymarket Theatre in Boston. This theatre was opened in

1796 by Democrats to compete with the Federalist biased Federal Street Theatre. The manager of the Haymarket, Charles Powell, saw to it that many patriotic and anti-British dramas were put on to appeal to the anti-Federalists. *Bunker Hill,* played during the first season, construes the British as lawbreakers and murderers, a depiction which would have been welcomed by a Democratic audience. The rivalry must have worn thin by 1798, for on April 16 of that year was produced Everett's *Daranzel,* a play that reacts against the extremetists of the French Revolution and praises the incumbent American government. Of course the "XYZ affair" and French interference with American shipping may well have caused sufficient Democratic anger against France that David Everett's play could use history to point an anti-French moral to the Haymarket audience. While in the prologue Everett admonishes "Columbia's sons" to prize their land "where rules a chief, whose power is all your own", he closes the play by having Daranzel offer the vanquished tyrant life in return for an equitable rule. The tyrant refuses, duels with Daranzel, then kills himself. The playwright wished to point up the uselessly violent deeds of Danton, Robespierre, and the extremetists which led to the *Directoire* and Franco-American schism.

Marmion by James N. Barker, the most interesting play of the historical group unfavorably depicting men who upheld tyrannous forms of government, appeared under the guise of a British play at the Park Theatre in New York, April 13, 1812. In his preface to the second edition of 1816, Barker mentions the deception as necessary, since plays received recognition not as a result of intrinsic merit but according to which side of the Atlantic the author called his home.[12] (The complaint of many early American playwrights and authors since the late 1780's.) Marmion, as in Scott's poem, is the British scoundrel-nobleman who defeats the Scotch pretender, James IV, at Flodden Field. In the 1812 version of the play, Barker causes Marmion to confront James with an offer for com-

---

[12] Public taste accepted British judgment as arbiter in matters of fashion and art, a condition which existed especially in the eastern American cities until after the War of 1812. American authors, in particular, thought themselves unjustly treated by Anglophilic critics. See Chapter Five for a further discussion of this phenomenon.

promise. James replies rather mildly: "In vain you lure me with these airy scenes." Yet in 1816, after the play proved a success, after Barker admitted authorship, and after Jackson's victory at New Orleans, James' defiance takes a different tone:

> I know it all. The nation the most selfish,
> Presuming, arrogant, of all this globe,
> Professes but to fight for others' rights,
> While she alone infringes every right.
>
> * * *
>
> England insults us with the true complaint
> That we are partial; for she shows by this,
> She thinks our senses are too dull and blunt
> To know who wounds us and who gives the balm.

Marmion's maleficence does not change that much between the two editions; he still schemes do work his will on innocent womanhood and plots to outmaneuver James. The difference lies, of course, in the strength of republican sentiment present in the sympathetic characters. The ratio mentioned in connection with *Female Patriotism* holds valid for this play. Once Barker showed his colors – after public opinion about the British had shifted because of the War of 1812 – he waved the Stars and Stripes with a vigor consonant with his Republican political affiliation. Britain as much as Marmion serves as antagonist.

Isaac Harby continued and strengthened the vogue for history-twisting with his *Alberti* (1818). This play takes place in fifteenth-century Florence, where Alberti defends the de Medici "republic" against Naples and Rome until all the states unite to fend off the Moslems who threaten the peninsula. Isaac also complains bitterly about the critical climate which will not permit American plays laudatory of American virtues to receive their full due.

To regard the place of an author's birth as necessarily connected with the merits or demerits of his productions – to view him through that medium alone, in which smoky war – not cheerful literature – presents her victories – may be very spirited and very national; but it would be rather difficult to convince the world that *Criticism*, under such banners, can be either just, useful, or liberal.

One year later Fanny Wright saw her *Altorf* produced. In the preface she orates:

England pretends to an unshackled press; but there is not a stage in England from which the dramatist might breathe the sentiments of enlightened patriotism and republican liberty. In America alone might such a stage be formed; a stage that should be, like that of Greece, a school of virtue; – where all that is noble in sentiment, generous and heroic in action should speak to the hearts of a free people, and inspire each rising generation with all the better and nobler feelings of human nature.

Probably a modicum of truth peeps past Fanny's passion, for she had arrived in America not long before its republican freedom inspired her to write *Altorf*. The play treats the same subject matter as Dunlap's *The Archers;* only in Frances Wright's work a love story concerning the fatal passion between already married Captain Altorf of the Swiss army and Rosina, daughter of Austrian Count de Rossberg, takes precedence over the battle for independence. Yet the Count and the Austrians are antipathetic primarily because the Count manages to bring about Altorf's defection through his love for Rosina, and secondarily because they attempt to subjugate Switzerland to tyranny. Fanny's republican sentiments ran a poor second to her romantic instincts.

American playwrights not only turned to the distant past in order to find monarchy, aristocracy, oligarchy, and tyranny to juxtapose to illustrious democracy, but sought the stuff for lessons in the present and near-past. Plays such as *The French Revolution* (1790), Sarah Pogson's *The Female Enthusiast* (1807), Edward Hitchcock's *The Emancipation of Europe* (1815), and Jonathan S. Smith's *The Siege of Algiers* (1823) all contain foreign governments, governors, or aristocrats who become antagonists in the drama because of their enmity toward egalitarian and democratic ideas. *The French Revolution,* previously discussed, serves as a ready example. *The Female Enthusiast* interweaves a love interest and the story of Charlotte Corday, who stabbed Jacobin terrorist Marat in his bath on July 13, 1793. Pogson dramatized Marat as vicious and bloodthirsty, Charlotte as sensitive and patriotic. The Jacobins, once Charlotte's deed has been discovered, pillage her father's home. The Corday family leaves for America to escape the excesses of the Reign of Terror. Hitchcock, in *The Emancipation of Europe*, views all anti-Napoleonic factions sympathetically. Bonaparte and Marshal Ney are represented as genocidal atheists who gleefully order conquests despite the decimation of the French male population.

> *Bonaparte:* This world was surely made for me
> to rule
> But if 'twas not, by me it shall be ruled.
> If this required each drop of blood in France
> It matters not. What are men's lives to me?
> The same as is a revenue. The rabble
> Were ever meant to be so used as best
> Convenience suits – just as we use a coin.

The Siege of Algiers is a tedious polemic of one hundred and forty pages. Smith levelled his disapprobation at the entire Algierian situation. American and foreign consuls, Algierian governmental offices and officers, the Dey, the paying of tribute to the Barbary pirates – all receive broadside upon broadside of inaccurate but heavy satire. In the playwright's words: "In this drama will be . . . strongly exemplified the great contrast between the government, custom, and manners of unlettered despotism, and those of the more free and enlightened nations . . ." Self-righteous vanity, a trait not universally admired, seems the one characteristic to dominate this drama of the early republic.

To reiterate, let it be emphasized that in the majority of the post-Revolutionary plays which present a political moral through the medium of some sort of historically foreign anti-tyrannical conflict, it is impossible to discern – as was present in the patriotic drama of the Revolution – the figure of a foreign type whose characteristics stemmed solely from antipathetic opinions and biases held by the American populace. Yet these plays reveal a mode of thought which persisted long into the nineteenth century. The American viewed himself as having created a political paradise that had no equal anywhere else on the globe. So taken was he with his accomplishment that he cried out for a native literature and culture which would express his ideals. While playwrights as early as Dunlap, in *The Father* (1789), deplored the apparently unfair critical practice of judging European plays, *prima facie,* the better, there nevertheless existed in the United States a climate favorable enough for the nurture of the near-chauvinism exhibited by these plays. The playwrights' attitudes toward oligarchies, monarchies, and aristocracies define a general notion of the foreigner as either oppressed (if he were one of the lower classes) or oppressing (the governing class). Exuberant over the success of the American experiment, people in the young Republic refused to concede any beneficence to a form of government different from their own. Not content to crow among themselves, they attempted to proselytize anyone who would listen. That previously unsuccessful conflicts between freedom and oppression had occurred prior to their own Revolution served to point the favorite moral: men are created equal naturally, and democracy is therefore the natural government. Even fairly contemporaneous European and African history, slightly strained to suit the message, assisted in reassuring Americans that every man would enjoy democracy if only he could manage to convince his despot of its benefits.

Along with the political differentiae noted by the playwrights discussed just above, Americans also thought they possessed a more lustrous set of mores than others of their world. Living in a democracy not only gave one the political advantage over one's foreign contemporaries, but the liberation from trammels and restrictions enjoyed by early republicans, startlingly enough, did not result in a wave of immorality and crime. This realization, coupled to the commentary of post-Revolution travellers from abroad such as Isaac Weld, Frances Wright d'Arusmont, or Captain Hall, nurtured an already thriving sense of difference between the new and old worlds. Theories about the superiority of American mores over those of older and more degenerate countries burgeoned. Americans sought to set themselves apart by every means available, and their comparisons did not reflect unfavorably upon the new Republic.

Commencing with David Humphrey's *The Widow of Malabar* (1790),[13] American playwrights sought for the entire period

---

[13] That Humphrey translated and adapted the play from Le Mierre's *La Veuve de Malabar* (1770) raises no valid objection, since he saw in it a comparison to be drawn.

under scrutiny, to dramatize the shortcomings of other codes of ethics and mores (at the same time reaffirming the transcendent excellence of their own!). Humphrey's prologue serves well to initiate one to the strength of self-satisfied sentiment expressed by early American authors.

> Oh! born to bless, and meliorate mankind,
> With manners winning, and with taste refin'd,
> What wrongs, ye fair! your gentle bosoms bore,
> In each rude age – on ev'ry barb'rous shore!
> Doom'd the mean vassals of unfeeling lords,
> By Western Savages, and Tartar Hords!
> Through Asian climes, see custom reason braves,
> And marks the fairest of their sex for slaves:
> Hearts form'd for love, but doom'd in vain to glow
> In prison'd pomp, and weep in splendid woe: –
> Or see their fate in India more severe,
> The sad companions of a husband's bier! –
>
> Not such their doom where genial science shines,
> And Heav'n-born freedom, human souls refines;
> Where polish'd manners social life improve,
> And teach us to respect the sex we love;
> Confirm their claims in equal rights to share
> Friends in our bliss, and partners in our care: –
> And hail, ye fair, of ev'ry charm possess'd –
> Who grace this rising empire of the West;
> With better fates, and nobler genius born,
> Your sex to honour, and your land adorn;
> In this blest age, to share our fond regard,
> The friends of heroes, and their blest reward! –
>
> Yet when o'er foreign woes ye shed a tear,
> And find your bliss by contrast still more dear;
> With humble joy adore th'Almighty hand,
> Which fixed your birth in this auspicious land!

Forty years later early suffragettes such as Fanny Wright would disagree not with the spirit, but with the letter of Humphrey's prologue – but for the first decade after the establishment of the United States, the sentiment does it author credit. The play hardly equals its preamble, being an exposé of the Brahman custom of suttee. The beauteous widow, Lanissa, after many hesitations, refuses to immolate herself. The presence of her French lover as commanding general of the besieging army provides the strongest motive for her choice.

In 1798 Charles Stearns had five hundred and forty pages of exemplary dialogues published. Among these may be found such cautionary playlets as *The Gamester, The Female Gamester,* and *Bernard of Berlin.* Significantly enough, each of the plays in which Stearns unfolds some vice for the enlightenment of his American audience has its scene set in a foreign land. The gamester is a Dutch husband who, unlike wiser American spouses, refuses to heed his wife and gambles away their fortune (happily to his brother-in-law, who returns it with the proper admonitions). In *The Female Gamester* Mrs. Ombre holds an open gaming table for women during her soirées in Brighton. The delicate gamblers come to no good. They lose their money, their suitors, and their husbands. Bernard of Berlin spreads his money and favors too profusely. In the end his friends turn on him and he perforce retires to an honest, even frugal life on his one remaining farm.

Duelling, the chase, immorality, slavery, loose morals, and alcoholism are treated by, respectively: Charles L. Adams in *Favelle, or the Fatal Duel* (1809), Charles Breck in *The Fox Chase* (1806), William C. White in *The Clergyman's Daughter* (1810), David Everett in *Slaves in Barbary* (ca. 1797), Lemuel Sawyer in *The Wreck of Honor* (1824), William Gilmore Simms in *A Dramatic Dialogue* (1827). Worth notation is British Lord Sindal in *The Clergyman's Daughter.* The consummate evil of his villainy in duping the clergyman, the son, and seducing the daughter must have sent chills of loathing across the nerve endings of the Federal Street Theatre audience in Boston. *The Wreck of Honor* chronicled for an interested spectator the type of manners and morals he might have expected at French courts of the Empire period. Satirically, Sawyer points out how political preferment depended mainly upon one's wife's ability to kiss and, if necessary, follow up the salutation. A courageous American naval Captain works the Boccaccian trick of causing a French Marshal and his wife to spend a night together under the mutual assumption that each had an assignation with another. The Captain dies in action off the Irish coast in the War of 1812, and the tricked and wiser Marechal Folard and his wife decide to leave Napoleon's court for the Land of Promise. Nearly at the end of the period covered by this study, William Gilmore Simms wrote a temperance dialogue. He placed it in Italy, where Chlorine and her child suffer while Ghiraldi, the husband, carouses with his betters.

Britain and the British people furnished a continual source for comparison to America and Americans; especially since many British travellers were far from hesitant about expressing in print their usually unpleasant opinions concerning the natures of the more outstanding Columbian types. In Lord Sindal of *The Clergyman's Daughter* may be discerned a current counter-attack upon the mores of British nobility. Maria Pinckney's *The Orphans* (1818) contains Sir Spendall and Lady Flinty. The scene is laid in England, as in many of these "morality plays", because there the direct reverse of American virtue may be seen. Sir Spendall personifies the weak husband. Although he has all the best intentions in the world about maintaining his younger sisters, he lets his wife dictate the kind of treatment the girls receive. Lady Flinty, representing the shrewish and grasping harridan who refuses to harbor his orphaned younger sisters (and for a reason, since she has been spending their income, and fears they will ask for it), is a study in avaricious womanhood. But let the authoress describe the good lady and her spouse:

The character of Lady Flinty may appear gross and exaggerated, but there are such persons. Violence of an ungoverned bad temper in an ignorant person, with a malevolent heart can do much mischief and compel an husband of a good natured indolent disposition, to act even against his will and so inflict through criminal passiveness, evil upon others and misery on himself.

Lady Flinty manages to have the orphaned sisters removed from the castle, but not until they discover her "reading" the newspaper upsidedown. In the end, the girls find solace and fortune in marrying two rich young men, one of whom, a nobleman and therefore immoral, had first to undergo a change of morality. Specifically, Maria Pinckney wished to point out the difference between European lack of sensibility and the charitable behavior on the part of

American women, whose virtue reciprocally guides and shields them. To this end she not only characterizes the erring Lady Flinty as grasping, shrewish, and lacking in sentiment, but makes her illiterate as well. For had she been able to read, then sentimentalism would have doubtless stamped its impress on her mind. The only people who do not receive a large share of disapprobation are the commoners, such as Freeman, Sir Spendall's brother, and Frederick, the son of a miser. The authoress spent so much of her play depicting the rewards for goodness and perseverance, that she neglected to show Sir Spendall and Lady Flinty in the grasp of poetic justice. Perhaps the audience was meant to reflect that the pair create their own punishment.

A more explicit comparison than that found in *The Orphans* appears in James K. Paulding's *The Bucktails* (ca. 1815).[14] A mine of character types, the play sets off two American brothers and a rich young American lass, living in England, against Obsolete the antiquarian; Lord Nolan the debauched aristocrat; Admiral Gunwale the salty, peglegged, besotted gaffer; Threadneedle the small-souled banker who can not see past his vaults; and Sir Christopher, M. D., knighted for killing – as Lord Nolan puts it – as many of the King's subjects as the Admiral has his enemies. Paulding also continues the comparison between the New England Yankee and his foreign counterpart started by Tyler: Jonathan Peabody and Paddy Whack engage in the servant-exchange, popular since Roman times.

Lest the impression be given that all Americans during the first forty-five years of the Republic imagined that their country could harbor no vice, immorality, or evil, let John B. White and George Watterson speak. Watterson, in *The Child of Feeling* (1809), remarks,

Most of the *few* dramatists of this country seem to have mistaken the principal object of comedy, and have, accordingly, laid their scenes in foreign nations. To satirize the prevailing vices and follies of mankind, is evidently the design of this species of dramatic composition. It becomes, therefore, the peculiar duty of those who devote

[14] In the preface to the 1846 collection, Paulding states that *The Bucktails* was written "shortly after the conclusion of the late war with England".

their attention to the comic muse, to confine themselves particularly
to their own nation, and to satirize such vices and follies as are there
the most frequent and common. . . . Men are too apt to laugh at those
follies, or frown at those vices to which the inhabitants of other
countries are addicted, though they themselves possess them, because
the satire is not particularly levelled at them, or directed at their
countrymen; while they, of consequence, are freed from the apprehension of being made the marked objects of ridicule.

Unhappily, Watterson's play does not show the same assiduous
adherence to the requisites of good comic dramaturgy that his
preface does to perceptive theorizing. John B. White, in 1812,
heeded Watterson's warnings, for in the prologue to *Modern
Honor,* A Friend states:

> No tales of wonder bid the curtain rise
> And point a spectre to your straining eyes:
> No royal crimes, in sable colours shown,
> Make you detest, who never saw a throne;
> Truth, homely truth, directs our Author's plan;
> Life is his picture, and his portrait, man.

White lays the scene "In any part of the *civilized* world". The
action adheres to that of the usual romantic tragedy containing a
villain, a hero, and a long suffering heroine whose brother erroneously kills her lover (the hero). Yet despite the similarity of these
plays to the very drama decried by Watterson, the existence of a
counter-current eddying through such chauvinistic American
drama and rippling its influence out into the lettered population,
marks the exception which either may or may not prove the rule
that Americans thought all iniquity foreign – the proof depending
upon one's susceptibility to apothegms.

C. FOPS, DANDIES, AND TRAVELLERS

The dandy, another type of foreigner whose dramatic vogue endured long past 1830, first simpered onto that institute of fashion,
the post-Revolutionary stage, as a mark for censure in the anonymous *Sans Souci, alias Free and Easy* (1785).[15] Objecting, some-

[15] The play is sometimes attributed to Mercy Warren, but one would

what in the manner of *The Adulateur,* to the imitative British excesses of a portion of Boston society, the playwright includes a catalogue of dandydom in the male characters: Mr. Importance, Jenny Satirist, Doctor Gallant, Mr. Bon Ton, Young Forward, and Little Pert. An allegorical figure, Republican Heroine, complains to the protagonist of the piece, Mrs. W[arre]n:

> I did not carry my enthusiasm so far as to expect to find the rigid Spartan principles practised; but I did conceive to be introduced into societies of frugality and economy ... I am greatly disappointed. British gewgaws – etiquette and parade are too prevailing to be easily eradicated, unless some immediate exertions are made to turn this destructive current.

Dandies, were they foreign or American, grew to stand for the effeminate, un-American excesses of a degenerate and enervating society. Especially during the first few decades of the Republic, when Americans sought dissimilarities between themselves and other peoples, did the epithet "dandy" carry a full measure of pejorative meaning.

The most influential play to contrast an American dandy to his patriotic opposite, the second American play on record to be acted by a professional company in this country, and the play which contains the progenitor of all Yankee characters, Royall Tyler's *The Contrast* (1787), exposes the American fop influenced by unwholesome British manners, suffering from too much Lord Chesterfield. The title of the play gives away the intentions of its author. Tyler carefully contrasts foreign and American manners and customs on a variety of levels. Passing from the lowest on the social scale to the highest, the couples compared are: Jonathan, the natural New England "waiter" (not servant) who can not understand or learn the tricks of fashion, and Jessamy, the overly-fashionable servant of Dimple; Charlotte, the vain, pert belle, sister to Colonel Manly, and Letitia, against Maria the serious American lass; Colonel Manly the true American patriot, and Billy Dimple, wastrel and fop, too widely travelled to know the homey

---

hardly expect that model of Boston propriety to write herself into one of her own plays – no matter how strong her feelings about society's shortcomings.

value of republican sentiment and sensibility. The prologue not only reflects the then powerful movement toward an indigenous culture and theatre, but also presages the attitude struck by the author. It denounces foreign customs, titles, dress, and letters at the same time it attemps to inculcate an attitude of benevolence toward American society, manners, and mores. The contrast, explicit and implicit, in all the previous American drama containing foreign characters, culminates in this play. Tyler, choosing comedy of manners as the form to hold his criticism of foreign attitudes and customs practiced by Americans, supplies a good argument for Americans to cleave to their own republican ways. One must understand, though, that the fullest condemnation falls upon an American who does not follow the dictates of republican sentiment and sensibility, but choose to adhere to effete and decadent foreign customs in his behavior and belief. The travelling European, or even the Britisher against whom Americans had recently fought, did not receive such a large measure of forthright post-war censure. Yet foreign customs are nonetheless condemned, since they may lead a Columbian to pursuits other than those approved of by Americans interested in preserving native mores and manners.

The most important comparison in *The Contrast* sets Dimple, the dandy, against Colonel Manly, rough-hewn American patriot. The first indication that the audience receives concerning Dimple's character occurs almost as soon as the action commences. Letitia describes Dimple before he took his European tour as "a good natured, decent dressing young fellow, with a little dash of the coxcomb, such as our young fellows of fortune usually have". During his tour, the sensible Maria, affianced to the rapidly "dandifying" Dimple, read Richardson and Sterne, became imbued with the uplifting principles of eighteenth-century sentimentality, and fell out of love because "the contrast was so striking betwixt the good sense of her books and the flimsiness of her loveletters". To citizens of America's early republican era, the antipathetic aspect of Dimple's characterization would have been immediately apparent – especially since they soon learned that the travelled and misguided dandy reads a few pages from the immoral Chesterfield each day, then attempts to put those principles into practice. Not only does Dimple affect effete manners and speech, dress *à l'outrance,* behave flippantly toward women, squander his inheritance in vice and game, but he also intends to jilt Maria, marry Letitia for money, and keep Charlotte around as "companion to my wife". Effeteness compounded by extravagance surmounted by immorality!

Colonel Manly, Charlotte's brother, Tyler opposes diametrically to Dimple. Whereas Dimple scoffs at American customs, Manly espouses the virtues of sentimental attachment to country, parents, morality, plain dress, and simple speech and manners. The audience's first sight of Manly sets him against the giggles and trivial gossip of Letitia and Charlotte. Charlotte attempts to gibe at her brother's seriousness, but he answers each comment with common sense designed to exemplify the speech and manners of a true American.

Manly: Forgive me, my sister – I hope I am no enemy to mirth; I love your sprightliness; and I hope it will one day enliven the hours of some worthy man; but when I mention the respectable authors of my existence, – the cherishers and protectors of my helpless infancy, whose hearts glow with such fondness and attachment, that they would willingly lay down their lives for my welfare, you will excuse me, if I am so unfashionable as to speak of them with some degree of reverence and respect.

Manly wears the clothes that served him during the Revolution and Shay's Rebellion, from which active duty he has just returned. He intends to hold on to his commutation notes rather than sell them to speculators, trusting in their eventual redemption by the federal government. His good faith and sentimental nature carries so far as to forbid his attentions to Maria, whom he loves, so long as he thinks that she is betrothed to Dimple, whom he loathes. Manly's curt manner and his obvious dislike for Dimple's flippant attitudes result in clashes whenever they meet. At the end of the play, when Dimple had been exposed for what he is, Manly refuses to answer the call to a duel: "The reputation of my life does not depend upon the breath of a Mr. Dimple." Dimple departs, ironically calling attention to the differences between himself and Manly:

Dimple: ... ladies and gentlemen, I take my leave, and you will please to observe, in the case of my department, the contrast between a gentleman, who has read Chesterfield, and received the polish of Europe, and an unpolished, untravelled, American.

Tyler sets off the sentimental, common-sense Maria against Letitia and Charlotte in the same way that he compares Manly and Dimple. The frivolous pair, minds always on the latest fashion or the most recent ball, bother their heads with no serious thought. Charlotte's brief comment on Maria's sentimentality furnishes an example of their gossip.

Charlotte: A mighty pretty story! And so you would make me believe, that the sensible Maria would give up Dumpling manor, and the all-accomplished Dimple as a husband, for the absurd reason, forsooth, because she despises and abhors him. Just as if a lady could not be privileged to spend a man's fortune, ride in his carriage, be called after his name, and call him her *nown dear lovee* when she wants money, without loving and respecting the great he-creature. Oh! my dear girl, you are a monstruous prude.

Maria, on the other hand, the audience discovers seated at a table strewn with books, disconsolately singing a sentimental little American air about the constancy and stoicism of an Indian. She then soliloquizes on the comparative merits of true courage and the false values attibuted to men of fashion. She can not bring herself really to rejoice that Dimple will be her spouse, even though she acquiesces in the abrupt and ill-natured demands of her father that she prepare herself for the impending nuptials. Maria's ready acceptance of parental will marks the behavior considered exemplary on the part of young women of that era. Letitia and Charlotte, enamored of Dimple as a result of his polished foppishness, almost fall prey to his dishonorable intentions, and in the closing scene are verbally chastised because of their attitudes. Maria, on the other hand, finds a reward in her betrothal to Manly.

The contrast between Jonathan and Jessamy repeats on another social plane the comparison between the Colonel and the fop. Jessamy causes the gullible New England Yankee servant constant social pain. Yet despite Jonathan's position in the drama as the most ludicrous of the comic characters, he strikes a chord of sympathy because his wholesome simpleness of mind make him susceptible to Jessamy's schemes. Were Jessamy to have made Jonathan over into his image, or had Jessamy's schemes been utilized to point up the foibles of the New England Yankee type rather than those of the foppish servant who apes his already ridiculous master, then an audience would have been led to assume that those attributes of Dimple's which were to be condemned, would operate successfully on another level. Jonathan tumbles into each ludicrous situation because his Yankee nature trips him up. When he attends the theatre, his naive reaction (he assumes he was eavesdropping on a family) causes Jessamy to go into gales of laughter. Far from satirizing only foreign peculiarities, Tyler poked fun at the strait-laced Americans whose puritannical proclivities kept them fomenting against all forms of entertainment. Jonathan points up the ludicrous nature of the country bumpkin faced with the marvels of the city as well as he operates in contrast to the social pretensions of Dimple's servant. Yet it must be emphasized that Jonathan's laudable characteristics of patriotism, loyalty to Manly, honesty, constancy, and frugality are never seriously questioned by rendering them ridiculous through jest.

The Contrast is a key play in the portrayal of foreigners and the conveyance of attitudes concerning people and customs of other lands. It includes all the antiforeign elements that Americans thought would set off their splendid and shiny idealistic new government and ethics against the outmoded systems operative in other countries. It was reviewed favorably upon its opening, the critic in the *Daily Advertiser* stating that it was "the production of a man of genius".[16] It played in all the major theatrical centers of the United States, and was finally published in 1790 with an impressive list of subscribers headed by President Washington, and including among others, Aaron Burr, Charles and James Carroll of Maryland, William Dunlap, David Humphreys, Benjamin Harrison, Henry Knox (Secretary of War), Thomas Mifflin (President of Pennsylvania), Baron von Steuben, and Jonathan Trumbull.

The reading and playgoing audiences of the era were aware

[16] Odell, vol. I, pp. 256-257.

of the foreign elements Tyler considered anti-American. They would have immediately extracted the following ideas from *The Contrast* as being those which an American should despise: titles and aristocracy; affected civility and social manners; equation of taste in dress with excellence of character; slavish imitation of European fashion; ridicule of sentimentality and all its attributes; loss of American virtues while travelling abroad; marriage for convenience or cash rather than for love; excessive frivolity; depravity of morals and sentiment; a "heart-insensible to the emotions of patriotism", that "dilates at the plaudits of every unthinking girl"; specious behavior; drinking and gaming; inconstancy; seduction; "bribery, corruption, and force from abroad"; duplicity in manner; the prattle of inconsequential gallantry; outworn and depraved usage and custom; holding foreign culture superior to American; spending time at a frivolous occupation; the substitution of a decadent set of mores acquired abroad for those arising from the natural goodness found in the simple life and ethics of the new Republic. Of course the opposite of each of these un-American vices was to be understood as worthy of acceptance by a citizen of the new democracy. The author, to push home his lesson, specifically reminds the audience in the last two speeches of the play, that everybody can learn how to act in an ideal and natural manner.

Charlotte: ... I now find, that the heart of any worthy man cannot be gained by invidious attacks upon the rights and characters of others; – by countenancing the addresses of a thousand; – or that the finest assemblage of features, the greatest taste in dress, the genteelest address, or the most brilliant wit, cannot eventually secure a coquette from contempt and ridicule.
Manly: And I have learned that probity, virtue, honour, though they should not have received the polish of Europe, will secure to an honest American the good graces of his fair country-woman, and, I hope, the applause of THE PUBLIC.

The ramifications of Tyler's contrast spread through the succeeding decades and affected Americans' conception of themselves. The progeny of characters like Jonathan and Colonel Manly, appearing in such plays as *The Politician Outwitted* (1789), *Jonathan Postfree* (1807), *Tears and Smiles* (1808), *The Yankee in*

England (1815), and *The Forest Rose* (1825), set up an American vs. foreigner kind of comparison. Dimple, Jessamy, or any later contrasting foreigner or dandified American might fulfill the qualification. Such conscious nationalism aided the American from that time forward to differentiate himself from the foreigner; especially from the British, with whom he had been identified before the Revolution. The portrait of the person adhering to British custom or loyalty passed within five years from hateful Tory to a caricature of the Europeanized fop.

In time, the source of the bad example acquired by American dandies removed from Britain to other European countries, the choice of nationality dependent upon the political sympathies of the author. Worthnought, in Federalist Samuel Low's *The Politician Outwitted* (1789), became a fop in France: "Sir, I have the hanor to be, with the profoundest respect and esteem, your most obedient, most devoted, and most obliged humble slave, *foy d'Homme d'Honneur,* – Tol lol, &c. (sings)." Fluttermore, in *Tears and Smiles* (1808), by James N. Barker, also shows the sorry effects of a French influence. Barker's adherence to Jefferson and the Democrats caused him to preface his play with remarks indicating the currency of a low opinion among a coterie concerning value of American customs, goods, and letters: when compared to European counterparts "in fine, this unaccountable prejudice extends to every thing here; the farther, therefore, you remove from America, the nearer you approach to their favour." Washington Irving, on the other hand, complained in 1802 that American youth no longer aimed at that refined nicety of manner that was the rule when he (in the guise of Jonathan Oldstyle) was young.[17] The manners against which Irving inveighs resemble the ones objected to so strenuously as unnatural by Tyler and the author of *Sans Souci*. Not as exaggerated and as gross as Dimple's behavior, the manners described by Jonathan Oldstyle are still far from the ready and brusque forthrightness of Manly's deportment. Behavior once open to censure because of its foreign origin became antipathetic due to its own nature.

[17] Washington Irving, *Letters of Jonathan Oldstyle*, ed. Stanley T. Williams (New York, 1941), p. XIX.

In 1825 Samuel Woodworth repeated in the operetta, *The Forest Rose,* a contrast between British fop and American hero similar to Tyler's Dimple and Manly. Woodworth, indebted to American history for the material in most of his plays, wrote into his comic operetta a British dandy, Bellamy, and an American worthy, Blandford. He also included Jonathan Ploughboy, one of the progeny of Tyler's creation. Bellamy, effete and affected, attempts to carry off a wholesome country lass. He is tricked into a ridiculous situation and upbraided by his onetime friend, Blandford, for his fashionably immoral actions. As Odell says in the third volume of his *Annals of the New York Stage* (p. 203), the play represents "one of the first attempts . . . at the still popular American rural drama". Woodworth contrasts the naturally chaste and moral country life to the less desirable, overly civilized urban existence.[18]

"Everything in nature, when once transported to America, will degenerate", maintains British traveller Captain Flash. Appearing in *The Better Sort* (1789), an operetta by an unknown author, derived from a character in Garrick's *Miss in Her Teens* (1747), the Captain ridicules anything and everything American until his miraculous conversion just before the last duet. Along with Ranter, the servant disguised as an English captain in Dunlap's *The Father* (1789), Flash marks the initial appearance of the travelling foreign dandy in American drama. Destined to a long career, this variety of foreigner, existed not only in drama, but in real life journeyed from town to city. From Weld to Mrs. Trollope, the English traveller – not to mention those from other European countries – came to gape, remark, then publish the peculiarites of Americans. Although an early urban inhabitant would gladden when he learned of the dissimilarity between, in his opinion, a downtrodden citizen of a monarchy and himself, he burst into picturesque epithet when his foibles were ridiculed or criticized.[19]

---

[18] For other treatments of the American dandy as antipathetic see Beach, *Jonathan Postfree* (1807); Watterson, *The Child of Feeling* (1809); Hutton, *Fashionable Follies* (1815); Taylor, *False Appearances* (1819); and for a strange admixture of fop and bumpkin, Brice, *A Country Clown* (1829).

[19] Charles Mathews, *The London Mathews* (London, n.d.), pp. 15-16, and William W. Clapp, *The Boston Stage* (Boston, 1853), pp. 211-212,

In retaliation, playwrights created satires of travellers, by and large British. Murdoch, in 1800, includes the Briton Vainly, "a young foreigner on his travels, carried away by national prejudice, but naturally of a good heart", in *The Beau Metamorphized*. In the end, the ministrations of two charming American damsels bring Vainly to donate two hundred dollars to charity and promise not to ridicule American manners again. Paulding's *The Bucktails,* in which appears the catalogue of English types noted above, stands as the most pointed play to turn a caricaturist's pen against the English.

D. ROMANTIC MOTIVES AND POLITICAL VILLAINS

So emphatically did the Americans of the early Republic estimate that their own way of life held for mankind an ideal to be attained, that to find in drama of the period a native antipathetic character taxes the abilities. Much more available, of course, are the dandies and foreign villains noted in the previous pages. The downright antipathy of the foreigner, however, began to change form under the pressures of time and events. The reaction against the British as a result of the Revolution became tempered by the feelings about the French after 1793. So varied were the sentiments depending upon Federalist or Republican affiliation, as has been previously stated, that a dramatist of that era would be prone to choose his villain in accordance with his own politics.[20] The depiction of Americans in drama, though, remained fairly constant in this period of political turmoil. Seldom, if ever, did one appear as an unsympathetic character whose aberration might be traced to proclivites solely native. The result of it all may be seen in such plays as *The Battle of the Eutaw Springs* (1807),[21] Charles S. Talbot's *Paddy's Trip to America* (1822), Samuel Woodworth's *The Widow's Son* (1825), and Henry J. Finn's *Montgomery*

---

contain two accounts of a reaction to supposed anti-American satire.

[20] See Howard M. Jones, *American and French Culture* (Chapel Hill, 1927), pp. 533-543; and Beard, pp. 366-376.

[21] Erroneously attributed to William Ioor; if this play is compared with his *Independence* (1805), one must conclude that the same man could not have written both.

(1825). These pieces include antagonists whose foreign birth
and attachment serve only as partially unsympathetic qualities
among stronger reasons for their antipathy. In *The Battle of the
Eutaw Springs*, which dramatizes an engagement between British
and Americans in the South during the Revolution, the most mem-
orable character is a comic British trooper by the name of Oliver
Queerfish. He acts with loyalty to his homeland, but decides to
settle in America after peace is declared. A British officer, about
to have his men cut down an American, reacts to a Masonic signal
by calling off the soldiers. The British still tend to be automatically villainous – yet this type of antagonism is of less importance
than the unnatural acts of the local Tories who pillage and murder,
and the amusing antics of Queerfish.

Charles Talbot wrote both sympathetic and villainous Irishmen
into his play. Immigrant Paddy saves Lucy, abducted by the trig-
amist Whelan. Both men hail from the land of potatoes, only
Whelan possesses the patently evil traits of all melodramatic villains. The other three plays treat Revolutionary topics. In *A Tale
of Lexington,* the falsity of British Captain Ethlinde depends upon
his bigamous nature rather than his nationality. An audience condemns him more for leaving his American wife in Britain (whence
she arrives in Lexington) to take up with her sister in this country,
than it does for fighting against the Americans at Lexington.
General Clinton, in *The Widow's Son*, swears: "Yes, I am resolved. This rebel chief shall rue the day he injures a hair of
André's head. Unless he restore him to me, safe and uninjured, I
will hang every rebel prisoner . . . The gallant, the amiable André:
I have not the patience to think of his present situation." The
reason for Clinton's proposed but unimplemented threat no romantic would ever deny: affection for a noble friend.

In *Montgomery* – a far cry from Brackenridge's treatment –
the British entertain the Americans with kindness, going beyond
what would be considered sufficient courtesy to prisoners of war.
L'Araignée, Frenchman, attempts to abduct the heroine only to be
foiled by American soldiers (Sgt. Welcome Sobersides, a son of
Jonathan, and Cpl. O'Shamrock). L'Araignée, as did Ethlinde,
acts from purely melodramatic motivation. He covets Altamah,

the beauteous, blank-verse speaking, Indian wife of La Valle.

By the third decade of the nineteenth century, the feelings engendered by the Revolution and reawakened by the War of 1812 had quietened in a measure sufficient to allow audiences to call for more than mere alien nationality as grounds for villainy. Romantic and melodramatic motivations spurred the antagonists on to deeds dark and despicable.

Concomitant with the type of play which contained the foreign villain appeared a group with none but Americans in the *dramatis personae*. The authors of these plays, so strongly pro-American in thought, held viewpoints emphatically antagonistic toward foreign ideas and people. This type of drama occurred as early as 1785. *Sans Souci* and *The Contrast,* already discussed, react violently to British fashions and manners, although not a Briton speaks from their pages. *Jefferson and Liberty* (1801), by Horatio N. Nichols, indicts ex-President Adams as the seditious Duke of Braintree (Adams' home) who nearly sells his country back to Britain. Nichols, elaborating upon a publicized affair, depicts Hamilton as a rake with a taste for ferryman's wives, and with insufficient brains to keep from being caught with one and put in a potato sack. Anyone Republican, therefore partial to the French and to Jefferson, can do no wrong; those with weaker convictions are vilified. John Minshull extolled the validity of the American system of business in *The Sprightly Widow* (1803), and praised America as the best hope for immigrants in *Rural Felicity* (1801). In the former, the American fop, Dash, reforms half way through the play and promises to tend more closely to business than to British fashion. In *Rural Felicity* an Irishman a Scotchman, and a Cockney argue about the merits of their respective sections of Britain, yet agree that their adopted America is the place for them. William Dunlap's *Yankee Chronology* (1812) celebrated the victory of the *Constitution* over the *Guerriere* less than a month after the actual engagement. Seaman Ben Bundle returns to recount the particulars of the battle, finishing with the air, "Yankee Chronology", which tells of the victories won by American derring-do. Needless to mention, British character, as well as British naval armory, receives a drubbing.

In retrospect, strong anti-foreign sentiments appeared in American drama at the time of the Revolution. The need for an immediately apprehensible villain towards whom patriotic hate would be directed led to the rise of the automatically evil Briton. Almost as soon as the gunfire died down, Revolutionary drama – as with all propaganda polemic – ceased, to be supplanted by plays containing foreigners whose antipathy grew from sentiments unfavorable to American democracy, manners, or mores. At first the British formed the nucleus of this corps, but as the excesses of the Girondists, the Jacobins, and the Reign of Terror spread alarm among all but the most rabid of American Democrats, French antagonists began to appear in the drama. During the same period – prior to the War of 1812 – the steadily increasing strength of nationalistic sentiment in the United States led to a drama which sought historical origins and parallels for the noble experiment in democracy which was apparently succeeding so well. Foreign politics, manners, and mores were inveighed against through romantic historical dramas, a genre whose vogue did not pass until long after 1830.

The urge to differentiate those things distinctly and admirably American from all things appertaining unto others led to caricatures of the American and the foreign dandy. An explicit comparison was erected by setting off the American possessed of natural purity and uprightness with the fop who practiced artificial punctilio. Differentiation between American and European thereby grew more marked, with local characterizations abetting the conception of the naturally and simply good American. Following the patriotic fervor engendered by the War of 1812, and the consequent return to chauvinistic polemic in dramatizing anti-foreign sentiments, American playwrights turned, with an exception or two, toward the more popular romantic motivations for antagonists.[22] The foreign antagonists prodominated in large numbers over

[22] At no time did the American dramatists of the early period create what today would be called a "realistic" foreigner. Yet the intensity of hate with which the Revolutionary playwright endued his British villains, the overly-nice mincings of the fops, and the blatant immorality of the Empire courtiers and courtesans seemed real to our forebears. Psychological verisimilitude had different criteria then (see Maria Pinckney's preface, p. 58):

those of native birth and traits. Americans still believed that anyone who would only take the trouble to understand the nature of
democracy and its practitioners could not help but see that in the
United States lay man's last, best hope for political, economic, and
moral salvation.

---

audiences shuddered for Theresa abducted by the villain, as present-day
theatregoers quake when the heroine in *Dial M. for Murder* struggles with
her would-be assassin.

III. THE SYMPATHETIC FOREIGNER

A. THE PERIOD OF THE REVOLUTION

An awareness among colonists of the eastern seaboard that their interests did not necessarily coincide with those of Britain burgeoned first, as has been pointed out in Chapter One, during the early 1760's. After the cessation of the French and Indian War, prior to the Earl of Hillsborough's proclamation removing colonists from the upper Ohio territory and the Parson's Cause litigation – both in 1763 – a period of comparative calm pervaded the Crown's colonies. Following Hillsborough's proclamation and the Parson's Cause, further fuel was fed the smoldering colonial temper through the Sugar and Currency Acts of 1765. To reiterate, Britain's colonial policy led to the Stamp Act Congress, the Sons of Liberty, the Letters and Committees of Correspondence, the First Continental Congress, Concord, Lexington, Bunker Hill, and the Revolution. The events and battles mentioned in the preceding sentences, as has been discussed, aroused a patriotic fervor in the breasts of colonists inclined to find fault with Britain, which in turn brought on recognition among the insurgents of a politico-economic identity separate from that of the fatherland.

But not all colonists of British extraction sympathized with the discontented contingent. There naturally existed a group which retained a great deal of pride in its British ancestry and ties. These people remained in accord with Crown policy. While there have come down approximately half as many Tory pieces in comparison to the "patriotic plays", the existence of at least eight, in addition to the few known titles, indicates that the Whigs were not able to muzzle completely – because of strength in Tory numbers and sentiment – Loyalist dramatic literature.

Prior to colonial knowledge of Hillsborough's proclamation, and before the Parson's Cause case reached the docket, Nathaniel Evans wrote a pedestrian dialogue for the commencement of May 17, 1763, at the College of Philadelphia, blessing England and rejoicing in the recently ratified peace between Britain and France. Insignificant as a Loyalist piece, since it was first published prior to any real reason for a separation of interests between Tory and Whig, Evan's exercise acquires significance through its republication in 1772. Evans had been dead since 1767, so the reprint served no personally commemorative purpose such as a decennial memorial. It reappeared to oppose Whig literature, by that time beginning to differentiate between interests colonial and Parliamentary.

Reverend William Smith, first provost of the College of Philadelphia, wrote an exercise in 1766 that differed slightly in subject matter from Evans' earlier effort. News of the Stamp Tax repeal reached New York on April 26, 1766. Rejoicing spread through the colonies. Part of the joy found expression in Smith's commencement dialogue, which praised Pitt and other "patriots" who had espoused the American cause in Parliament, and then soared in a paean to the colonies' re-found freedom. Smith was a Whig, and by 1775 his sentiments were reversed. In that year he reissued the exercise, leaving in the portions about Pitt, Burke, and Parliament, but changing the general tone by exhorting self-sacrificing American patriots to continue the battle for liberty already begun on colonial territory. Tory writers, of course, held on to their loyalty.

Loyalists could well have rejoiced over the production of George Cockings' *The Conquest of Canada* in Philadelphia's Southwark Theatre on February 17, 1773.[1] One of the two American plays to be produced professionally prior to the Revolution, it "has the further distinction of being the first play written in America which obtained the honor of a second edition".[2] Cockings composed the play in Boston while working for the British government. It was

[1] Pollock, p. 123.
[2] Hill, p. 17.

published at London in 1766, Baltimore and Philadelphia in 1772, and Albany in 1773. The later publications place it in the list of pre-Revolutionary Loyalist literature, although its author had not intended it for that purpose (he later styled himself "poet-laureate of Congress"). Quinn finds the play far from dramatic, and the bias of its author decidedly British.[3] The prologue praises highly Britain's rectitude, power, and policy, and extols the colonial troops which helped to fight the battle of Quebec. The play deals with Wolfe's selfless patriotism, noble sentiments, and untimely death. It follows in fair detail the progress of the battle as popularly reported. At no point, though, are the French guilty of cowardice, scurrility, maleficence, or of harrying the British with the same ungentlemanly actions that later and more fervid Whig writers accused the English of committing.

Wolfe speaks with lofty and idealized sentiments that concern the defense of hearth and homeland through personal sacrifice and heroic action. He leaves behind him a fiancée, Sophia, to whom he utters his noble ideas on duty and victory. The pair decide to await Wolfe's triumphal return before marrying. Once the British confront the walls of Quebec, the language grows, if anything, more turgid than in Wolfe's earlier speeches. To the French defiance, Wolfe replies:

> *Wolfe:*   Say they thus?
> They shall e'er long, hear *Britain's* thunder roll!
> And feel the Bolt! Our Troops and Tars shall roar
> Them such a Concert, as shall shake the strong
> And lofty base of their *Quebec*!
>   * * *
> I cannot boast twelve thousand Regulars,
> With many savage scalping Bands; my Troops
> Will scarcely to eight Thousand rise; but these
> Are gallant Fellows; and I have seen them
> Try'd: They're Britain's Troops, and from *Old
>   England*,
> *Caledonia* and *Hibernia* drawn.

Sentiments which would not rest easily with the patriots of 1773 appear even in this brief extract. To put on a play containing pas-

[3] Quinn, p. 30.

sages that extolled Britain to the degree found in *The Conquest of Canada,* would be to fling a gauntlet straight into the faces of colonial sympathizers. Yet, as was mentioned in Chapter One, no records of a reaction to the play seen at the Southwark Theatre on February 17, 1773, have been transmitted across the years, leading one to believe that the Loyalists commanded a good deal of agreement in pre-Revolutionary Philadelphia, at least.

The Tories did not rest tranquilly while Whigs stirred up anti-British feelings. In addition to producing plays, they wrote dialogues scoring Whig attempts to act against the Intolerable Measures of 1774. *The Debates at the Robin-Hood Society in the City of New York* (1774) deals with a meeting of the New York Committee of Correspondence. The anonymous author acridly satirizes the proceedings of the meeting by reducing its participants to the ridiculous and causing them to dispute unimportant points of a few of the resolutions. The cast of characters participating in the "debate" also indicates the way in which a colonial audience was supposed to judge the events chronicled: "Fight-the-good-fight-of-faith Peter, Moderator; Captain Holland; Mr. King; Mr. Make-do-all; Matt-of-the-mint; Mr. Instep; Mr. Smart-Cock; Mr. Silver Tongue; Mr. Sledge." Few citizens attended the meeting, even though notification of the resolutions and the date and hour of convening had been previously advertised. In the *New York Journal; or, General Advertiser* for July 21, 1774, the proceedings of the Committee were noted, along with chairman Isaac Low's complaint that, "altho' the said resolves cannot with certainy be said to correspond with the sentiments of the major part of the citizens, tho' in all probability they do, yet as they contain *our* sentiments, it is further ordered, that they be immediately published". The ten resolutions follow.[4] In an epilogue to the satire, the author states

[4] A summary of the resolutions might aid in ascertaining patriotic ideas of mid-1774.

1. That George III is the colonists' liege and must be upheld; but that the colonies view with concern the late acts of Parliament.

2. All acts of Parliament imposing taxes on the colonies are unjust.

3. The New York Committee sympathizes with the sentiments expressed by the Boston Tea Party, and thinks the British embargo on Massachusetts unfair.

4. All colonies should aid Massachusetts.

his viewpoint. A few salient excerpts will serve to indicate the bias.

> ... The affairs of this immense continent are now arrived at a crisis, when they are no longer to be *sported with* – and the virtue and good sense of its inhabitants must be rouzed to vindicate that honour, which has been so greatly sullied by the insidious arts of its pretended friends. ... But happily, the bold career of faction, stimulated by the wicked designs of a few and led on by the arrogance of others is at length defeated by the *feebleness of its votaries*. ...

In the fall of the same year as the New York "debates", the First Continental Congress met in Philadelphia. This gathering, too, had its opponents. One pseudonymously identified herself (or himself) as Mary V. V., and wrote *A Dialogue between a Southern Delegate and His Spouse* (1774). The dialogue disseminates a feeling prevalent among those condemning the Congress. The wife first berates her husband for taking part in the Congress, then argues vehemently with him against the implementation of such Congressional resolutions as the Courts of Inspection, the embargo on trade with Britain, the withholding of taxes, and the formation of militia.

> Wou'd! instead of Delegates, they'd sent Delegates Wives;
> Heavens! we couldn't have bungled it so for our lives!
> * * *
> Your Non-Imports, and Exports, are full fraught with Ruin.
> Of thousands and thousands, the utter Undoing.

Reduced to their essence, the reasons for inaction presented by the delegate's wife claim that such procedures would work untold hardship upon the people of the colonies.

---

5. The idea of a Continental Congress is excellent.

6. The colonies should decide what action to take at a general Congress Philadelphia.

7. The preservation of colonial rights means that right-thinking British citizens will cooperate.

8. If a non-importation of goods from Britain agreement be voted approval by Congress, it should be adhered to be all colonies.

9. Delegates "for the good of the colonies" should be chosen for Congress.

10. A tribute to sympathetic Members of Parliament and friends in Britain.

Above summarized from *New York Journal*, July 21, 1774.

In response to Whig outbursts during 1775, and occasioned by the commencement of hostilities, the well-known Tory, Jonathan Sewall, wrote *A Cure for the Spleen* (1775). A Harvard graduate, Sewall served as attorney-general for the colony of Massachussetts from 1767 until his embarkation for England in 1775. He was purported to have inclined at first toward the rebel cause, but his playlet refutes the endurance of any such sympathies.[5] The piece is truly a Tory apology. Sharp the country parson, Bumper the country justice, and Trim the barber uphold Tory views, while Puff (lately of Congress) and Fillpot the inn-keeper hesitantly attempt a defense of Whig logic. To weak protestations that Parliament and the King have been treating the colonists unjustly, Sharp replies that British troops always protected colonial interests, having recently driven out the French and subdued the Indians to make America once again a fit and safe place to live. Sharp reviews colonial history back as far as 1650, calling to the defense Parliamentary acts and laws of aid to the colonies, explaining that the colonies have been well represented, and maintaining that they possess a requisite amount of sovereignty. Puff and Fillpot, far from quickminded, finally admit that the Tories espouse the right cause. One perceives the way the chaff blew as far as Sewall was concerned: all the intelligent and responsible citizens regretted the hotheaded action by the Minutemen at Lexington and the patriots at Bunker Hill.

Shortly after the American rout from Long Island and Washington's retreat from New York City, an anonymous Loyalist farce entitled *The Battle of Brooklyn* (1776) treated the patriot army and its leaders to the same sort of satiric vilification accorded the British by Whig playwrights of the same period. The play contains the full roll of American generals active in New York – Washington, Putnam, Sullivan, and Stirling – each more cowardly and incompetent than the next. The satire opens upon a crapulous Lord Stirling. He fears the British, but categorically refuses to entertain any idea but his own misguided notion of surrounding them in order to recoup the losses of the previous day. He commences to condescend to a Joe King, but then remembers that he must treat

[5] Quinn, p. 57.

the man well, for they have been partners in the business of counterfeiting paper Continentals.

The American officers state that they intend to have the regiments containing the most foreign troops bear the brunt of the attack, in order to spare the "native" colonials. Remsen, a Pennsylvania or New York Dutch colonel, takes fright at a British maneuver, and dashes up to the staff for advice, only to discover that he ordered a retreat because he imagined rather than saw a British attack, and left a hole in the American lines. The next scene contains what Quinn erroneously calls, "a vileness of slander against Washington, that is absent from any of the other dramas upon either side".[6] With satiric method similar to that found in Brackenridge's *The Death of General Montgomery*, or Leacock's *The Fall of British Tyranny*, the playwright causes Lady Gates and her maid, Betty, to discuss in unflattering detail the behavior of Washington and other American officers while in bed with Betty. Just prior to the crucial battle, Washington, Sullivan, Putnam, and Stirling display their incompetence in conference. In the same way that Howe in Brackenridge's *The Battle of Bunkers-hill*, and Hutchinson and Gage in Warren's *The Adulateur* and *The Group* all lament their anti-American deeds, Washington regrets his anti-British actions.

Wash: . . . My apprehension from the King's troops, believe me, are trifling, compared with the risque we run, from the people of America at large. The tyranny, that our accursed usurpation has made necessary, which they now feel, and feeling, I fear, will soon make them see thro' the disguise. Their rage, no doubt, will be heightened, by the slaughter that will probably ensue; and we, as members of the Congress, fall the first victims of it. – O Sullivan! my heart never consented to this ruin of my native country.

The main line of argument in the satire appeals to the sensibilities of the American populace. According to Loyalist thinking, Washington, Congress, and the patriots were rebels who had usurped power in the colonies. In an attempt to reverse that seizure, Tories proceeded to employ every piece of evidence that their logic told them would have an effect upon an audience. Therefore they, as

[6] Quinn, p. 58.

did the Whig satirists, depicted the opposition as immoral, cowardly, indecisive, scurrilous, barbaric, and ridiculous.

The war continued for more than a year after Cornwallis' surrender at Yorktown, with sporadic British and Loyalist skirmishes
the length of the seaboard and inland. Even after both the colonies
and the mother country realized that the United States had won
its independence, pro-British sentiment remained a force to be
reckoned with as Americans strove to evolve a policy of direction
and firmness. Not a few brand new citizens of the infantile United
States of America sought a reestablishment of ties with Britain.
Many factions stood to lose livelihood, business, and trade through
the new relationship with Britain. Among these factions appeared
the Yankee shipowner whose vessels and cargoes were shut out of
the West Indies and required to pay tariffs Britain formerly had
not demanded of its colonists.

The anonymous author of *The Blockheads* (1782) was a spokesman for that group of Loyalists which, just prior to the end of
hostilities, saw more beneficence than harm in once again uniting
British and American interests. Quinn discerns in the allegorical
drama a reflection of confused political ideas. The play, though,
does not indicate any prevalent pro-British sentiment; it could be
Tory propaganda.[7] The force of the attitude put forth by *The Blockheads* may be partially measured by the amount of resistance it
provoked, even though this particular play was apparently published in New York prior to the British evacuation in 1783. Mercy
Warren, Royall Tyler, Peter Markoe – to name a few dramatists
– inveighed against a decided tendency among members of the
upper class to continue to adhere to British sympathies, customs,
and manners, despite stringent anti-Tory governmental sanctions.
Had, as Quinn maintains, the sentiment in favor of England been
so minute, then there would have been little need for the continued vigilance of post-Revolutionary Whig satirists.

The Blockheads deals harshly with those who favored a Franco-American union after the rebellion. As much allegory as play,
the piece boasts a cast containing a Prodigiator (in the obsolete
sense of one who promulgates portentious omens), the symbolic

[7] Quinn, p. 59.

English sailor, Dutchman, French and English Physicians, an Old Wig (Whig), Americana (America personified), Liberta, and Amita (liberty and friendship personified). The allegory opens in the Temple of Peace, where the Prodigiator prognosticates (from a point prior to 1772) the coming of Revolution, then foresees a post-Revolutionary reunion between Britain and America. Liberta and Amita conjointly bewail the loss of liberty and friendship through civil strife, and Old Shaver describes several of the wigs (Whigs) in his shop with far from flattering terminology.

The fourth scene of the first act contains an allegorical treatment of the Dutch plight, symbolized by the behavior of Mynheer Van Braken Peace. Mynheer wishes a set of French spectacles to improve his eyesight, but Meanwell, the English physician, exhorts him to refrain from anything that will distort his vision. Then Deception, the French doctor, arrives, places a black bandage over the Dutchman's eyes, and leads him away. In the second act, a British sailor finds Mynheer wandering about blindfolded looking for Brest, since he has lost Ceylon and the Cape of Good Hope. The sailor takes Van Braken Peace in tow, and steers into port. The play ends with Congress in an uproar. The Prodigiator places French cockades on the members, which awakens them to the true state of affairs. Eventually Congress decides to ally with the British rather than the French. The final scene contains Liberta, Amita, and Americana. Americana declares that the French restrict relations among the three of them, and calls for Albion to "haste and destroy this Gallic chain". The author, who most likely evacuated New York with the British, left behind a strong dramatic statement of Loyalist ideas. To him, as to the approximately 100,000 British sympathizers displaced by the Revolution, events had truly taken a tragic turn.

While internecine strife engaged those on the American continent, and while the ban on entertainment initiated by Congress remained in force, many members of the acting profession plied their trade in the British West Indies. One of the plays produced for the British was written by an actor who returned to the continent in 1782, then joined with Hallam's Old American Company at Albany in 1785. John Henry, that actor, adapted *A School for*

Soldiers from "*Le Deserteur* of the French". Henry rearranged the incidents to please a British audience during the Revolution, then, upon his return to the United States, reworked the play so it would appeal to an American audience. (A handwritten note on the page containing the dramatis personae says, "This piece is now performing in America (with many alterations) adapted to the Meridian of the U.S. and the scene laid in Philadelphia.")

The drama, as performed in Kingston, takes place in Revolutionary America. The action concerns one Bellamy, forced to desert the British army years prior to the Revolution, his father who enters the city with the occupying British regiment, and Mrs. Mildmay, a Loyalist who runs a boarding house. Young Bellamy has been staying at the Mildmay home, where he has fallen in love with Clara Mildmay. Hector, a middle-aged American rebel, desires to marry Clara. When she refuses, he carries on about the Mildmays' ingratitude in the face of all the money he has spent on Clara's upbringing. Henry portrays him as antipathetic, for he attempts to thwart the course of true love, eavesdropping when young Bellamy confesses his desertion and his fear of recapture now that his old regiment marches into the city. Hector compounds his villainy by reporting young Bellamy. The dramatist, of course, depicted Hector as much less than a gentleman because of the sympathies of his Jamaican British audience. More than likely, when the play was put on in America after the Revolution, Hector either became sympathetic, or his politics were changed to those of a Tory.

At the boarding house are quartered Major Bellamy and Captain Valentine. The Captain is an irrepressible rake and dandy. The Major constantly admonishes him to behave himself: "*Major*. I am astonished, Valentine, that with so noble a heart, you can have so light a head! You seem to think of nothing but the pleasure of triumphing over women, in a country where we have come to combat"; and again, "My dear friend, consider, you represent the English nation: and by such behavior will give strangers an ill impression of your country." Eventually Valentine recalls his British upbringing and reforms his behavior.

The rest of the play concerns the impending execution of young

Bellamy, the Major's battle with his conscience over freeing his son (who has been paroled into his custody prior to fateful dawn), and the last-minute pardon. As played in Kingston, the play extols the magnanimity and honor of the British troops, while it reproves the rebel cause and its adherents. Henry would not have experienced a great deal of difficulty in rearranging the elements of the drama to please a post-war American audience. He could easily have exchanged British for Americans, and reversed the sympathies of the participants, laying the action at the time of the American recapture of Philadelphia for the play's New York opening on April 24, 1788. While the play unmistakably promotes the British cause, it does not do so in an aggressively polemic manner. Henry's piece can not be considered part of Tory propaganda, as were the other plays scrutinized in this section. In fact, it came to be looked upon as a popular patriotic piece, being played on July 4, 1799, 1800, 1801, and in honor of Washington's birthday on February 23, 1800 (Washington issued the pardon in the "Americanized" version).

B. ENEMIES OF THE REPUBLIC

Each of the dramas to be discussed below contains characters who were considered enemies of the United States. The playwrights pointedly rendered those enemies as characters whose degree of dramatic heroism or villainy did not depend upon their political beliefs. The attitude propounded in each of the plays is one that reacts against the factious sympathies of the era. The plays refuse alignment with any belief not based in a fundamental humanity. One must differentiate between these dramas and the types strongly pro-British, pro-French, or pro-American that have been treated in this and the preceding chapters. The playwrights Robert Munford, William Dunlap, and Mary Carr Clarke resisted easy acceptance of the violence and injustice promoted by rabidly partisan activities during a time of actual or ideological conflict. Even though Dunlap adhered closely to his Federalist bias, one might say that all three, in the dramas to be studied, wage war on both war and its unpleasant by-products, so adamantly does each resist the attractions of puerile patriotism.

Colonel Robert Munford, officer in the American army during the Revolution, wrote the first of these plays, *The Patriots* (ca. 1785). Munford's son brought out both this drama and *The Candidates* in *A Collection of Plays and Poems by the Late Colonel Robert Munford* (1798). The events mentioned by Munford in the play, however, dictate a much earlier date of composition; probably in the middle 1780's, while families suspected of Tory sympathies during the Revolution were subjected to persecution and property seizure. Quinn correctly estimates the play to be pacifist in outlook, representing the opinions of many colonials who first vacillated, but eventually fought for the Revolutionary cause.[8]

Trueman and Meanwell act as raisonneurs in the play, which is set in the South in 1777. Both stand accused of Tory partisanship, while the only real Tory remains on the Whig committee investigating Loyalists, until exposed through Trueman's disclosure of his activities. The committee calls before it three Scotsmen living in the area. The Caledonians, McGripe, McSqueeze, and McFlint, comprise the only foreign contingent in the drama, and they receive the maltreatment objected to so heartily by Trueman and Meanwell. When the Scabbies (as the Whigs term the Scots) appear before the committee, McFlint asks the nature of their offense. Colonel Strut, fervid Whig, replies:

Strut: The nature of their offence, gentlemen, is that they are Scotchmen; every Scotchman being an enemy, and these men being Scotchmen, they come under the ordinance which directs an oath to be tendered to all those against whom there is just cause to suspect they are enemies.
McGripe: I've gi'en nae cause to suspect that I am an enemy. The ordinance says, ye must hae just cause. Bring your proof gentlemen.
Brazen: Proof, sir! we have proof enough. We suspect any Scotchman: suspicion is proof, sir. I move for the question, Mr. President.
Trueman: In the catalogue of sins, I never found it one before to be born on the north of the Tweed. (Aside to Meanwell.)
Meanwell: In nature's lowest works, I never saw before such base stupidity. (Aside to Trueman.)

[8] Quinn, p. 55.

The committee agrees that all Scotch harbor sentiments hostile to the Whig cause. McFlint then asserts that he was born but not bred in Scotland.

McSqueeze: What, Sandy, do you deny your country mon, tak shame to yoursel, Sandy.
McFlint: It is time to deny man, when they make it a crime to be born there.
McGripe: I'll lose my life for dear old Scotland, before ever I'll blush for it.

Munford elicits sympathy for both the man who denies his country and the two who admit their loyalty for Scotland. An audience could not help but understand the desire for self-preservation that would drive a man despicably to deny his land of birth, as an equally strong but more patriotic sentiment could impel another into a willingness to die for his country. Munford intends to underline the sort of blind chauvinism that leads to such situations. The voice of the author speaks through Meanwell.

Meanwell: What a pity it is that all heads are not capable of receiving the benign influence of the principles of liberty – some are too weak to bear it, and become thoroughly intoxicated. The cause of my country appears as dear to me as to those who most passionately declaim on the subject. The rays of the sun of freedom, which is now rising, have warmed my heart; but I hope my zeal against tyranny will not be shewn by bawling against her enemies; and never may I signalize my attachment to liberty by persecuting innocent men, only because they differ in opinion with me.

The remainder of the play exposes a variety of unsavory types who have associated with both extreme factions; from Tackabout, the Tory on the investigatory committee, to the Irish recruiting officer who gambles, then dips into public funds to pay his debts. Munford's outright criticism of misguided and unprincipled wartime patriotism maintains a unique position between the extremes of Whig and Tory propaganda. The Colonel, although he joined the fray on the side of the colonists, did not permit personal animus to negate the principles for which he considered the Revolution had been fought.

One year before Dunlap produced the patriotic *Darby's Return,* he wrote *The Father, or American Shandyism.* September of 1789 saw *The Father* on the boards in the John Street Theatre at New York, with a line in its prologue alluding to the continued hassle over the Constitution and Bill of Rights: "... what's good, our sages still amend." This play, like *Darby's Return* (to be discussed in Chapter IV), may be classified as a patriotic piece – but with a difference. Colonel Duncan, the father in the title, and his batman, Cartridge, have served in the American army, and exemplify ideal American male maturity. The Colonel has journeyed to New York City in search of the two daughters of an old friend. One of them is married to Racket, whose attentions have wandered afield; the other, the yet unwed Miss Felton, lives in the same household. Mrs. Racket flirts with the British rake, Captain Ranter, in order to arouse her misguided husband's jealousy and secure his attentions once again. Ranter has eyes for both her and Miss Felton. The Colonel forms an immediate and vocal dislike for Ranter. The situation worsens, until the dénouement exposes Ranter as the onetime servant of Duncan's lost son, Henry. When Henry was sick, Ranter had stolen his belongings and left him for dead in England. Henry recovered, traced, his erring servant to America (Henry was a British officer, since Duncan had been forced to give over his upbringing to an old English friend), and regained his fiancée, Miss Felton. So far, the play appears to take inception in a desire to compare British and American manners, as did its famous predecessor, *The Contrast*. Yet at that point the similarity ceases, for Dunlap adapted Sterne's Uncle Toby and Trim to the exigencies of drama, renaming them Colonel Duncan and Cartridge.

The Colonel's unabashed sentimental streak conveyed a message to American audiences of the era, who professed a sensitivity to the finer feelings aroused by the British sentimental writers.[9] Duncan can not view any poverty, unethical or immoral behavior, or sadness without being immediately moved by a practically uncontrollable urge to correct the situation. He works to save Racket and his wife from "a gulph of poverty, misery, and reproach",

---

[9] Compare Maria in *The Contrast*, who has supplemented her native goodness by reading Richardson and Sterne; or Colonel Manly, who reveres his parents as no callous rake ever did.

serves notice to Ranter that his addresses would be more welcome elsewhere, and, most significantly, urges aid for an old English soldier. Duncan, upon hearing a knock, asks Cartridge who stands without.

Car.: An old soldier, Sir, he says, an English soldier, your honour.
Col.: Not the worse for that, Cartridge.
Car.: No, your honour. I think not the worse of a soldier, or a man, for being English: we are no longer enemies, your honour; and if we were – he is in distress, and blind.
Col.: Then we will be his friends, Cartridge, bring him hither.

The precepts of true sentimentalism dictate a sensitivity to the plight of distressed humans that finds satisfaction only when misery has been alleviated. Adherence to those precepts, as in the case of Duncan, leads to a reward. The Colonel, through chastening Ranter, befriending the soldier (who is his lost son, Henry, in disguise), and straightening out the affairs of the Racket family, prepares the path to a happy closing. For shortly after the incident with the disguised old soldier, Henry arrives to reveal that the English rake had been his servant, Racket promises to behave in the future, and Ranter swears he will reform.

Quite contrary to *The Contrast,* Dunlap's play contains no member of the upper class whose manners are so unprincipled and British that reformation could not possible occur. Ranter has sprung from the serving class, and Racket perceives his error. Staunch Federalist, Dunlap could not completely sever himself from the conception of class, decried so heartily by the Democrats. The main message promulgated by the sentimentalists carried a burden of humanitarianism. Dunlap, despite the precepts propounded by earlier playwrights, applied that message to Anglo-American relations, and concluded that neither nationality nor politics should act as primary motivation in human associations.

In 1806, Dunlap revised *The Father,* renaming it *The Father of an Only Child.* The major changes concern a clarification of motivation for the actions of the various characters, an exchange of names for principals, and a few excisions and additions among the minor agents. Despite the British depredations upon American shipping and the Anglo-American hostility engendered by them,

Dunlap causes Colonel Campbell (Duncan in the 1789 version) to censure the rake quite early in the play.

Col.: Hold, sir! Do you nothing to disgrace your country or your profession, and you will find a friend in every enlightened American. Though now separated from your country, we revere it as the source from which we sprang, and whence we derive the dearest blessings we enjoy. We claim the same kindred as yourselves with the heroes, the poets, and the philosophers of England; and, though we will not submit to be treated as inferiors, we cordially receive every Englishman as a brother.

Such sentiment, anathema to Americans at that time incensed over the British Orders in Council forbidding commerce with France, and angered by English impressment of seamen from American war- and merchantships, makes an excellent reason for having kept the revision from the boards.

But the changes in epilogues from 1789 to 1806 show a significant shift in the winds of upper-class literary infatuation. In the earlier edition, no emphatic mention appears of an attitude among the literate which derogated American letters. A reliance upon and reverence for British models, however later impelled Dunlap to revise the epilogue in order to satirize the widespread uncritical acceptance of all products of English letters, and possibly caused him to include Campbell's speech quoted above. In the epilogue he says:

> Who is this author, and from when his play?
> Who ever heard of him before to-day?
> Born among woods and bears, a country noodle,
> A gawky lout, in short a Yankee doodle!
> > * * *
> And can he write a play? Can he have wit?
> Believe it or not; 'tis neither right nor fit.
> Than for the thing itself; why you'll be undone
> If you approve a piece not play'd in London.
> > * * *
> > ... Then ne'er applaud
> A play that has not travelled from abroad.
> In Drury Lane or Covent Garden tried,
> (Or e'en Haymarket) we th' award abide,

With awe receive what's sanctioned by their appeal.

* * *

Why risk your judgment by your approbation
Of mushroom products of our mushroom nation!
No, no, condemn. Nip in the bud the evil,
And frown all Yankee poets to the devil.

Nearly twenty years after first writing the play, Dunlap still argues for an enlightened outlook. But by this time, although the Anglo-American foreign policy was in a state of distress, the fashionable attitude required an adherence to British literary precepts and preceptors that eventuated in a storm of protest from American authors.

Dunlap did not hesitate to write other dramas containing notions that might disrupt the public equanimity. In the spring of 1798 his tragedy, *André*, played to New York audiences. Choosing a subject of much controversy for the center of dramatic interest, Dunlap wrote a play concerning the friendship between the doomed Briton and Bland, a young American officer. Sensible of the reaction that might arise, Dunlap included a statement of purpose in the preface.

... Still further difficulties has the Tragedy of André to surmount, difficulties independent of its own demerits, in its way to public favor. The subject necessarily involves political questions; but the author presumes that he owes no apology to any one for having shown himself an American; ... the author has adorned the poetical character of André with every virtue; he has made him his Hero.

Farther along in his prefatory comments, Dunlap mentions that during the initial performance Bland's heated renunciation of the American army raised such a hurricane of audience remonstration that he gladly changed the play, permitting Bland to retrieve his symbolically removed cockade.

Whoever penned the prologue – Dunlap or another – realized the risk entailed in handling material that might inflame old sores:

A native Bard, a native scene displays,
And claims your candour for his daring lays;
Daring, so soon, in mimic scenes to shew,
What each remembers as a real woe.

* * *

> O, may no party-spirit blast his views,
> Or turn to ill the meanings of the Muse:
> She sings of wrongs long past, Men as they were,
> To instruct, without reproach, the Men that are;
> Then judge the Story by the genius shown,
> And praise, or damn it, for its worth alone.

The final verses contain what may be considered Dunlap's purpose in writing *André*. He intended to utilize events still retaining the poison of political partisanship to teach a humanitarian lesson. Much of the drama concerns human motivation: Bland's justifiably angry reaction to André's impending execution; André's patient acceptance of the fate brought about by his acts; Washington's dilemma when faced with the choice between duty and his own humanitarian beliefs. Even though Dunlap intended to focus interest upon the tragic figure of André – the honorable, upright, and virtuous British officer who erred only once, and because of the strictures of a wartime code of ethics, must undeservedly die – the quandary faced by young Bland as he attempts to reconcile patriotism with true friendship demands a central position in the drama. The play well might have been entitled *Bland* as readily as *André*.

Dunlap astutely sets the tone of the entire play during even-tempered and wise Melville's opening speech.

> *Mel.:* – In vain the enlighten'd friends of suffering
> man
> Point out, of war, the folly, guilt, and madness.
> Still, age succeeds to age, and war to war;
> And man, the murderer, marshalls out in hosts
> In all the gaiety of festive pomp,
> To spread around him death and desolation.

Bland arrives almost at once, and the audience catches the drift of attitudes a second time.

> *Bland:* The south teems with events; convulsing
> ones:
> The Briton, there, plays at no mimic war;
> With gallant face he moves, and gallantly is met.

The British will not be characterized as blatantly evil warmongers, attempting to extend their tyranny over an unwilling people, but as human beings trapped in the toils of war and forced to face out the conflict. Bland soon learns that a British spy has been caught. He rejoices that Arnold's plans have been thwarted and his instrument apprehended. But glee turns to sorrow in the next tick of time, when Melville informs Bland of the spy's identity.

> *Bland: André!* – O no, my friend, you're sure
> deceiv'd –
> I'll pawn my life, my ever sacred fame,
> My General's favor, or a soldier's honor,
> That gallant André never yet put on
> The guise of falsehood. O, it cannot be!

A long explanation of how André saved Bland and other Americans from the lethal confinement of a British prison ship at New York ensues, at the close of which the first scene ends.

Within the space of some one hundred and fifty lines, Dunlap has prepared all the dramatic and ideological conflict in the entire play. The Americans fight, unwillingly but gallantly, the equally unwilling yet gallant British. War does not solve anything since it, as Melville soliloquizes, can not prevent or eliminate evil, being evil itself. One's enemies in war often do not deserve to die, as André's case shall prove. No clear-cut demarcation between enemy and friend exists, for the bonds of true and deserved friendship bridge the gulf between warring factions. The complications of civil strife disrupt the simple virtues held so dear by men of sensibility. These ideas, at odds with the usual easy partisanship encountered in dramas of the early republican era, recur constantly throughout the play. Dunlap organizes his action to illustrate the many problems created by the conflict between ideology and humanity.

The second scene of the first act introduces the two generals, Washington and McDonald, and the staff officer Seward. The three of them converse about the causes of the war, its progress, and the eventual results related to freedom and man's earthly goals. McDonald asserts that men fight not for motives of honor and glory, but to defend home, hearth, free-hold, and to redress past injuries. Again Dunlap introduces an idea not usually present in

pro-American literature of the period. He adds, utilizing Mc-
Donald as his spokesman, a conception that would recur constantly throughout the next century: America as mankind's earthly
paradise; a continent of democratic tranquillity separated by a
vast ocean from the unstable Old World.

> *M'Donald:*   Now I see in this new world,
> A resting spot for man, if he can stand
> Firm in his place, while Europe howls around him,
> And all unsettled as the thoughts of vice,
> Each nation in its turn threats him with feeble malice.

Dunlap must have composed with the Napoleonic wars fresh in
mind, as the third verse in the preceding quotation signifies. Mc-
Donald, in the second act, responds to Seward's condemnation of
Europe as a breeding ground for mankind's ills, by pointing out all
the benefits that flow from the old to the new land.

> *M'Donald:*   Prophet of ill,
> From Europe shall enriching commerce flow,
> And many an ill attendant, but from thence
> Shall likewise flow best Science. Europe's knowledge,
> By sharp experience bought, we should appropriate;
> Striving thus to leap from that simplicity,
> With ignorance curst, to that simplicity,
> By knowledge blest; unknown the gulf between.

Knowledgeable simplicity extracted from the tempering experience
of others, the dream of those who believed in a race of modern
Adams to people the paradise of America, Dunlap also includes
as one of the ideas that teem from the pages of his drama.

The second act introduces André. The young British adjutant
acknowledges his error, and soliloquizes in a manner that would
endear him to an audience.

> *André:* Kind heaven be thank'd for that I stand alone
> In this sad hour of life's brief pilgrimage!
> Single in misery, no one else involving,
> In grief, in shame, and ruin.

The irony of his thankfulness strikes home as soon as Bland enters
and involves himself in André's fate. Bland argues with his friend
that the dictates of duty demanded he should exchange his uniform

for civilian clothes. André disagrees, admitting that he gave in to the sin of ambition by accepting the commission to contact Benedict Arnold, and that he how reaps the bitter harvest of his error. He asks Bland to arrange a firing squad rather than a hanging party, since he would prefer to die an honorable death. Bland rushes out swearing to save André or defect to the British. He hurries to Washington and entreats for André's life. The commander-in-chief admits André's virtues and the personal injustice accompanying the execution, but argues that the general weal demands his death. Stymied, Bland heatedly tears the cockade from his hat, forswearing an army and a country that could perpetrate such a deed. After he leaves, Washington murmurs to himself that had a witness been present, he would have been forced to have Bland arrested. Back at the prison, Bland tells André of his failure, and of the British threat to kill the captive Bland Sr. in retaliation for André's execution. André begs him to forgive the British for intending such an act, and writes a letter urging Clinton not to avenge his death.

In the fourth act Bland's concern for André spurs him into an argument with McDonald, who replies to the young officer's insistence upon André's personal merit and undeserved death with the equally irrefutable logic of greater benefit to greater numbers made necessary by a state of war. Bland attempts to provoke McDonald into a duel, but the General refuses, realizing the young man's state of mind. Dunlap piles on the pathos by bringing in Honora, André's fiancée, to plead his case. Washington almost relents, but news that lawless British scouts have hanged the gallant Hastings after a kangaroo court trial impels the commander-in-chief to reaffirm his original decision, "Why, why, my country, did I hesitate!" The British then release Bland Sr., Mrs. Bland arrives to care for Honora, Bland accepts his cockade back from McDonald, and André marches across the stage to his death.[10] The play ends with McDonald's caution to remember always the mo-

---

[10] As addenda to the play appear letters from André to the people, dated 1769, a poem by André, correspondence between Washington and Congress relating to the young British adjutant, and the proceedings of the trial in synopsis. Dunlap took no chances, weighting heavily sympathy for André.

tives that caused the war, but at the same time to reflect that those who actually planned and carried out the deeds have passed on; "Never let memory of the sire's offence / Descend upon the son." [11]

Seventeen years and one war after *André* caused a furor in the Park Theatre, one of the gentle sex pleaded to her countrymen the universality of virtue and gallantry in time of war. Hill calls Mrs. Mary Carr Clarke's *The Fair Americans* (1815), "A Federalist criticism of the War of 1812", while Quinn preceives in it an "undercurrent of Federalist criticism of the War".[12] Certainly the Federalists disagreed with Madison's decision to fight against Britain, but no expression of their discontentment peers from the pages of Mrs. Clark's play, even assuming that it might have been written during the course of the conflict. The play is interlarded with patriotic songs and sentiments. Even though Ensign Freelove, the American fop, behaves as a coward, General Trueman's valor and devotion to the welfare of his country offsets the Ensign's conduct. The American army departs with the unanimous good wishes of the populace, and emerges victorious from the battle.

Mrs. Clarke's attitude toward the British, although the play does not contain sufficient evidence to assign it a Federalist bias, finds expression through the heroism of Captain Belford and Major Clifford, both English. They save two American girls from Indians, and are reciprocally harbored at an American farm. They discuss politics with Harley, the farmer, and Belford proffers the comment that in his opinion America is an excellent example of what a good republic should be. Despite wartime factions, Mrs. Clarke contends, men still retain an individual sense of mental balance. Belford asks Sophia to marry him, but she hesitates because of his nationality. At that juncture Freelove arrives with an entire company of troops to capture the British, but Harley helps the Major to escape, Belford having elected to remain behind and

---

[11] In 1803, Dunlap gave in to the popular demand for easily palatable patriotism, and rewrote *André* as *The Glory of Columbia*. Dunlap excised much of the meaning in the original, substituting songs for soliloquies, and Dennis O'Bogg, the comic Irish soldier, for much of the pathos aroused by the apparent reprieve. The results of the rewriting may be livelier, but hardly as momentous.

[12] Hill, p. 16; Quinn, p. 154.

press his suit. Certainly, any author intending to criticize American participation in the War of 1812 would not have a British officer freely choose to remain in his enemies' land. At the close of the comedy, Belford marries Sophia while the other girls select their husbands from available American suitors. The honor and gallantry of the British opposes the usual sort of treatment an enemy receives in wartime propaganda, possibly leading Hill and Quinn to judge the piece a Federalist tract. Yet if Mrs. Clarke criticizes the war, she does so in the same manner as her predecessors, Munford and Dunlap. She objects, as do they, to the state of bellicosity that blinds men to the possibility of basing personal evaluations upon moral or ethical assessments rather than political sentiments, which can never lead to valid conclusions.

C. FOREIGNERS WITH AMERICAN IDEALS

Despite the efforts of some playwrights to employ devices other than pro-American utterances in order to notify an audience that a stage foreigner could be viewed with sympathy, there remained throughout the period under discussion a strong predilection for delineating sympathetic foreigners by liberally endowing them with American ideals. What better method quickly to align the good versus the bad than by enduing one faction with democratic and the other with monarchical or tyrannical beliefs? For example, as if the name of LaFayette would not suffice to cause the immediate rapport between character and any American audience, the author of *The French Revolution* (1790) makes certain that nobody will mistake where LaFayette stands in the lists, for or against democracy.

> *LaFayette:* Here, Sir, we boast the name,
>   assume the air,
> And ape the manners of the truly great,
> While poverty internal speaks us wretched;
> Duped to the nod of a despotic court.
> Not so Columbia! There no tyrant's power
> Sways nor annuls the general mind.

The play finishes with the Bastille fallen and Louis, advised by La-

Fayette and Necker, offering the country a constitution based upon democratic doctrines. The author, obviously a Federalist who disliked Jacobin excesses both in France and America, solved the problem of presenting a compassionate monarchy by causing both LaFayette and Necker to argue vehemently for a constitution and greater rights for the populace. Samuel Elliot, in writing *Fayette in Prison* (1802) sometime immediately prior or during 1800,[13] can not permit merely LaFayette's unjust imprisonment to carry the pathos, but has the protagonist further endear himself to Americans by praising their Revolution and ideal lack of cynically complicated motives and mores. LaFayette thereby expresses the current American conception of the unadulterated excellence of ethic and custom springing from a closeness to the primevally good land and from naturally benevolent democracy.

> *LaFayette:* When the brave yeomen of Columbia's
> fields,
>
> Impell'd by ALBION's insolence, arose,
> And led by WASHINGTON, their shackles broke.
> * * *
> 'Twas there I found and serv'd a gallant people,
> Of manners unaffected, souls sincere.

John Murdoch, a playwright whose politics in 1798 agreed totally with late eighteenth century Federalist isolationism, wrote *The Politicians* (1798) as a polemic against any anti-Adams factions. The play serves to present a series of political arguments concerning the pros and cons of allying with France or Britain. Written while the Alien and Sedition laws were in effect, it concludes that any alliances would be dangerous to American security. Both pro-British and pro-French factions receive a share of dramatic disapprobation. The French had just insulted the American ambassadors during the "XYZ Affair", and the undeclared naval war with France had created a good deal of discontentment. Yet there remained a staunch Democratic contingent which argued that America had ill used the French, to whom she owed so much. To this faction the Scotsman Sawney Biscuit, Caledonian by birth but American by choice, objects. Adz, American Democrat, misconstrues the situation and misplaces his affections.

[13] According to Hill, p. 37, Wegelin lists an 1800 edition of the play.

Sawney: Ye may ca them allies, and your beest freends: If they are yeare beest freends, they have a very extraordinary way of shewing it, by roobing and insoolting you.

Adz.: We have used them damn'd ill, by making a treaty with the English.

Sawn.: O canna kin what they ha to do wee that; youre gouvernment surely has a right to make its own bargains; if they canna do that, ye need nae mare make a boast about yeare independence.

Adz.: Hell take our government! I shall always dislike it, for making such a treaty.

Sawn.: Upon my word, if you was in England, and to mutter such sentiments against their gouvernment, you would be ganged awaw to Boutany Bay; for my part, I am veery weel satisfied with leeving under your gouvernment.

Adz.: The treaty, I am talking of.

Sawn.: Have you ever read it?

Adz.: Have I ever read it!

Sawn.: I asked you the question.

Adz.: Hem . . . (confused) . . .

Sawn.: Is it right fair in you to censure and condemn what ye ha na seen. . . . Ye hee the freest gouvernment in the world; and if ye dinna continue to be a free people, it is in your ain faults, all that ye hae to do, is to be true to yoursels, do nae suffer English of French factions to influence you. . . .

The burr characterizes the canny Scotsman to an audience, immediately identifying him as a foreigner. Usually that group was anti-American, hence Sawney's appeal and credibility are heightened when he utters ideas dear to patriotic breasts. Sawney not only objects to what would soon be called by Jefferson "entangling alliances", but can not abide the uninformed prattling of people who speak from ignorance. The play closes on an appeal by O'Callaghan, who argues as vehemently against the French as did Adz for them:

O'Call.: God save us, what a combustion? here is a subject for the most shallow-pated to moralize upon: Americans enrolling themselves under the banners of foreign powers . . . I think the sons of Columbia should observe more dignity, than to suffer themselves to be divided by governments across the Atlantic; . . . I trust the people will know how to prize their singular happy situation among the nations of the earth, and join heart and hand, in supporting the tried patriot, who is at the head of their great national affairs.

The Federalist lesson intended to be drilled into Americans of the era could not have been more patent, especially since it takes foreigners to teach them that foreign alliances would benefit only foreigners.

As late as 1829, when the thoughts of Americans had turned homeward from the burning foreign issues of previous decades, loyalty to an affection for America uttered by John and Charles Bull in Richard P. Smith's *The Eighth of January* (1829), served to enlighten citizens of the United States as to the correct manner of judging foreigners. Quinn states: *"The Eighth of January* contrasts Charles Bull, the American soldier who is willing to sacrifice himself for his chief, with his father, John Bull, who as a loyal Englishman will not fight against either his native or his adopted country. . . It celebrated ostensibly Jackson's victory at New Orleans in 1815, but in reality it celebrated his triumph of 1828." [14]

Jackson has been trapped behind the British lines. Charles Bull, loyal to the country in which he has matured, draws the British soldiers away from his father's mill, where Jackson has been secreted. When Jackson inquires of John Bull why he refused to grind corn for the British, the old Englishman answers: "True, they are my countrymen, and as such I regard them, but as long as America feeds me may my mill stand still, when I become the traitor who would feed her invaders." His feelings oppose those of the Scotch traitor in Grice's *The Battle of New Orleans* (1816), who attempts to betray the Americans in New Orleans to the approaching British forces. (Notice that no American would be portrayed as sinking low enough to betray his country. Grice employed a foreigner for the dastardly deed.) By 1829 the edges of anti-British feeling had worn sufficiently smooth to allow Richard P. Smith to create an obviously symbolic Briton whose loyalty remains with his homeland, but whose behavior marks a man of good sense. In that manner, the play contains, partially, the meaning intended by Munford, Dunlap, and Clarke, who objected to zealots of any persuasion. John Bull's ideas should agree with those of an enlightened American – so went the thoughts of his creator.

[14] Quinn, pp. 207-208.

Another classification of foreigners, who after exhibiting initial antipathy came to espouse American ideals, has been previously discussed. The travelling foreigners, first vehemently outspoken concerning the barbarism of the New World, come to realize that what they mistook for lack of civility and culture could in actuality be ascribed to forthright simplicity of manner and defensible pride in an ennobling political system. An early, but not easily reformed traveller appears in the anonymous operetta, *The Better Sort* (1789). Captain Flash, more than likely borrowed from Garrick's *Miss in Her Teens,* popular both before and after the Revolution, clashes almost constantly with Yorick, a Yankee whose articulate arguments make him the equal of the British officer. Flash and Yorick disagree on many topics. When Yorick avers that America needs a native musical literature, Flash replies: "Who is there to make songs or musick in this country? Or what is there to make songs about? Or if they were made, what would they be good for?" A later disagreement springs up over the subject of loyalty. Flash, goaded by Yorick, states that "everything in nature, when once transported to America, will degenerate". And in final refutation of Yorick's complaint that not enough respect and recognition is being accorded America's great ally, France, the Captain maintains:

Flash: I look upon America as nothing more than a *cats paw*, which the ambition of France, prompted by diabolical antipathy to Old England, has made use of to stir up the embers of sedition. America, it is true, is independent, but in my mind she will soon rue the time she withdrew from the protection of the parent country. How happy it would be then, for both countries if America were to return.

The playwright had a body of fact on which to base the characterization of Flash, for after the Revolution an influx of European travellers curious about the new Republic so bumptiously declaring itself a political power peered at American politics, manners, and customs, then returned to their countries to write of what they saw. Many could not discover one item that pleased them.[15] Therefore the author naturally expected his audiences to

[15] See W. Matthews, *A Historical View of America*, 2 vols. (Dublin, 1789); Isaac Weld, *Travels through the States of North America* (London,

THE SYMPATHETIC FOREIGNER

hold the reverse of Flash's opinions. After a long conversation
with Yorick and other characters who exhibit good sense and
proper appreciation of France, Flash remarks: "As I have great
faith in the conversation this evening, I now say, if it were possible I could forget my King and country, I would settle in Boston and leave off my old pranks." The main interest in the plot,
though, does not lie in the Flash-Yorick conflict, but in the reformation of Mrs. Sententious, an American fashion plate who slav-
ishly copies British custom. She receives her comic punishment,
and Flash agrees that America offers more to a traveller than grist
for his complaints. He elicits a greater degree of sympathy at the
end of the play than does Mrs. Sententious, for he had been, after
all, reared abroad, where he learned the wrong precepts; his reformation shows his susceptibility to democratic – e.g., the correct – ideas. Since he remains loyal to Britain, his pro-American
sentiments become the more admirable.

Miss Sprightly, in John Murdoch's *The Beau Metamorphized*
(1800), describes the travelling British dandy, Vainly:

Miss S.: He is well enough as to personal accomplishments; but the
creature is so full of prejudices in favour of his own nation, he wont
admit that the Americans have any genius or taste; he is constantly
ridiculing the American character; – faith, if I had my will of those
foreigners, who affect to dispise our country, I'd make them all march
out of it, to the tune of yankee doodle.

After being subjected to a series of corrective pranks, Vainly
reforms, donates two hundred dollars to charity, and promises not
to ridicule American ways again. As a reward, the playwright
honors him with Miss Sprightly's worthy American hand. Americans were not so prejudiced against the foreigners, they believed,
that proper forgiveness could not be arranged upon receipt of
sincere apologies.

The same sort of comic lessons change young Mr. Wentworth
from sarcastic calumniator to willing admirer of American won-
ders in Dunlap's *A Trip to Niagara* (1828). Dunlap mimicks any

---

1799), among others. One must also realize that the travellers who did not
commit their opinions to print complained to Americans orally, in the
manner of the later Mrs. Trollope.

one of a number of travelogues complaining about primitive American travel and scenery that had been published by 1828.

Wentw.: I wish I had never seen it. I should have taken warning from others, and not have commenced my travels in this fag-end of creation. I should have gone to Rome, and looked with delight on the ruins of greatness. But here everything is new – no ivy crowned towers! no mouldering monuments – nothing worth a traveller's crossing a kennel to see – all fresh – all bright as a brummagen button.

Wentworth's sister and John Bull, both of whom admire what they have seen in the new world, undertake to cure the young Briton's complaint of traveller's jaundice. After John Bull perpetrates a series of American disguises, during which he constantly upbraids Wentworth, the blinders fall. Wentworth's prejudices transform into openmindedness, and he agrees that America's newness does not constitute a detriment, but an advantage.

The initial bias against items, customs, habits, mores, and goods because of their strangeness – among foreigners from any portion of the first fifty years of American post-Revolutionary history – changes to admiration once they learn to employ the right yardstick for measurements. Similarly, their wrong-headedness finds rapid forgiveness among the citizens of the United States when they profess approval rather than contempt. The transformations were important, for they showed Americans that not even former enemies and vilifiers could long withstand the attributes and appeal of the new democratic system and all its concomitants.

D. WEAKENED AMERICAN IDEALS

Following the policy of dividing the sympathetic foreigner into groupings according to the major impetus motivating his compassionate treatment, a category which includes foreign agents in early American drama formulated according to function performed in the plot may be observed. Thus a British officer or French aristocrat would not be placed in a play solely to orate principles pleasant to American ears, but would appear because the exigencies of form or genre might call for a sympathetic character; whereupon the author, for the sake of differentiation or because he had layed the play in a foreign country, would choose a foreigner. Admittedly, a case could be briefed, accusing the majority of agreeable foreigners in early American drama of presenting pro-American sentiments so the author would be assured of their warm acceptance, but some applaud America more than others. The difference in degree rather than in kind engages our attention at this point.

For instance, Colonel Mellfont in Judith Murray's *Virtue Triumphant* (1795) is an English officer. He and Maitland, the son of the comic protagonist, are about to set out on a tour abroad. The authoress carefully leads her audience to understand that the Colonel will be only a good influence on Charles. Of upright mores, Mellfont even attempts to correct Maitland Sr.'s aberration: he lives by "the medium", which means that one should strive for equality between extremes. Maitland Sr. so stubbornly observes his guiding principle that he refuses to permit Charles and Eliza Clairville, a penniless but virtuous waif, to wed. Since he believes in equality, Maitland Sr. maintains that no rich young American should marry a destitute, partly-French orphan. Colonel Mellfont argues valiantly, but to no avail, that Eliza possesses a share of virtue equal to Charles' worth in cash. Maitland Sr. refuses to listen until some documents turn up that prove Eliza a wealthy heiress and a relative of the Colonel. The play is intended to propound the idea that virtue triumphs over the detriments of a poor birth; but the moral goes astray because it turns out that Eliza has had the advantages of gentle parturition and liberal patrimony. Colonel Mellfont serves as the raisonneur in the piece, his nationality is *secondarily* of importance. The play establishes that the British can act according to the right values: "*Col.* I always feel compassion for persons in a state of servitude and dependence, Mr. Maitland."

Two more examples shall serve to supply the variety of treatments accorded to sympathetic British foreigners up until 1830. Charles Breck wrote *The Fox Chase* (1806) to illuminate the maxim that the simple virtues to be learned through the bucolic life may reform even a dandified profligate. Although he states in the prologue,

> The wish inspires me, and the hope beguiles
> For native efforts to engage your smiles,
> For them to wake your patriotic zeal,
> And then embolden'd to your taste appeal:

he set the play either in England or in a previous American era, since the characters speak of guineas. The play concerns disinherited sons, fortunes stolen by villainous partners, and fops who reform. Henry Lunewell, a dandy who loves the chase as well as the lesser vices to be indulged in the city, has a heart fashioned from the proper stuff. Under the wholesome influence of country life, he throws off temptation, reinstates his father's long-lost fortune, reforms the villain, and marries Julia, the villain's daughter. The play might just as well have taken place in America as Britain – in fact that seems to be what should happen according to the prologue. The characters possess no uniquely British qualities. They support the preference among American authors to endow those needing correction with the nationality of another land. That tendency led Breck into making his characters either British or placing them in an earlier epoch.

Twenty-four years after Breck's play had been produced, George Washington Park Custis wrote *Pocahontas* (1830). By that time the differences between America and Britain had been settled to the extent that an author could feel secure in presenting British characters loyal to Britain. Thus Custis, more interested in writing a good romantic history play than promulgating republican politics or mores, created dramatic agents rather then mouthpieces expounding some theory of the evils to be found among foreign social systems; a possibility available to anyone writing an historic Indian play, since the British did usurp much Indian territory during the early years of colonization. The British in the play act from motivations of honor, love of country, and gallantry with respect to the opposite sex. No disapprobation attaches to their actions because the author might have been interested in turning a political or moral grindstone.

The same sort of statements may be applied to a certain class of French foreigners in American drama of the early post-Revolutionary era. In the second decade of American freedom, John

Murdoch – the same man who three years later vilified the French through the caricature of Monsieur Aristocrat in *The Politicians* – placed Beauchamp and his sister Clementina, French colonists, in *The Triumphs of Love* (1795) as objects of interest and compassion rather than for factious propaganda purposes. In 1795, the French had managed to rebuild a new constitution calling for a bicameral legislature and a multiple executive, or *Directoire,* of five members. This indicated to the American Democrats that France had finally straightened out her twisted politics. But by 1798, the *Directoire* had proved to be as incompetent as its predecessor. This political ineptitude coupled with France's treatment of American ambassadors in the "XYZ Affair" and her attacks on the American merchant marine, led many authors to criticize actively the French. Clementina and her brother have lost their fortunes through the native revolt in French Santo Domingo. George Friendly, American profligate who reforms because of his love, marries Clementina, "one of the late sufferers of St. Domingo". Friendly's marriage changes his ways, and he captures the audience's admiration for recognizing virtue and intrinsic worth as more important than dowry. The catalyst, of course, is Clementina – French refugee and object of compassion.

Thirty years later, the Chevalier La Valle appeared as melodramatic hero in *Montgomery* (1825), by Henry J. Finn. The author had no intention of engaging in dramatic polemics concerning the relative merits of foreigners, but placed a French Canadian hero *and* villain in his Revolutionary melodrama to achieve variety from the usual play of that type. La Valle has married Altamah, a beauteous Indian. L'Araignée, the villain, harbors a grudge against La Valle, and attempts to revenge himself by kidnapping Altamah. La Valle serves in Carleton's army against the Americans, and acquits himself as befits the hero of a melodrama. The only difference between La Valle and other melodramatic heroes of the era lies in his nationality and marriage to an Indian, two elements incidental to character formulation.

When one attempts to separate popular pro-American sentiment from romantic motivation for actions by sympathetic characters in early nineteenth century drama, a fundamental similarity between the two devices of characterization prevents easy division. Quite often, as in Maria Pinckney's *The Young Carolinians, or Americans in Algiers* (1818), what was intended to further American ideals, in actuality depends upon romantic notions of behavior. Ellinor and St. Julien, betrothed to one another, have been captured by Algierian pirates; Ellinor several years later than her fiancé, since she has gone east to find him. Achmet, an Algierian engaged to Selima, acquires a romantically villainous passion for Ellinor, and neglects his intended. Even though Selima realizes that Ellinor is the object of Achmet's passion, she can not – although a Mohammedan – abide the thought of Ellinor's captivity and enslavement. Her romantic, Christian ideals overrule her strong reason for disliking Ellinor, and she aids the Americans to escape. The Algierians are moved not so much by the necessities of verisimilitude, but by the dictates of romantic notions. Selima functions in accordance with Christian precepts. The golden rule, compassion for those in trouble, and an innate nobility of sentiment serve to motivate her.

Compassion also forms the main reason to accord LaFayette's captor, Lohrstein, audience sympathy in Samuel Woodworth's *La Fayette* (1824). The Austrian General, even though he has been ordered to imprison LaFayette, permits the French patriot to take a walk about the countryside each day, and to enjoy the freedom of his library. Lohrstein esteems above all else "wisdom and integrity" in a human being. Huger, the young American allied with Bolman in the plot to rescue LaFayette, falls in love with Ellen, the General's daughter. The General shows his good sense by, later in the play, judging the titleless American to be worthy of his daughter. Huger's capture and his impending execution thwart the marriage plans. A pardon from the Emperor settles affairs, and Huger and Ellen wed while LaFayette goes free. Although Woodworth could easily have made the General villainous, he chose to render him, his sister, and his daughter foreigners who recognize intrinsic merit in a country and its citizens not their own.

Nationalism grew to function as one of the characteristics of

European romanticism, and it served the same purpose in plays written by Americans prior to the 1830's. Romantic nationalism and chauvinism differ mainly in degree. In Woodworth's play, the General, his sister the Duchess, and Ellen all arrive at conclusions agreeable to Americans. They admire, after first meeting the gallant Huger, the products of American democracy; Lohrstein has informed his daughter that she may pick her own husband; the three noble Austrians all value a person because of his immanent worth. To exhibit such qualities exclusively would lead to labelling the character one whose dramatic purpose leaned more toward the side of promulgating chauvinistic ideas. But each of the characters in this play, as in many during the first thirty years of the nineteenth century that resemble it, manifests other romantically sympathetic traits. The combination creates a non-polemic foreigner; one whose American ideals serve in a capacity subsidiary to his romantic motivations.

E. THE IRISH

Although the Irishman most often appeared in early American drama as a caricature meant to enliven a farce, melodrama, or comic operetta, occasionally a displaced native of the Emerald Isle would be sympathetically characterized through traits other than his stereotyped ludicrousness. For that reason, rather than placing them in the chapter dealing with humorous characterizations, this group of Irish protagonists has been entered under the classification of sympathetic foreigners. Of the six plays to be discussed, three will be mentioned in the chapter containing comic Irish immigrants, and one stands apart, unique for its treatment of the Irish character at this period. An early American employment of other than humorous antics to delineate the Irish may be perceived in Dunlap's *Darby's Return* (1789). To be mentioned in connection with early post-Revolutionary outbursts of chauvinism, *Darby's Return* supplies the first indication that an Irishman appearing in American drama can be taken seriously even though his behavior evokes much humor.

Asked by Thomas Wignell, the eminent actor of Irish roles, to write a benefit piece, Dunlap borrowed the character of Darby from the English-Irish playwright John O'Keeffe, who had placed the perigrinating trooper in *The Poor Soldier* (1782) and *Patrick in Prussia* (1785). In the first play, Darby comically wooes the country lass Kathlane, to marry her at the close of the drama. In *Patrick in Prussia*, Patrick, now a captain, discovers Darby in his troop. Darby, jilted by Kathlane, got drunk in Dublin and embarked on a ship for the Baltic rather than on the packet-boat for London. He enlisted in the Prussian army, where his farcical antics have nearly been his undoing. Dunlap utilized Darby's popularity with American audiences to assure himself and Wignell of a ready welcome for the Irishman's patriotic comments.[16]

Dunlap elaborates upon Darby's experiences in Prussia, sending him to Austria, to America, and to France before he returns to relate his adventures to Father Luke, Kathleen, and Dermot – all characters from O'Keeffe.[17] The manner in which Darby makes his observations elicits laughter, but his sentiments agree with those of the post-Revolutionary patriots.

> *Darby:* A man who'd fought to free the land
> from woe
> *Like me* had left his *farm a soldiering* to go;
> But having gain'd his point, he had, *like me,*
> Return'd his own *potatoe ground* to see;
> But there he couldn't rest; with one accord
> He's call'd to be a kind of –, not a Lord –
> I don't know what – he's not a great man, sure,
> For poor men love him, just as he was poor!
> They love him like a father or a brother.

Dunlap, a devout Federalist, could not resist an opportunity to

---

[16] Pollock lists eleven performances of *The Poor Soldier* in Philadelphia prior to the New York opening of *Darby's Return*, and fifteen from then until the nineteenth century. Dunlap's play was produced three times as a benefit for Wignell and Morris. In addition, *Darby and Patrick*, and *Dermot and Kathleen*, both based on characters from *The Poor Soldier,* had six and nine Philadelphia performances, respectively. The Irishman was a popular character on the American stage.

[17] Substance of the preceding material drawn from George C. Duggan, *The Stage Irishman* (London, 1937), p. 142 ff.

take a crack at the Jacobins either in France or America. Although he agreed with the idea of a French Revolution, he did not approve of the methods employed.

> *Darby:* They caught the fire quite across the
> ocean,
> And to be sure, they're in a nice commotion:
> (Down with the bastile – tuck up the jailor.
> Cut off my lor's head, then pay his taylor.)
> Oh bless their hearts, if they can but get free,
> They'll soon be as fat and as jolly as we;
> Some took the *liberty* to plunder others,
> Because equality is more like brothers.
> You may be sure I didn't stay there long.
> So here I am boys, hearty hale and strong!
> But oh, New York's the place to get a wife,
> Aye, that's the place to lead a merry life.

Since it was meant to be a piece for Wignell's benefit nights, the entire dialogue depends upon the Irishman; he does not operate in a position secondary or tertiary to the main story.

Over thirty years elapsed after the production of *Darby's Return* before the appearance of an American play dealing sentimentally with the plight of the Irish – and then the drama takes the form of a moral lesson for schoolchildren. No prior American or British drama dealing with the problem in such a sympathetic manner has endured to this date. The tribulations confronted by destitute but gently reared Irish Catholic refugees engages the playwright's compassion. Almira Selden's preface to *The Irish Exiles in America* (1820) states her ideas much more completely than any synopsis.

The following little dramatic piece was written by the author, for the purpose, of having it represented by her youthful pupils. ... The situation, of the unfortunate Irish Emigrant, is too well known, for any one to suppose, that the scenes here delineated are mere dreams of fancy – The American, (though in the full possession of his darling Liberty) can never fail, of commiserating the destiny of the Irish Exiles, when he thinks of what would have been his fate, had, the plans of our Washington and the fortitude of our revolutionary patriots failed.

Not one humorous son or daughter of Erin appears in the cast.

The play takes place on the fourth of July. Evelina and her mother, Mrs. Balfour, have been harbored by an American farm family. They were forced to flee from Ireland during its civil troubles, leaving the male contingent of their family behind. Although invited, Evelina can not take part in the annual celebration of American independence because she sorrows for Ireland and her trapped relatives. Miss Armyne, a rich American socialite, has previously aided the Balfours, but now that the novelty has diminished, she makes her excuses and refrains from returning. When the pathos has accumulated to the point of saturation, news that Evelina's brother has escaped the clutches of the British, retaining a large segment of the family fortune, revives Evelina and her mother. A sentimental reunion ensues, and Evelina, now on a social par with Miss Armyne, refuses to forsake the humble but refined farm family who stood by her in her adversity. The drama closes on a prayer for enslaved Ireland.

Obviously, the play was meant as a moral-pointer for Almira Selden's students. One of the romantic-American rules by which the young ladies were to organize their lives concerned a correct evaluation of the native worth of a human being. Social status, of course, could not affect intrinsic merit. Therefore it would behoove all students to remember that during later life one of their duties and privileges would consist of relieving the distress of deserving paupers, among whom were numbered the unfortunate Irish immigrants.

Almira Selden's play probably influenced few outside the coterie of students she taught. Yet within three years after she published *The Irish Exiles*, two other plays which placed Irish in positions pivotal to the development of plot complication and dénouement had been written. The first, by Charles S. Talbot, contains Patrick O'Flaherty. The protagonist of *Paddy's Trip to America* (1822), Patrick foils a plot to kidnap an American girl by another Irishman. Paddy, as shall be pointed out in Chapter Four, continually involves himself in scrapes that result in comic drubbings, but at the close of the play he emerges an undisputable hero. The same holds true for Darby, the comic Irish porter in Mrs. Mary Carr

Clarke's *The Benevolent Lawyers* (1823). Despite his ludicrous antics, devotion to the bottle, and general lack of perception, Darby manages to foil the villain, Lovegold, and save the two children he had been hired to drown.

These instances, isolated and uncharacteristic though they be, indicate a weak yet perceptible undercurrent of opinion toward the Irishman that decreed he should be depicted as other than ludicrous. The numbers of Irish caricatures surfeited the American drama until, in the search for originality and a moral, sentimentally romantic characterizations exploited another possibility in the formulation of stage Irishmen. The characters in *Irish Exiles* anticipate the more honorable Irishmen of Talbot and Clarke, and lead almost directly into the historical Irish drama typified by James McHenry's *The Usurper* (1827), and George Pepper's *Kathleen O'Neill* (1829). These two authors follow in the tradition of a temporally long but numerically short line of plays on historic Irish subjects. Commencing with James Shirley's *St. Patrick for Ireland* (1640), and ending with Francis Dobb's *The Irish Chief* (1773), Duggan treats seven dramas that base their action on an important event in Irish history. Both the American plays, as did their transatlantic predecessors, take place in a distant and more glorious era of Ireland's past. When the setting of a drama moves back in time, and a truly romantic view of its action and agents may be taken, then the characters follow more closely the dictates of nobility prescribed by elevated rules for courtly behavior in love and war. The Irish lose all caricatured elements of portrayal, and resemble most closely their later non-Irish counterparts in romantic American plays by Robert M. Bird, Richard P. Smith, and George H. Boker. The six plays treated in this section serve as a preamble to John Brougham's *Temptation* (1849) and the later sentimental characterizations by Dion Boucicault, in which the Irish find a full measure of sympathy, their rightful due after so many decades of caricature.

While the Revolutionary War raged, Loyalists as well as Whigs wrote propaganda polemics abusing the efforts and partisans of the opposition. Since the colonial patriots (a post-facto appellation of approbation) won the Revolution, Tory propaganda plays are now termed sympathetic to foreigners. Had the issue produced another outcome, then the foreigner in American drama would have appeared at a later date. In New York, a stronghold of the British, many a Tory tract peeled from the presses. Among the pamphlets appear a number of plays or dialogues: *Debates at the Robin-Hood Society, A Cure for the Spleen, The Battle of Brooklyn*, and *The Blockheads*. In these the Tories heaped as much abuse on the Whigs as, in their plays, did the Whigs on the Tories. The patriots were condemned as rebels, immoral rabble, traitorous wretches worthy only to be executed. This highly factious expression of sentiments sympathetic to a group the Whigs considered foreign, naturally ceased as soon as the rebels won the Revolution and the Loyalists left for other British territories.

After the Revolution and into the nineteenth century, the attitudes toward foreigners which appeared in American drama may be broken into three categories: foreigners viewed and depicted sympathetically because of their innate humanity, because they accept American precepts, and for reasons more closely tied to form and genre than to political predilections. Robert Munford, William Dunlap, and Mary Carr Clarke led the dramatic vanguard against a partisan alignment of wartime sympathies. These three dramatists were essentially cosmopolitan in a society which tended to be strongly prejudiced in its own favor. They sought and found similarities and nobility in all men, placing their plays in time of war to take advantage of the violent tempers and sentiments then operative against a sanely humanitarian outlook.

Almost in opposition to this attitude appears one which accepted foreign viewpoints so long as they agreed with American standards. Stronger at periods of political turmoil precipitated by tense foreign relations, this attitude tended to fade after the War of 1812. It found dramatic expression in foreigners who espoused American precepts. Thus, a Frenchman in an American play might argue in 1793 that France was in the process of dissolving into anarchy. The author would be affiliated with the Federalist party of that period. The same applies to the British during any period up to and including that of 1812-1815, and immediately thereafter. The American system, if viewed by a foreigner initially antipathetic to what he saw, could work a metamorphosis of opinion if that foreigner would choose the correct values in his judgment. An idealization of the situation, this attitude sprang from the idea current after the Revolution that the American system of government, free competition, and mores would function superbly anywhere, to the admiration of all, if only the world would remove its blinders. So the travelling foreigners would initially decry all they saw, later to veer their opinions one hundred and eighty degrees to utter admiration.

The final category of sympathetic foreigners to appear in early American drama did not exist primarily to grind a political or moral axe. Any proclivities for espousing attitudes sympathetic to American ideals appeared secondarily to an interest in working out the exigencies of form and genre. A French hero believing in universal freedom would, in a melodrama, function heroically primarily because of his nobility of character, purity of intention, and ingenuity of outlook, rather than as a result of his pro-American expressions. The basically patriotic precepts of post-Revolutionary drama later became sentiments tinctured with romanticism and the rose colored dye of time and distance.

Foreign settings toward the close of the first fifty years of independence began to assume a few of the characteristics of Shakespeare's Forest of Arden. The Barbary Coast, Italy, France, the German principalities, and, to a minor extent, Britain, grew to represent different and peculiar places to a large segment of the population. The romanticism of foreign countries and exotic settings affected the behavior of foreigners in the drama until they became romantically stereotyped. The stage Irishman benefitted from precisely that transmutation of outlook. Even though Dunlap made a funny Irishman speak serious thoughts in 1789, it was not until 1820 that the Irish immigrant had become settled, and the Irish stage caricature sufficiently stereotyped, that a divergent and sentimental treatment of the Irish plight in Erin and America could be undertaken. But the effects were not widely perceptible, for even though Irishmen did find themselves in the position of protagonists, they nevertheless retained many of their earlier comic characteristics. Finally the complete romantic metamorphosis of the historic Irishman occurred just prior to 1830. This prepared the way for Brougham and Boucicault later to romanticize the contemporary Irishman.

IV. COMIC FOREIGNERS

A. THE IRISH

The Irishman had enjoyed an extended career in the British drama prior to his appearance in an American play. In 1600 an Irish servant complete with dialect had been written into *Sir John Oldcastle*. In the seventeenth century such eminent playwrights as Shakespeare, Jonson, Beaumont and Fletcher, Shirley, Ford, Otway, and Farquhar had included a variety of Irish characters in a few of their plays and masques. Yet not until the late seventeenth and early eighteenth centuries does the frequency and popularity of Irish parts point to the beginnings of the stage Irishman in British drama. Dramatized and stereotyped characters of one or another nationality depend upon caricaturization. The playwright exaggerates supposed national proclivities, traits, or qualities and utilizes them to delineate his stage character. For example, in Shakespeare's Shylock may be seen an Elizabethan caricature of the avaricious Jew. The forerunner of the Irish servingman appeared in Richard Howard's *The Committee, or the Faithful Irishman* (1665). Teague, the servant of an English Colonel during the Interregnum, manages to keep his master's lands from being confiscated by confounding a Presbyterian committee formed to investigate holdings of former Cavaliers. His brogue, capers, garrulity, and tricks rendered him so popular that Farquhar placed a Teague in his *The Twin Rivals* (1702). As late as 1779, John Moody, the famed enacter of Irish roles, played Teague in a revival of Howard's play.

The popularity of Charles Shadwell's five plays depicting Dublin life gave renewed impetus to the stage portrayal of the Irishman in the early eighteenth century. Thomas Sheridan – father of Richard Brinsley – produced the next notable stage Irishman, Captain O'Blunder. The Captain appears in a one-act play which takes its title from his name, *Captain O'Blunder, or the Brave Irishman* (1738). Irish from his shillelagh to his boots, O'Blunder exaggerates everything he states. Sheridan employs dialect and "bulls", or "Irish-isms", as the means for much of the amusement in the Captain. O'Blunder is treated as the butt for foolish situations, but in the end he marries the girl of his choice. Charles Macklin may have remembered O'Blunder when he placed Sir Callaghan O'Brallaghan in *Love à la Mode* (1760). O'Brallaghan's brogue is liberally peppered with figures of speech drawn from a soldier's vocabulary.

Sentimentalism affected the portrayals of Irish soldiers in 1771, when Richard Cumberland created Major O'Flaherty in *The West Indian*. Denis O'Flaherty assumes the role of general benefactor, helping a fellow officer to regain his estate, aiding that officer's son in a duel, and bringing about universal happiness by making the plot end happily for everyone. Lucius O'Trigger, in Sheridan's *The Rivals* (1775), stands next in the line of caricatured Irishmen. Fooled constantly by Mrs. Malaprop, herself the butt of many a jest, O'Trigger topped in downright boorishness his many predecessors. So strong was the caricature that the public outrage of Hiberniophiles caused Sheridan to rewrite the role into its present form. By the time O'Keeffe wrote *The Poor Soldier* (1782) and *Patrick in Prussia* (1786), whence the omnipresent character of Darby originated, the Irish stage caricature had become well established on the British and American stages. Patrick descends from O'Flaherty, and his sentimentally brave action in saving Fitzroy's life in America leads to his commission and marriage – the reward for his admirable qualities. Duggan, in his incomplete listing of British plays containing Irish characters, enumerates fifty-three from *Love à la Mode* (1760) until 1800. The stage Irishman became popular in America almost as soon as in Britain: Macklin's play was produced as early as 1768 in Philadelphia, *The West Indian* by 1772, *The Poor Soldier* by 1785. Each of

these plays received numerous performances, often being repeated
as many as four or five times in a single season at one playhouse.[1]
Indeed, *Love à la Mode* played on the night in 1785 that the
Americans opened the post-Revolutionary theatre in New York.[2]
With increasing frequency the stage Irishman appeared in both
English and American drama through the late eighteenth and
into the nineteenth century.

American playwrights emulated the prevalent fashion when it
came to including comic dialect parts in their pieces. The one
foreign type most consistently ludicrous throughout the early history of American drama was the Irishman. His brogue could be
heard in practically any comedy that included farcical action.
As servant, fresh and fearful immigrant, awkward soldier, porter
or ditch digger, the Irishman more than any other national
stage type caused American audiences to break into unrestrained
laughter. The continued emigration of Irish to the New World
furnished living examples for literary likenesses to the populace
of the larger American cities.[3] The ready laughter and boisterous
mannerisms of the immigrants reinforced what readers and play-
goers knew from the dramatic literature of the day.

A prevalent kind of Irishman, proportionately as numerous in
dramatic literature as in American life, was the indentured servant. While the British drama contained, toward the end of the
eighteenth century, considerably more Irish servants than at any
previous time, their peculiarities were not identical to the American stage servant of Irish birth. The British caricatures of the servingman depended upon a liberal use of the brogue, the ability of
the servant to get into then talk himself out of awkward situations,
and a readiness of tongue that allowed him to make many comic
observations about his surroundings. These qualities resulted from
a line of Irish stage servants starting in the seventeenth century.
The Americans, although British in ancestry and culture, never-

---

[1] The above material concerning the Irish stage character in British
drama has been drawn from Duggan, p. 117 ff.

[2] Seilhamer, vol. 2, p. 185.

[3] The famines of 1740-41 and the decline of the linen industry around
1771 sent larger than usual numbers to this continent, according to the
Encyclopedia of American History, pp. 444-445.

theless depicted a somewhat different Irish servant. Possessed of an ability for avoiding work surmounted only by his capacity for whisky and potatoes, the American comic Irish servant seldom performed any role closely involved with the working out of the plot.

Patrick O'Neal in Judith S. Murray's comedy, *The Traveller Returned* (1796) may be used as an example. In Patrick may be discerned several of the major characteristics found in Irish servants of early American drama. Patrick arrives during the Revolution, attending Mr. Rambleton, who had been an unwilling expatriate. Almost as soon as servant and master disembark, the play divides into plot and sub-plot. In the main plot the fortunes of Rambleton wax and wane as he is called before the Committee of Safety under suspicion as an English spy, manages to clear himself by proving that he is a citizen who has returned to seek a wife and daughter, then finally retrieves both family and fortune. Patrick, an overly-cautious New York Dutch innkeeper, and the innkeeper's recklessly avaricious wife, operate in the sub-plot. The Vansittarts plan to steal Rambleton's trunkload of valuables, guarded by Patrick. To that end they scheme first to overfeed Patrick, then get him drunk while they raise the alarm about Rambleton's nationality and escape during the furor.

The main elements of Patrick's characterization render his actions comic: he possesses a rapacious appetite that the Vansittarts can barely satisfy; he responds quickly to alcoholic temptation, growing boisterously drunk and finally passing out; he readily admits his gullibility and joins in the chase after the fleeing Vansittarts to recover the trunk his laxity lost. His brogue serves to illustrate another comic element of character delineation.

Patrick: Ow, may I never see my own sweet country again, if I did not think this land of America had been all salt water, d'ye see, we were so long in finding it. Arrah now, while we are standing here, by my soul we may as well be looking after a place to rest ourselves in, so we may.

The proclivity for comically misconstruing and exaggerating whatever confronts him is a quality playwrights included in almost every Irish servant in early American drama. These characteristics could suffice for a rudimentary description of nearly all comic Irishmen in British and American drama of the era. The name might differ from play to play, and the action in which the ludicrous character partook could vary from drawing room to soldier's tent, but these essentials of comic Irish caricature acquired from British drama remained substantially the same for nearly a century.

John Beete's *The Man of the Times* (1797) contains James and Katy, indentured Irish servants. They and an English servant comprise the foreign element in a play set in the new Republic and dealing with such un-American business practices as injurious speculation and usury. The author calls the play a farce, although the most pronounced farcical elements are supplied in a secondary manner by Katy and James. The exposé of unethical business practices bears upon the love interest between Charles Screwpenny (son of the usurer) and Lydia Upright (daughter of Major Upright, one of Colonel Manly's successors). The honest Upright will not permit Lydia to marry anyone named Screwpenny, and old Screwpenny threatens to disinherit his son if he weds Lydia. Charles solves the problem by taking the name of Upright, and his father tries one too many business tricks and impoverishes himself. The servants function on another comic level. James' gullibility surmounts even that of Judith Murray's Patrick, for he complains that he was tricked into emigrating to a country whose customs he can not learn.

James: Larn your customs! To be sure, I shall. Ah, poor James, to what a devil of a scrape have your brought yourself: three years to serve, for a bit of a passage to this fine country, where to be sure the captain told me, the streets were paved with dollars, and every branch of pine was loaded with kegs of whisky, guggling out of their bungs, and singing 'come drink me;' Well 'twas a devil of a lie, to be sure it was.

James' unfamiliarity with American idiom, another comic device, Beete compounds with a streak of unabashed amorousness.

Katy: Come, James, what are you doing here? They want you to wait at table.

James: Arrah! you're out there now: – Didn't I hear the Major say he'd wait on his daughter himself?

Katy: No such thing: He is calling you.

James: Well then, I'm going: But, Katy – give me one kiss, and then –

Katy: What then?

James: Why then fait, my jewel, another, another, and another.

Part of the reason why James can not acclimate himself to strange American customs, such as the dislike of titles, lies in his unwillingness to attempt a program of familiarization; he stubbornly intends to maintain his Irish customs and habits. Katy exhibits characteristics different from those of her fellow servant. She possesses greater perception when it comes to adjusting herself to foreign custom. Apparently, Katy does not mind bettering a situation by using her charms, for even though James must marry her to receive the full benefit of the colleen's endowments, the captain of the ship on which they travelled might already have given them a head start on a family.

James: To be sure human nature is human nature, isn't it, Katy? – So give me your hand, my girl, – never fear, lit, – James O'Connor shall do your justice; and now you are mine, why, you shall do an odd job for me, as you did for the captain, won't you?

It is entirely possible that she was intended to be portrayed already pregnant.

In another scene, James refuses to answer an insistent knock on the main door because he has seated himself to enjoy the Irishman's mid-morning repast, a potato.

James: Aye, knock away; I can't do two things at once: – *Fait* these American potatoes are almost as fine as little Ireland's, but then they have not such a sweet smack of the sod . . .

On the comic servant plane, James' exchange with William, Screwpenny's English servant ("*James.* 'Tis to Englishmen alone that we are allowed to speak twice, *becaise* they are so dull they can't understand plain English the first time"), parallels verbally and on another level the financial drubbing Screwpenny receives. The comment holds two-edged humor, for neither William nor James utters what an American would consider plain English. Despite

James' shortcomings, the Major recognizes the inherent goodness in an Irish nature, consents to his servants' wedding, and promises them a farm at the end of their indenture. The servant, who in many ways resembles the Elizabethan jester, receives a reward for supplying the master with so much amusement. The Irish servant also shows, through the character of James, the first stages in a peculiarly American dramatic technique: that of mixing sentiment with ridicule, despite their apparent immiscibility. That all men possessed immanent worth was believed by early Americans. The new Republic, with its naturally beneficial catalyst of a simple and straightforward society, could bring out that worth. The Major perceives in James and Katy the first indications of just such a change, so he supplies them further incentive to complete the transformation.

A reluctance to admit anything on the American continent the equal of a comparable item or custom in Ireland; a garrulity that taxes the patience of listeners ("*Major Upright.* This fellow's prolixity would almost make me think him a fool"), an incontinent attachment to whisky, a gullibility that causes the Irishman to fall into many a ludicrous situation, the constant desire to return to his homeland, a boisterous amorousness, the readiness for physical engagement in a situation likely to result in a comic drubbing (Patrick chasing the Vansittarts), the unwillingness to relinquish Irish ways, a naive reaction to the marvels of the New World – these elements all operate to a greater or lesser degree in every ludicrous stage Irishman from the date of his American birth sometime after the Revolution. The ubiquity of the Irish servant's comic characteristics does not mean that all playwrights agreed to employ them after observing the Irish immigrant. It indicates, rather, that the elements of farcical comedy were as well known to the American dramatists of the late eighteenth and early nineteenth centuries as they were to their French and British counterparts, and as they were to Plautus and Terence, Aristophanes and Menander. For that reason, the comic Irish servant, most numerous of the early brogue stage parts, may serve as a basis for the rest of the ludicrous and humorous dramatic characterizations of the sons of Erin.

American playwrights utilized Irish caricatures other than the servant alone. The Jameses and Patricks, indentured for servitude in a household, began to acquire incidental characteristics which provided a superficial variety. Loony McGra, in Joseph Hutton's *The School for Prodigals* (1809), returns to England from Dresden disguised as a gentleman. He ostensibly brings news about his self-exiled prodigal master, but spends most of the time at the family manse misguiding everyone and answering with a sharp tongue the jibes of salty Admiral Darnly.

For *The Fair Americans* (1815), Mrs. Mary Carr Clarke picked the shore of Lake Eire during the War of 1812 on which to place Dermot, Irish servant who turns soldier. Combining the possibilities for amusement contained in the Irish servant's reactions to domestic situations, with the wider latitude of laugh-provoking incidents created by Dermot's response to war, Mrs. Clarke draws a stage Irishman whose true courage transcends his braggadocio. Far from a coward, Dermot replies with humorous courage to a warning that the British will hang him for a deserter if he enlists, fights, and is captured: "Hung, say you, sure there's never an Irishman fears that death, when he has a good musket on his shoulder; and any death is better than living with two scolding women." Mrs. Clarke's Irish servant-soldier retains many of the characteristics previously mentioned in connection with the servant alone. The humor in a scene between Dermot and his intended, Hetty, depends upon the misconstructions and malapropisms each commits in discussing their notions of a last will and testament ("will and power") that Dermot intends to prepare against the possibility of his death in battle. Dermot returns alive, pretends to be his own ghost to Hetty, and imagines that he has killed her when she faints. Yet, despite his ludicrousness, Dermot has stood in battle for the American dandy, Freelove, who hid his cowardice behind a toothache. Dermot's Irish steadfastness is readily apparent.

In British drama the comic Irish soldier appeared both long before and in greater numbers than the Irish servant. The O'Blunders, O'Brallaghans, and Darbies – the caricatured soldier – remained popular just as long in America as in England, if frequency of appearance in plays serves as any indication. John Moody, Jack (Irish) Johnstone, and Spanger Barry acquired fame in Britain as actors of Irish parts – as did Wignell, Wallack, and Henry in America – and their popularity maintained the public interest in the roles which they portrayed. The dichotomy between the sentimentally depicted Irish officers and the caricatured soldiers and servants carried over onto the American stage, since both O'Keeffe's and Cumberland's plays were perenially popular in theatres of the new Republic. Indeed, O'Keeffe's Darby, although he instigates many a joke at the expense of others, and tumbles into situations revelatory of his own lack of perception, does not belong in the category of vicious satires. His morals are lax, he drinks too much, he attempts to cheat the priest (who deserves it), and his involvement in a mock-duel borders on the inane. Yet when his antics are compared to those of Bagatelle, Fitzroy's French servant, the sympathy accorded Darby becomes apparent. Bagatelle attempts to force his dubious charms on Norah, a girl beyond his social level. In addition, he attempts to call out Patrick in order to avenge his supposedly injured honor. Darby, although he assists Bagatelle, does not receive directly the dressing down that Fitzroy gives his servant for attempting actions beyond those permitted persons of a menial's rank. Fitzroy upbraids Darby, but his caution to the Irishman that duels are the privilege of the gentry does not contain the amount of acid it did when he castigated Bagatelle. Darby, however, shares in the opprobrium attached to the Frenchman. To that extent he represents a somewhat softened caricature of the Irish lower class, akin to the servant.

American playwrights early utilized the latent comic possibilities in an Irish characterization not only to cause laughter because of typically Irish mannerisms, as did the British, but to speak out in sympathy for American ways and freedom. An Irish brogue lent to recurrent patriotic outbursts a piquancy that alleviated their repetitive uniformity. Dunlap, before any other, recognized the chances for originality inherent in panegyrics spoken with a brogue. *Darby's Return* (1789) resembles remarkably the pre-Revolutionary exercises and dialogues by Freneau, Smith, and Brackenridge discussed in the second chapter: all overflow with unabashed chauvinism. Dunlap's acute sense of the dramatic caused him to seek a more unique way to couch his encomiums. Quinn mentions that Dunlap, "borrowing Darby from O'Keeffe's *Poor Soldier,* had given a more sympathetic interpretation of the wandering Irishman's character",[4] but neglects to point out that the sympathy results from Darby's strong pro-American sentiments. Dunlap may have borrowed Darby, but the manner in which he employed the Irish character removes the onus of plagiarism. The piece resembles more a monologue than it does a play, since Darby responds in long segments of rhymed couplets to brief questions by five other characters. Darby's return to Ireland from a trip to Austria, Prussia, America, and France furnished Dunlap's dramatic excuse for the little comic monologue. Of the monarchies Darby speaks no good; of the two revolutionary democracies no ill.

> *Darby:* Well Neighbours, now by destinies and
> fates,
> See me safe landed in the United States;
> And now I'm at the best part of my story,
> For there poor Darby was in all his glory
> From north to south, where ever I appear'd,
> With deeds and words, my spirits oft they cheer'd;
> * * *
> There too, I saw some might pretty shows;
> A revolution without blood or blows;
> For as I understood the cunning elves,
> The people all revolted from themselves;
> Then after joining in a kind consession,
> They all agreed to walk in a procession;
> So turners, taylors, tinkers, tavern-keepers,
> With parsons, blacksmiths, lawyers, chimney
> sweepers
> ... March'd thro' the town – eat beef – and
> drank strong beer.

Darby continues, describing George Washington who, "like me, / Return'd to his own *potatoe ground* . . .", and completes the comparison between the Americans and the French "bag and tails"

4 Quinn, p. 375.

of the Revolution. Dunlap's derogatory name for the French rebels refers to the part of Bagatelle in O'Keeffe's *Poor Soldier*. As the previous discussion of Bagatelle indicated, O'Keeffe treats the caricatured French servant with absolutely no sympathy. Bagatelle attempts to transgress on the domain of his betters in a manner not only unpermissible in the person of a menial, but vicious when attempted by any human being. Bagatelle is presumptuous, conniving, licentious, and lacking in any sense whatsoever. In fact the part so derided the French, that prior to the French Revolution, in a 1787 production of O'Keeffe's play, an American audience refused to permit Bagatelle, as the British caricature of a French ally, upon the stage. Dunlap refers to the event, quoting from *McLean's Journal* of March 21, 1787, " 'It is with real concern the subscribers learn that a character in the *"Poor Soldier"* has given umbrage to any frequenters of the theatre: it is both their duty and invariable study to please, not to offend, as a proof of which, they respectfully inform the public, they have made such alterations in the part alluded to, as they trust will do away every shadow of offence.' The part alluded to was Bagatelle." [5] By 1789, when Dunlap wrote *Darby's Return* as a benefit piece for the comedian Wignell, the French Revolution had broken out and the Jacobin-Democrats of America were in full cry, demanding that anything not highly reverent of the French be censored. Staunch Federalist Dunlap, along with others of his party, could not see the beneficence in closer ties with France, and in reply to Democratic outbursts wrote into his play the derisive, "And all the *bag and tails* swore they'd be free."

A decade after Darby returned to Ireland, Patrick and Timothy sang the praises of their adoptive mother country in John Minshull's comic opera, *Rural Felicity* (1801). Employed cutting wood for a New York farmer by the name of Clover, the two sons of Erin turn from their task to reply to their employer's behest to behave properly toward the government which has given them shelter.

Patrick: By my soul, you shall see, that an Irishman has a heart corresponding with a noble disposition. To be sure, I was a little mellow,

[5] Dunlap, p. 74.

as a body might say, and no harm to it neither. Your good advice is much like my honest father, who said, gun-powder balls, made with water, was like politics in the mind of fools; when touched with fire, pleased the eye, then blow them to the gibbet; there to dangle for the good of nations. I fought for liberty, and have found Columbia's shore; and if you hear me sing a song, hurtful to the feelings of my friend, and benefactors, then never trust a poor Irishman of honor, who is proud in heart, though poor in purse.

Probably written during Adams' Presidency, the play reflects the chauvinistic set of mind that decreed as seditious outbursts against the incumbent party, since it is shot through with sententiae similar to the preceding quotation. In accord with the sentiments of the era, Minshull's Patrick had the good sense to know when he was well off.

While many of the ludicrous Irish in early American drama extricated themselves from one farcical situation only to plunge into another, the characteristics of honest, proud, poverty which would cling to later sentimental Irish personae were part of not a few of their personalities. These characters also reflected the major difference between British and American stage Irishmen, first noted in the servants from Beete's *Man of the Times*. The cast of mind expressed by Patrick in Minshull's comic opera originates in the Rousseauistic notion that the natural life brings out the good in man. Patrick and Timothy have been working on an American farm, as close to the primitive as possible for them. As a result the two Irishmen acquire a portion of the same libertarian and democratic ideals that Americans, loath to trace their political heritage to Britain, claimed they inherited from the new land with its lack of artificial restraints.

Two years after the publication of *Rural Felicity*, Dunlap took the plot of *André* (1798) and reworked it to make the commemorative operetta, *The Glory of Columbia* (1803). Dennis O'Bogg, comic Irishman in a red coat, deserts the besieged British army for interesting reasons: ". . . finding how your general Arnold is treated by sir Henry Clinton, at York, with honor and command, I though I might as well get rid of my *little inconveniences,* for they will be springing up round an irishman, like mushrooms round a dunghill". The "little inconveniences", Dennis eventually reveals, are two wives left behind the British lines. At Yorktown, O'Bogg learns that his spouses are within the city under siege by the Americans.

O'Bogg: I shall get out of the fire into the frying pan. A pretty day's work I shall make of it! We shall silence the redoubts, carry the lines, take the town, and then I shall have two batteries open'd upon poor Dennis alone, that the devil himself couldn't silence.

Dennis does not lack for courage. He behaves reprehensibly in moral rather than combative pursuits.

A definite and strong trend toward any depiction of the Irishman as more serious than ludicrous can not be charted, for weighed against each sentimental or sensitive man of Erin are enough farcical Irish to steady the pointer. In 1828, for instance, Dunlap placed Dennis Dougherty on *A Trip to Niagara.* Dunlap wrote the play to accompany a moving panorama of the Hudson River and Erie Canal. The plot concerns the reformation of Wentworth, a worldweary and skeptical young English traveller. Dennis arrives in New York worried about the "faver" caught only by Irish immigrants, imagines that Negroes have the black plague, loses his way, mistakes the Bowery Theatre for a church, and works his passage on a canal boat by walking the horses. At the close of the play he is unreconstructed, and returns to Ireland. Even though the part of Dennis was tailored for John Wallack, Dunlap's ludicrous Irishman evinces the stock stage reactions which travelled across the sea in the eighteenth century, became a part of American depictions of Irish characters, and remained elements of Irish personae right past the close of the early period of American drama.

When it came to portraying the Irishman as an American, though, much of the glory attached to those who fought for freedom transferred to the immigrants who exchanged their shillelaghs for muskets. It took a while, but when the first blush of independence had paled and playwrights were casting about for ways in which to enliven their patriotic pieces, several of them followed Dunlap's lead by creating humorous but not ludicrous Irishmen. These were inserted into the patriotic drama in a variety of ways – each designed to invigorate what would otherwise have been the same old material. In brief, by the beginning of the nine-teenth century, American playwrights had begun to find more and more possibilities inherent in the funny Irishman. Oliver Queer-fish, in the anonymous *Battle of the Eutaw Springs* (1807), was mentioned in Chapter Two as one of a number of characters whose foreign birth served as partial purpose for their antipathy. More important than Queerfish's foreign birth is his nationality, York-shire Irishman.[6] Queerfish served as the author's means to show the ridiculous nature of the British cause. In one instance the recal-citrant Red Coat calls an officer of the guard to report a cow that had failed to answer a challenge. The officer had previously been curt while instructing Queerfish in his duties. The author com-bined the Yorkshireman, who in English drama served as the butt for ludicrous characterizations, with the popular Irish stage nationality in order to create a loquacious mock-hero who even though he fights on the side of the English, eventually settles in America (i.e., he shows both a sense of humor and good sense).

By the time the War of 1812 had passed, stage Irish characters were appearing regularly as soldiers. Possibly because of his citizenship, the Irish comic soldier began to acquire some charac-teristics other than those which caused laughter or amusement. As Americans grew more familiar with the Irish, a tendency to draw away from strictly ludicrous depictions appeared in *some* of the playwrights. C. E. Grice wrote *The Battle of New Orleans* (1815), a play which rivals patriotic drama written during the Rev-olution in its anti-British imputations. Yet Grice included among the officers of Jackson's army an Irishman, Captain Brien O'Fla-negan, who had been previously nursed back to health by Colonel Oakwood, noble and generous American patriot. Grice's Irishman, far from being ludicrous or even slightly amusing, refuses to bear false information against Oakwood, for which he had been offered a bribe by a vicious and anti-American Scotsman. The humorous nature of the Irish soldier diminished as he climbed in the ranks

[6] Queerfish, although he does not resemble Sir Larry MacMurrough of Ballygrennanclonfergus, in George Colman's *Who Wants a Guinea, or the Irish Yorkshireman* (1805), doubtless owes his existence to the popularity of Colman's Irish baronet who takes refuge from creditors on a Yorkshire estate. (Duggan, p. 276).

of the American army. Mrs. Clarke, whose *The Fair Americans* (1815) was mentioned in the section of this chapter devoted to Irish servants, placed Dermot in the fight against British troops in Canada as a willing substitute for the American coward and fop, Freelove. Two years later, Dunlap finally published *The Glory of Columbia*, which he had produced in 1803. While O'Bogg's morals leave much to be desired, as has been pointed out, he fights with courage and daring on the side of the Americans during the Revolution.

Henry J. Finn, in *Montgomery* (1825), also treated Revolutionary material. Using the battle for Quebec as motivation, Finn wrote a standard melodrama in which the amusing Irish soldier, whose good intentions and hardy efforts counterbalance his farcical mistakes, replaces the humorous servant so necessary to early nineteenth century melodrama. Corporal O'Shamrock serves as comic assistant to Yankee Sergeant Welcome Sobersides. One of the most delightful scenes in the play occurs when Narcisse Malheureuse, a Canadian, attempts to teach the Corporal how to speak French. O'Shamrock creates cognates never previously suspected. Yet when the heroine needs to be saved, the Corporal ably and fearlessly assists his superior to pull her from an imminent plunge over the Falls of Montmorency. One of the Philadelphia playwrights, Richard Penn Smith, wrote *The Eighth of January* (1829) in celebration of Jackson's victory at New Orleans. Appearing in it as a comic Irish captain. McFuse represents one aspect of the degeneration apparent in the British army decimated by Jackson's troops. Yet no disapprobation attaches to his character, since his ludicrous antics and comments obviate the onus of his enlistment in the British army.

If any change in attitude toward the Irish as a nationality were to be gauged by using evidence found in the drama, plays in which Irish characters held positions pivotal to plot dénouement or appeared as protagonists might serve, along with sympathetic soldiers, as indicators. One could possibly perceive the beginnings of a sensitivity to the Irish as people rather than as comic types, were it not for the abundance of material pointing out the reverse. The only fair judgment which can be drawn is that the playwrights who utilized comic Irish characters in major roles realized the attractive values of a heavy brogue and a shock of red hair.

Charles S. Talbot dipped into his national origins for the material of *Paddy's Trip to America* (1822), in which the most interesting character is Patrick O'Flaherty, fresh from a potato patch on the Emerald Isle. Quinn finds the two-act farce "a poor affair".[7] Granted it resembles the numbers of similarly constructed melodramatic farces which preceded it, but the character of Paddy stands a cut above the usual stage Irishman; possibly because of Talbot's acquaintance with or sympathy for those of his nationality. Paddy's Irish cousin, Whelan, has left a wife and four children behind him, has married a woman in Philadelphia and one in New York, and wishes Paddy to help him abduct Lucy, the daughter of his New York wife. Paddy refuses to implicate himself, and even attempts to rescue Lucy from the boat in which Whalen's hirelings are rowing her off. He receives a dousing and a thwack across the pate for his pains. Paddy then learns where Lucy is being held. In the company of FitzClarence, Lucy's fiancé, Patrick steals into the house and distinguishes himself by rescuing her single-handedly – leaping from a window to sprain his ankle. Paddy refuses to stay in America, for indeed, as he tells his audience, he has had a fearful time of it while protecting the fair name of Ireland from degradation and saving American innocence from Irish villainy,

Paddy: Very well, your honour, we'll have Patrick's day, and Moll in the wad – but as I was coming along, the strangest thing of all came to pass; they tell me something has happened to Jack for having three wives – I always knew that three wives was too much for any man – I told him how it would be, when he wanted me to run away with Miss; but no, says I, Patrick O'Flaherty is not your man. And when I see you two made into one, I'll be after going back again to Ireland, for d---l take me, if I like this place, at all, at all – the first day, a fellow at the Lobster and Cockleshell stole my hat – the next day I got soused in water, lost my best pair of brogues, and got polthogned in the head into the bargain – and today, by the powers, jumping with Miss, from a two pair window, I sprained my ancle – Och hone! It wont do – Judy expect me directly, and tell the childer and Towser, and the cabin, and the neighbours, I'm coming.

[7] Quinn, p. 375.

Talbot's stage Irishmen cross the spectrum from villain to comic hero.

Mrs. Mary Clarke, in *The Benevolent Lawyers* (1823), created Darby the drunken Irish porter who, because of his innate humanitarianism, refuses to drown two children for enough gold to return him to that nirvana of Irish immigrants, Ireland. Mrs. Clarke composed Darby's character of practically all the ludicrous elements mentioned previously in connection with Irish servants. Darby expects an easy fortune in the New World, drinks to excess, exaggerates his lack of luck, yearns for Ireland, and becomes involved in a ridiculous situation from which he humorously extricates himself. Lovegold, the villain who offered Darby return passage to Ireland in exchange for the murder of the two children, Darby treats to, "Oh! you spalpeen of the devil. The hemp is ripe for you." Truly Darby stands out from earlier servants.

Charles S. Talbot, author of *Paddy's Trip to America,* wrote another two-act farce in 1827 entitled *Squire Hartley*. Modelled somewhat after Sheridan's *The Rivals*, the play contains instead of Fag, Dermot O'Dogherty, doughty servant to Squire Hartley. Dermot engineers a crucial trick, for which he masquerades as a gentleman in order successfully to dupe the father of Hartley's enamorata into permitting Hartley to marry her. Richard Penn Smith combined the romantic attraction of a Barbary pirate melodrama with the comic possibilities inherent in the actions of an Irish sailor in *A Wife at a Venture* (1829). Dennis O'Whack so amuses the favorite courtier of the Caliph that he is appointed royal jailor. This provides Dennis scope for humorous mistakes and comments greater than that afforded him by the exotic Moorish setting. By the third decade of the nineteenth century, American playwrights had managed to place the Irishman in nearly every circumstance productive of comedy.

The variety of situations and locales into which Irishmen were set is difficult to overestimate. This one comic type appeared more frequently than even the Indian in melodramas alone, not to mention farces, comic operas, and romantic *drames*. In 1798, the Old American Company acted a sort of *Impromptu de Versailles* called *All in a Bustle* (William Milns, author), placing it in the newly opened Park Theatre. Hodgkinson, the acting, manager, played himself, besieged by an importunate Irish actor just off the boat and determined to take only the best parts in the company's repertoire. John Minshull wrote *He Stoops to Conquer* (1804), a scatalogical little piece layed in Italy. Sir John Patrick and his amorous servant, Tickle Toby, are the Irish in this play. Sir John helps Signor Ludovico trick his reluctant wife into consummating their marriage. A sample of the dialogue will serve to set the tone of the play.

Sir John: My dear Signor, excuse my freedom. Tho' you have the appearance of a proficient in all things, I am sorry there is reason to think you are a delicate novice. My dear friend, who could have supposed that your genius was of a superior nature, and that your composition would have appeared as the works of a man that could bodly use a sentence in a parenthesis, in a style that would have honored you as a grammarian, for most assuredly it gives infinite pleasure to be correct in tickling the fancy, by putting in or taking out without injuring the sense.

Ludovico: To possess a fine art without the privilege of planting an acorn, is against the national interest.

James Workman, in *Liberty in Louisiana* (1804), uses the purchase of New Orleans as motivation for a rambling comedy with a pro-democratic moral. The comic protagonist of one of the parallel plots, Phelim O'Flinn, travels the Mississippi in the company of Scotsman Sawny McGregor, the two of them engaged in relieving gullible Americans of their money. Upon their arrival at New Orleans, the con men enter the home of Don Bertholdo, a lecherous old judge who intends to steal away with his beautiful young ward, Laura. Phelim learns of the plot, and attempts to masquerade as Captain O'Brien, beloved of Laura. In a wedding-of-errors, Phelim is united with a young girl he had seduced up-river, while Laura and O'Brien manage to defy Bertholdo and arrange their own nuptials. Workman sustains the amusement well throughout the one hundred and three pages of dialogue: after compounding mendacity with felony, Phelim has the gall to confess to a priest that only the weight of a few childhood pranks presses on his soul.

That the stage Irishman was considered a necessary ingredient for melodrama is borne out by his existence in many plays of that genre. John H. Payne's first play, the melodrama *Julia, or the Wanderer* (1806), produced when the author was fourteen years old, contains tavern-keeper O'Dennis and his shrewish wife. Payne's play follows the formula for successful melodrama of the era. It contains a heroine, bothered by a villain, saved by a hero, and finding father, a fortune, and a husband in the end. James N. Barker placed a comic Irish soldier in the first recorded Pocahontas play, *The Indian Princess* (1808). The piece is more properly termed, in Barker's words, "an operatic melo-drama". It closely resembles the French melodramas of the period. When Irish soldier Larry laments, the woe of all other keeners hushes beside the intensity of his wail: "Och! Hubbaboo – Gramachree – Hone!"

The ubiquity of the Irish comic character in early American drama can not be over-emphasized. Commencing with Darby in Dunlap's *Darby's Return* (1789), he appeared in every type of stage entertainment and dramatic situation that could be improved by humorous antics and accent. Nationalistic pieces, melodramas, comic operettas, romantic dramas – all had a red-headed son or daughter of Erin somewhere between first and final scenes. As the nineteenth century advanced, and the popularity of British drama drew angry outbursts from some American playwrights, authors in the new democracy seeking rapid recognition for their plays tried to emulate successful elements of popular English works. The stage Irishman was one of those elements. Yet the Irishman in American drama differed from his cousin in British drama.

Due to the immigrant to which Americans grew accustomed, the part which the Irishman played varied from the innkeeper, servant, or tiller of the sod usual in English drama. The wide-eyed and amazed immigrant served to enliven many a caricature. If a specific attitude toward the Irish were to be accepted, it would have to be one which assumed that a large majority of the American populace visualized the Irishman as a comic bumbler. Yet the existence of plays in which the plight of the laboring or indentured Irish immigrant was treated as sentimentally humorous

rather than ludicrous, and even portrayed with extreme under-
standing and sympathy (these were discussed in Chapter III), miti-
gates the harshness of his general caricature. In reality, to identify
the Irishman as he actually existed by attitudes dependent upon
extant early American drama for their support, would be to judge
from insufficient premises. The Americans inherited the stage
Irishman from English drama, a bequest that developed a proclivity among Americans for viewing him as a comic *stage* type.
The depiction of Irish immigrants in a variety of local situations
shows that playwrights adapted the British caricature to American
settings, changing him to the extent that he was susceptible to the
natural beneficence of the land, but it does not sustain an avowal
that Americans invariably viewed the real Irishman as comic, they
only tended to. One must not identify a caricature too closely with
its subject. A caricaturist selects certain traits to exaggerate.

B. THE ENGLISH

Far less numerous in early American drama than the comic Irish,
the stage caricatures of Englishmen, one might assume, would
be of a different cast. The British were, twice in the first half-
century of American independence, the armed enemies of the
young Republic. At other times the Crown's foreign policy caused
no small degree of animosity among segments of its one-time subjects. Yet American rancor toward the British was not the type
readily transformed in a comic purgation. The vicious enmity
which existed between the two countries in times of stress (and was
sustained among anti-British groups at other periods of American
history) found expression in the bitter depictions of the English
discussed in Chapter Two. Partially for this reason, and partially
because of the continued popularity of the Irish servant, the British comic servant never reached an importance in American drama
equal to that of his counterpart from Ireland. In those plays where
a Britisher and his servant function in an American setting, the
overriding reason for that choice of nationality lay in a desire to
point a moral through characterizations of ludicrous foreigners.

Their aberrations were studied in contrast with the more ideal American behavior. Both the English traveller and his servant were ridiculed, often with a degree of vindinctiveness that revealed the strong anti-foreign attitude of the playwright.

All the generalities that were stated in reference to the comic Irish servant, save those peculiar to his Irish nature, apply to the comic British servant. Usually, a British servant exaggerates one of his master's characteristics, carrying it to its ludicrous extreme. On the other hand, the servant might be delineated by a behavioral characteristic strong enough to be likened to one of Jonson's humours. In a comedy of manners, the stuffy English butler or the pert British counterpart of the soubrette could be counted on to enliven the scene. Seldom, though, does there appear enough evidence to state that the characterization of the British servant reflects an attitude toward foreigners not discernible in English plays by English authors. An exception to every statement may be found, and Finikin in John Murdoch's *The Beau Metamorphized* (1800) – to be discussed shortly – supplies that deviation.

In the genre of mannered farce and comedy, Mrs. Marriott's *The Chimera* (1795), furnishes the first of two examples of the comic English servant not expressive of an American attitude toward the British. The authoress was a member of the old American Company who had arrived in the United States from Edinburgh, and had joined the company two months prior to the opening night of her play, November 17, 1794.[8] To dub her an American authoress might call forth some denials, therefore she shall be categorized as a Briton writing a popular type of play for an American audience. The play deals punitively with Lord Aberford, an old rake who wants to marry the young and beautiful Matilda. Matilda is fond of invoking names of minor classical deities in her fits of madness, feigned to frighten Lord Aberford. Dolly repeats and mispronounces these names, which she has picked up from her mistress, at times when her mispronunciations emphasize the ludicrousness of someone pretending to a level of knowledge above her ability. Frolic, another servant in the piece, resembles closely his name. The two of them add an element of

[8] Hill, p. 62.

liveliness, albeit in a typical manner, to a farce undistinguished in song or dialogue.

In 1808, Joseph Hutton wrote *The School for Prodigals*. The play is a melodrama of the returned prodigal, and it contains a pair of humorous servants included solely as additive elements. Fidget, the housekeeper, has a propensity for consulting chronological tablets. She hurries everywhere, accomplishes little but to argue with Osbert, and speaks of any minor house-hold event as an epoch. Osbert is Fidget's opposite. Measured and careful, he never utters an opinion not prefaced by two reasons: "primo" and "secondo". He outlags the porter in *Macbeth*, whom he resembles more than a little. The servants in these two plays are English solely because the setting is England. In neither case can an attitude toward anything but comic character construction be discerned. Had the plays been placed in France or in America, the servants could have switched nationalities with ease, never losing a comic element in the process. The same does not hold true for Loony McGra, Irish servant of the prodigal in Hutton's piece. No matter what nationality the rest of the characters might profess, he would remain a loquacious Irishman.

The next two plays contain comic English servants appearing in American settings. Once an author places a ludicrous foreigner in a native setting, then it may be assumed that that author intends some sort of comparative judgment. Traits supposed to be inherent in the national character of the servant, traveller, or soldier are caricatured for the enlightenment of the audience. Thus William, English servant of Screwpenny in Beete's *Man of the Times* (1797), receives a verbal drubbing from James, Major Upright's Irish man servant. William belongs to the antagonistic faction in the play, so he receives his comeuppance along with Screwpenny. Only William, since he does not function on the same plane as his master, gets the worst of only a verbal duel. William has the habit of repeating short expletives or sentences, such as, "What, what". James, with whom the audience agrees, makes fun of William's idiosyncracy.

John Murdoch's *The Beau Metamorphized* (1800) contains the English travelling dandy, Vainly, and his servant, Finikin. As the title of the play indicates, Vainly eventually learns to see America as its inhabitants want him to – but not before his hair has been miscut, a tailor has chastised him, and a duel he wishes to avoid has been almost forced upon him. Finikin pays for his aberrations in a manner similar to his master. Affecting exaggerations of Vainly's airs, he receives several sound drubbings at the hands of American tradesmen to whom he attempts to condescend. In both of these plays, the servant possesses a caricatured peculiarity intended to be held up to ridicule. That peculiarity – an exaggerated English characteristic – measured against the American norm, identifies the existence of an attitude held by playwright and audience receptive to comic aberrations among foreigners.

The English soldier received more careful comic characterization than did his servant. Because the possibilities for variety were greater than among servants, because the soldier remained longer in the minds of Americans as an enemy both actual and potential, and because the type had its predecessors (Farquhar's *The Recruiting Officer,* for example), one finds ludicrous and amusing British soldiers at almost every period of American history. During the Revolution, the usual serious depiction of the British soldier by American playwrights was changed for the humorous in *The Blockheads, or the Affrighted Officers* (1776). The play ridiculed the British army blockaded in Boston, purportedly in response to the British satire, *The Blockade,* mounted and produced January 8, 1776, at Faneuil Hall in Boston. The play apparently satirized the American troops, for the opening scene represented Washington "as an uncouth figure, awkward in gait, wearing a large wig and a rusty sword", attended by a country servant with a rusty musket. The colonial troops attacked Charleston on the night of the first performance, and the alarm at the theatre was thought to be part of the play until Howe ordered the troops to their posts.[9] In *The Blockheads* Lord Dapper (Burgoyne) leads the Britons, yet is so spindly that he can scarcely make the proper advances to his mistress. The British troops are described as "looking like French cooks, in a hot day's entertainment". The army, from commander to dragoon, ineffectually attempts to pre-

[9] Seilhamer, vol. 2, pp. 20-21.

pare for battle. Eventually the British embark, but not before the author has reduced their efforts to insignificance by satirically exaggerating their reactions to the blockade.

Joseph Hutton, in *The School for Prodigals* (1808), mentioned above in connection with comic Irish and British servants, turned to the rolls of retired naval officers for his humorous Admiral Darnly. Hutton treats the foreigners in this piece as excellent material for a comic-sentimental melodrama. While the Admiral exchanges many a verbal broadside with Loony McGra, he never becomes ludicrous. His nautical language – "Yohoi! clear the gangway and man the sides you lubberly cockswain! heave a-head my girl another cables length and we are in safe moorings" – serves to amuse rather than point up and satirize a national characteristic.

The opposite, though, is the case with James K. Paulding's retired Admiral Gunwale and Major Longbow. Since *The Bucktails* (ca. 1816), in which the two appear, was intended to set off more desirable American manners against ridiculous British custom, the English characters act in ludicrous ways. The Admiral stumps about on his wooden leg, swearing salty and besotted oaths and attempting to marry the rich American heiress, yet drunkenly proposing to an old English spinster. The play tells the story of Frank and Henry Tudor, two American travellers who pass some time in England. During their sojourn they reveal the silliness of many a British idea. Paulding, however, does not satirize as viciously as did the anonymous author of *The Blockheads*. He treats his characters with a comic whimsicality which tends to lessen the impact of satire. The British in *The Bucktails* are not so stuffy they can not laugh at their own aberrations.

On stage at the Park Theatre, on June 21, 1819, appeared Captain Pendragon of His Majesty's Army, on duty in Canada. A product of Mordecai M. Noah's inventive mind, the foppish Captain marks the apex of three satiric trends evident in prior American drama: the British traveller, the British dandy, and the British soldier. Noah's *She Would be a Soldier* ostensibly deals with the War of 1812, but both American and British causes receive comic treatment, even though the Americans win the battle. The Captain is so unique a character, that to categorize him quickly as the caricature of a foreigner whose exaggerated opinions, dress, and soldierly mannerisms serve to mark out for ridicule a certain national type, would be to do him and his creator gross injustice. Noah certainly intended to represent the British soldier in a humorous light, but so completely did he personify Pendragon that the Captain acquires a personality that sets him apart from a flock of lesser predecessors.

Enter Captain Pendragon, dressed in the British uniform, but in the extreme of fashion – throws himself into a chair.
Pen.: O curse such roads! my bones are making their way out of their sockets – such vile, abominable, detestable – Waiter! – If my friends at Castle Joram only knew the excruciating fatigues which I am undergoing in this barbarous land – Why, waiter! – or if his highness the commander in chief was only sensible of my great sacrifices to – Why waiter! where the devil are you?

He asks the waiter for an anchovy, to learn that the sole fare is bear meat.

Pen.: Bear Meat! why what the devil, fellow, do you take me for a Chickasaw, or an Esquimaux? Bear Meat! the honourable Captain Pendragon, who never ate anything more gross than a cutlet at Molly's chop-house, and who lived on pigeons' livers at Very's, in Paris, offered bear meat in North America! I'll put that down in my travels.

Soon an Indian chief arrives, Pendragon's commander in the impending battle. Potentially, Noah creates a situation that ridicules the stature of British officers; but so completely comic, so humorously exasperated is Pendragon, that the satire never materializes. The chief informs the doughty Captain that battle is near, and that leggins, war paint, and a feather comprise the uniform of the day. Pendragon objects, but the Indian replies that his braves would never fight under such a silly figure of a man as cut by the Captain in his resplendent British regimentals. Again, Pendragon makes his reservations known:

Pen.: Why this is the most impertinent and presuming savage in the wilds of North America. Harkee, sir, I'd have you to know, that I am a man of fashion, and one of the fancy – formerly of the buffs,

nephew of a peer of the realm, and will be a member of parliament,
in time; an officer of great merit and great services Mr. – Red Jacket.
Paint my face, and fight without clothes? I desire, sir, that you will
please to take notice that I fought at Badaboz with the immortal
Wellington, and had the honour to be wounded, and promoted, and
had a medal for my services in that affair, Mr. – Splitlog. Put rings
in my nose? a man of taste, and the *ne plus ultra* of Bondstreet, the
very mirror of fashion and elegance? Sir, I beg you to observe that I
am not to be treated in this manner – I shall resent this insult. Damme,
I shall report you to the commander in chief at the Horse Guards
and have you court-martialed for unfashionable deportment – Mr. –
Walk-in-the-water.

Indian: Come, come, sir, enough of this trifling; I do not understand it; you have heard my orders – obey them or, after battle, I'll
roast you before a slow fire!

* * *

Pen.: I'm horrified! lost in amazement! but I'll resent it. Damme,
I'll caricature him.

Pendragon and his French servant, La Role, are captured in their
Indian finery; Pendragon with his opera glass in place. His off-
handed flippancy, and his affected witticisms lift him from the
ranks filled by mere satiric caricatures.

Adela.: Pray, sir, may I ask how you came to fancy that disguise?
Pen.: O, it's not my fancy, 'pon honour, though I am one of the
fancy; a mere *russe de guerre.* We on the other side of the water, have
a kind of floating idea that you North Americans are half savages
and we must fight you after your own fashion.
Adela.: And have you discovered any difference exists in the last
affair in which you have been engaged?
Pen.: Why, 'pon my soul, Ma'am, this Yankee kind of warfare is
inexpressibly inelegant, without flattery – no order – no military ar-
rangement – no *deploying* in solid columns – but a kind of helter-
skelter warfare, like a reel or a country-dance at a village inn, while
the house is on fire.
Adela.: Indeed?
Pen.: All true, I assure you. Why do you know, ma'am, that one
of your common soldiers was amusing himself with shooting at me
for several minutes, although he saw from my air, and my dodging,
that I was a man of fashion? Monstrous assurance! wasn't it?

Pendragon, as he steps toward the American officers' tent, reveals
that behind his foppish facade there functions a balanced mentality.

Pen.: Why sir, if war was not my profession, I'd sell it; but it's always my maxim to obey orders, whatever they may be: therefore shall be happy to have a brush with you in war, and equally happy to crack a bottle of Burgundy with you in peace.

The invitation and Pendragon's response show that gallantry operates on both sides. Pendragon's remarks about American fighting, his complaints over the abominable roads, and his reaction to the bear meat of the frontier mark him as the uninitiated traveller; his preoccupation with dress outdoes even the most finicky of peace time dandies; his willingness to fight in Indian costume – although he objects – and his jaunty attitude toward the fracas indicate the hardened soldier beneath all the affectation. Noah not only managed to caricature the British soldier, but to create a character whose innate ability shines through his comic aberrations.

The remaining humorous Britishers fall into the category of mannered gentility. These types, appearing in such plays as Hutton's *The School for Prodigals* (1808), Marriott's *The Chimera* (1794), and *The Comet* (1817), differ from the characters discussed above. Rather than agents whose comic behavior served to point a moral to Americans, the Lord Aberfords, Edward Darnlys, and Sir Credulous Testys were conceived in that atmosphere where an anti-social deviation deserving of correction is intended to illuminate a trait of behavior native to a one-sided or socially imbalanced man. But occasionally the plays resist classification, with the attendant result of confusion in the ascription of character traits. For example, the Honorable Edward Darnly and his cousin, Lady Sarah Darnly, are the height of unfeeling fashion when they meet the ragged prodigal under a tree in *The School for Prodigals*.

Edw.: 'Pon my soul la'y Sa'ah there is a concatenation of unmannerly smells issuing from that gentleman's wardrobe, I feel it most sensibly!
Lady S.: Give the poor mendicant a few pence for the sake of charity and let us be gone!
Edw.: 'Pon my soul, la'y Sa'ah there's no getting rid of these beggars! begging's a bad trade at the west end of the town, don't you find it so my batter'd bedlamite?

One would surmise that since the affected pair act in such an insensitive way toward a poor beggar, they would be eminently eligible for retribution at the end of the play. But the two fashionable west-enders appear at the happy reunion and describe how they were out for a drive one day, saw the curate's house, stopped for a chat, and were married.

Lord Aberford, in *The Chimera,* is treated as the butt of all the humor. An old man, he aspires to marry young Matilda. She feigns violent madness each time he broaches the subject, much to his fright. Finally she pretends to stab him with a fan, whereupon he thinks he has been mortally wounded and bequeaths a fortune to his disinherited nephew, who has fortuitously appeared in time to receive the benefit of Lord Aberford's will and Matilda's love. *The Comet* contains Sir Credulous Testy, who wishes to marry Emily for her ten thousand pounds, youth, and beauty. Lady Candour arranges that Sir Credulous should peer through a rigged telescope to see a monster in the sun, a comet in the heavens, and then receive a shock from a Leyden jar. In his fright, Sir Credulous signs a paper agreeing to a marriage between Emily and her beloved. These characters are not punished because their behavior is inimical to American mores and society, but because their comic aberrations break the rules of any normative western society.

In order to clarify the disposition of comic British characters in American drama, the distinction between corrective comedy, satire, and pure comedy must be kept in mind. While Americans utilized comedy and satire to point out the differences between themselves and the Britons, they did not turn to corrective comedy as readily as one might suspect. Comedies such as *The Beau Metamorphized, The Better Sort,* and *A Trip to Niagara* all contain Britishers who, once apprised of the virtues of American society, reform their opinions, morals and manners. Yet those three plays nearly exhaust the list of corrective comedies. One play, *The Blockheads,* utilized vicious satire to point up the ludicrous nature of the British army blockaded in Boston. Paulding employed a milder form of satire in *The Bucktails,* softening the incisive sarcasm by building into the British an ability to laugh at themselves. English servants do not appear in early American drama with anywhere near the frequency of their Irish counterparts, nor are they as uniquely delineated. While American play-wrights borrowed the stage Irishman from British drama, they embellished his character until he became a person distinct from his prior dramatic caricatures. The English servant, on the other hand, remained similar to his brother in British drama, with the exception of the few servants of travelling British in punitive comedies. The British soldier, traveller, and dandy, separately evident in American drama prior to 1819, combined in that unique figure, Captain Pendragon. Each of those types had previously been used to censure the behavior of real-life counterparts. Noah so effectively personified Pendragon that what would have been open to condemnation becomes an exaggerated yet believable part of the captain's own character. To understand the peculiar position of the ludicrous or amusing Briton in American drama, one must recall that where local attitudes toward strange mores and behavior were concerned, the early Republican generally had a most serious cast of mind. Therefore, an attitude concerning the British appears to be stronger in the plays which deal more serious-ly with English mores and manners.

C. THE FRENCH

Seven years after the American Revolution, Toupée, comic French barber, appears in Samuel Low's *The Politician Outwitted* (1789). Low ridicules the French sense of honor by having Toupée refuse to "frize" a man any more "becase he vas fronte me". When Trueman asks Toupée to explain the trouble, the Barber states:

Toup.: I vill tell your honare of the fracas. I vas vait on monsieur a – choses, and make ma compliment avec beaucoup de grace, ven monsieur vas read de new papier; so I say, is 'your honare ready for be dress? De great man say, "no–, d–n de barbare." I tell de persone, sare I have promise 'pon honare for dress out great man vat is belong to de Congress, 'bout dis time, sans manquer: De ansare vas (escuse moy, monsieur) "go to hell, if you be please; I must read about de Constitution". Dis is de ole affair, en verité.

The main interest in the play concerns the suit for Harriet Trueman's hand by a fop influenced unduly by French fashion, and his opponent, Charles Loveyet, whose father receives comic punishment for fulminating against the Federalists and their Constitution. Toupée furnishes farcical relief from the main story, as he refuses to leave a scene until jokingly threatened. But why, so closely following the Revolution which 44,000 French soldiers and sailors helped win,[10] did the French receive satiric treatment from an American author? Jones explains that French manners and French people were quite popular among the upper class between 1775 and 1790, ". . . the general picture that one forms of the period up to the French Revolution is one of peculiar concord – a period in which the ideas and manners of the French were extraordinarily influential in shaping American ways".[11] Yet in 1789, in Low's play, not only does a ridiculous French barber appear, but also an American fop whose excesses are committed in the name of French fashion (see Chapter III for a discussion of Worthnought). It is more than coincidence that Low placed both in the play, and ridiculed both.

In one sense, Toupée descends directly from a series of predecessors in the English drama. In fact, Low's comic French barber might be modelled after Mignon, the *friseur* in Garrick's *Bon Ton* (1775), first played in New York in 1780, during the British occupation.[12] Mignon objects in strenuous and practically incomprehensible Gallicized English to supposed insults upon his honor by one of the nobility who did not want his wig arranged at the precise moment the barber arrived. Satirization of French manners and types had been prevalent on the eighteenth century stage as early as the 1750's, when the irrepressible Samuel Foote was engaged in burlesquing everything from the aristocracy to social vagaries of the day. "Frenchified" Englishmen received a measure of Foote's sarcasm in *The Englishman Returned from Paris* (1756). The frequency with which English playwrights translated entire French pieces throughout the mid-eighteenth century also

---

[10] Howard M. Jones, *America and French Culture* (Chapel Hill, 1927), p. 128.
[11] Jones, p. 132.
[12] Seilhamer, vol. 2, p. 43.

rendered the Englishman familiar with French stage productions.[13] However, the Seven Years War led to a dislike of the French and reinforced the caricatures that many writers of farce and comedy created.

Just as some American drama later ridiculed the French through ludicrous characterization of American fops who had picked up too many French idiosyncracies of manner on a tour, English drama in the second half of the eighteenth century utilized the "Frenchified" gentry as a means of levelling disapprobation. The Gallic affectation of Lord Trinket's speech, in George Colman's *The Jealous Wife* (1761), immediately identifies him as ready for comic censure. The tendency to ridicule French manners did not die out of the British drama, even though it was never as strong as the proclivity for satirizing the Irish, Scotch, and Jewish.[14] As late in the eighteenth century as 1795 (the drama played in Philadelphia, 1799) John O'Keeffe included L'Oeillet in *Life's Vagaries*. L'Oeillet serves Lord Torrendel, a spindle-shanked old roué, by appropriating money designated for the Lord's son and by acting, complete with accent, the intriguing servant. This sort of characterization did not stop at the end of the eighteenth century, but carried over into the nineteenth in the still common farces and afterpieces, not to mention its place in melodrama. The continued popularity of British drama on the American stage throughout the entire early period can only indicate that audiences in the United States were as familiar with the French caricature as they were with the Irish. In part, public interest in the French type of character led to an increased demand, which American playwrights complied with by supplying

[13] See Nicoll, vol. 2, pp. 117-121 for a list.

[14] Richard Cumberland, the great sentimentalist, states in his *Memoirs*, "I introduced the characters of persons who had been usually exhibited on the stage as the butts for ridicule and abuse, and endeavoured to present them in such lights as might tend to reconcile the world to them, and them to the world" (Albert C. Baugh, *A Literary History of England*, New York, 1948, p. 1042). Those characters included the Irishman, the Scotsman, and the Jew. Cumberland either disliked the French himself, did not get around to sentimentalizing a French caricature, or did not think the type sufficiently numerous to warrant his attentions. The last assumption seems the likeliest.

their own French barbers, tailors, and fops. Yet the Americans had, part of the time, a good reason for satirizing the French affectations they perceived.

Despite the high favor in which some Americans held any person or item French, there was a post-Revolutionary movement to purge American society and mores of foreign and therefore debilitating influences. Among its more zealous adherents, the movement acquired strength enough to attack even those institutions which basked in the public approbation. Playwrights such as Mercy Warren, Royall Tyler, William Dunlap, and Samuel Low were in the vanguard of the movement. Therefore, Toupée, rather than serving as a presagement of dissatisfaction with the French revolutionary extremetists, represented a faction which called vociferously for a native American culture. People like Low were among the first to object once the Girondists and Jacobins committed post-Revolutionary excesses against the nobility. But to attribute to Low an early dislike of the French Revolution would not be consonant with the sympathies expressed in the play.

Since the French, after 1794, were rude enough to prey upon American shipping and insult her ambassadors, a strong anti-Gallic movement arose among the citizens of the United States. Frenchmen spoke a different language and possessed manners as well as political sentiments decidedly at odds with those of America; therefore, American dislike could find ready expression in ridicule. The derision was especially forceful when Federalist (anti-French) and Jacobin-Democrat (pro-French) political factions clashed, as they did in Boston. The product of their differences was the Haymarket Theatre, erected late in 1796. Dunlap describes the events in his *History of the American Theatre*.

... before the first of January, 1797, the Haymarket theatre, an immense wooden pile, proudly overtopping every other building in the metropolis, was completed. It is believed that the idea of raising a rival house was first suggested by C. Powell, or some of his friends, who thought him injured by the proprietors of the Federal-street theatre; but there was another and more potent principle exerted in producing the establishment than mere theatrical rivalry, and that was political feeling. Political excitement at that time, between the parties then denominated *Federal* and *Jacobin*, was high and furious.

Every man joined himself to one or the other of those parties, and each was jealous of the ascendency of the other. It was suspected, and not without some reason, that party politics, which pervaded almost every private as well as public concern, had some influence in the management of the Federal-street house; and that the trustees who were all of the Federal school of politics, had upheld and justified the manager, in the introduction of pieces tending to provoke the resentments and animosities of their political opponents. It was customary (and very naturally so), for the actors, who were all emigrants from the English stage, to interpolate jests and witticisms at the expense of the French, who were then at war with Britain; and these often gave great offence, excited disapprobation, and sometimes created great uproar in the house. The anti-Federal (or as it was then called, the Jacobin) party, were so exceedingly sensitive that they took great offence at the representation of the *Poor Soldier*, pretending that the character of Bagatelle was a libel on the character of the whole French nation. They were encouraged in this by the French consul, then residing in Boston. A pretty smart quarrel was excited between him and the editor of the Boston Gazette; and the controversy at last became so bitter, that a mob on one occasion attempted to stop the performance of this farce, and did considerable damage to the benches, doors, and windows of the offending house.[15]

Quite at odds with the more serious treatment the British and American differences usually received in American drama, the Gallic nature was more easily exposed to comic censure. An example may be discerned in John Minshull's *The Merry Dames* (1805). Monsieur Billows, captain of a French frigate visiting an American port, falls susceptible to a barber's impersonation of an English "Knight of the Comb." Billows detects the deception when he perceives Comb, the barber, plying his scissors in the Exchange barber shop. Billows remonstrates rather vigorously with Comb, "Sare – sare – sare –, you be no gentleman, by gar, but one God dam barber." Billows' comments grow more obscene as his anger waxes, until he finally attempts to run Comb through. Comb seizes Billows' nose with a pair of barber's tongs, putting the captain to ludicrous flight. Billows really commits no error in social behavior, prior to his anger, that might call for such retribution. He is French, and as such, fair game for both satirist and barber's tongs. His obsequiousness towards what he considers a

---

[15] Dunlap, p. 141.

titled Briton, and his later obscenity serve as two characteristics that were supposed to estrange him from the sympathies of an American of that era. But both these are elicited by the impersonation initiated by Comb. In order to emphasize the undesirable aspects of the French, Minshull chose to render the behavior of Monsieur Billows ludicrous by American standards. His profession, that of a naval officer, the author derides, thus dramatically mocking the very men who were commissioned to attack American shipping.

James N. Barker displayed yet another attitude toward the French in *Tears and Smiles* (1807). The play contains a Monsieur Galliard, who returns to America with the fop Fluttermore. The American dandy has picked up the worst of Gallic affectations, and Barker scores him unmercifully for such bad taste. But Galliard, as one might not suspect, does not evince the same lack of good judgment as his travelling companion. In fact, when asked his opinion of Europe, he answers, *"Eh bien!* For me, I tink Europe is like de old libertine, de courtesane; I am disgust vid her. Amerique is de lit demoiselle you point me in de street; vat you call?"* Fluttermore rejoins, "Ha! ha! A Quaker!" Galliard's attraction to the little Quaker, and his comments about American customs he mistakes cause some amusement, but Barker intends no rancor to be felt towards him. Some of the reason for Barker's treatment may be noted in the preface to the 1808 edition of the play. In it Barker complains that while people applaud foreign patriotism expressed in plays, they never permit a similar enunciation by Americans. "They can never pardon the endeavour to depict our national peculiarities, and yet they will listen with avidity to Yorkshire rusticity, or Newmarket slang." Barker, a Jeffersonian Democrat, vehemently argued for a native American drama, along with Dunlap, Noah, Wright, and others. His Frenchman therefore praises America, while his American fop commits moral upon social sin – all because of an immature and un-American acquisition of foreign culture on a grand tour.

By the second decade of the nineteenth century, the comic Frenchman had become a substantially stock figure in American drama. He had even been stereotyped sufficiently to appear often as a servant whom the following description could well suit: "A meagre fop, large ruffles and a huge neckcloth. Takes snuff immediately." The passage was written by Joseph Hutton to describe the manservant, Grenouille, in *Fashionable Follies* (1815). Grenouille serves Delany, American dandy who tries to abduct Maria Dorriville and keep her father from his rightful fortune – all because it is fashionable. Captain Dorriville arrives in time to thwart Delany's plans, and convinces the dandy to reform. Grenouille operates on the farcical level of the plot, taking messages back and forth and attempting to finagle his way into a pantry to assuage his omniverous appetite, ". . . suppose you hit moi on da belly, I vill sound all de same as von kettle drum, je suis hollow as von vind sail, by gar."

Two years later, Mordecai M. Noah supplied the resplendent Captain Pendragon with La Role, servant *extra-ordinaire*. La Role takes snuff, puts on exaggerated airs, and chases the chamber maid. He reveals his own character while attempting to impress the maid.

LaRole: Oui, ven I could not run away, begar, I surrender like von brave homme, and now I am jentiman to capitain Pendreagoon; I do brus his coat, poudre his hair, and pull his corset tight, and ven he was order to come to Amerique, and fight wis de Yankee Doodel, begar me come too. I arrive ici, I am here, to make a little de love to you.

La Role mentions his abilities in many of the areas that Americans grew accustomed to seeing French refugees and emigrés exploit. Those who fled to America had been forced to seek some sort of livelihood ever since the days of the Jacobins and the revolt on Santo Domingo. But by the time the nineteenth century was barely fifteen years old, the French and their jobs had become part of the comic stage caricature of the French servant, in the same way that the stage Irishman's reaction to "the faver", whisky, and American customs had become stock stage ingredients first observed among immigrants.

In the 1820's appeared two plays, each of which treated the Frenchman in a comprehensively different manner. Peter Puffem, the pseudonymous author of *Heaven on Earth* (1825), warmly disliked all foreigners, and Robert Owen in particular. In his play he viciously satirized the New Harmony venture, depicting Owen as a man who gulls the prospective New Harmonyites out of their arable land for his own advantage. The party travelling to Indiana contains a Monsieur Vestris who, at the cry of "painter", scurries up a tree, leaving a woman in the mud to fend for herself. When the alarm has been revealed false, Vestris offers to fight a duel with one of the travellers who called him a coward. Once the group arrives at New Harmony, they perceive their mistake after one look at the sorry site, and depart for the East.

George Washington Parke Custis, step-grandson of the first President, wrote the second play, *The Indian Prophecy* (1828). He chose an incident in the life of George Washington to dramatize. Washington, surveying West Virginia in 1772, meets an Indian chief whose braves had tried to kill him in the Monongahela debacle during the French and Indian War. The Indian chief prophesies a great future for the surveyor. In the play appears a French trader, Duquesne. He is amusing because of the attributes that became attached to American comic French stage characters after the French Revolution. He tries to get an Indian maid to succumb to his attractions, anachronistically describing himself as might an emigré twenty years later, "I am Monsieur Duquesne, I come for de sciance: I teach de musique, et de dance, to Lady of de Governeur." Custis included him solely to set off the natural sagacity and innocence of the Indian, who refuses to be fooled by Duquesne's whimsical airs. He serves as comic focus in an otherwise dry recount of a Washington legend.

It appears that even though Americans reacted violently to French policy at times during the early history of the United States, a steadily antipathetic dramatic depiction did not take place. French aid during the American Revolution, of course, caused much favorable reaction and tended to influence the views held by American society. But from the beginning of the Republic, a strong movement to initiate native customs and culture caused an attitude of disapproval toward slavish imitation of foreign manners. To disabuse Americans of their reverence for all things Gallic, Federalist Samuel Low included a ludicrous French barber in

The Politician Outwitted. When the excesses of the Revolutionary faction in France drove many refugees to America, and when the revolt in Santo Domingo accomplished the same, Americans grew accustomed to seeing French emigrés teach the dance, turn to trades, and attempt to bring French manners to American society. Those most familiar qualities became the basis for comic treatments of the stage Frenchman. Only when the author seemed particularly to dislike the French, especially when politics became involved, did a ludicrous Frenchman such as Minshull's Monsieur Billows receive harsh comic comeuppance. Howard M. Jones sums up several excellent reasons for discerning in the drama of the first half century of American independence a steady progression toward dramatically treating the Frenchman as a comic character.

To the average American . . . the most obvious facts about the French were, first, that they were politically unstable; and second, that their principal productions were articles of luxury, fashions, millinery, the dancing master, an exaggerated sense of punctilio, and various other things or qualities which seemed to him unworthy of serious consideration by a truly great and important people. What trust can be placed in a people who take so seriously the frills and little accomplishments of life? [16]

D. OTHER FOREIGNERS

Playwrights have constantly sought ways to create novelty among stereotyped characters. To that end, a stock melodramatic plot might be set in a variety of countries, depending upon the incidental effects the author desired to achieve. In the same manner, American playwrights invented comic servants of many nationalities in order to vary the stereotype. The funny slave or servant had been a stock figure in drama since the fifth century B.C., and his popularity had not diminished by the time of the eighteenth and nineteenth centuries A.D. Therefore, when a playwright such as Susannah H. Rowson decided that she needed a comic servant for *Slaves in Algiers* (1794), she made him Spanish rather than British or American. His characteristics, however, she pulled from that large stock which filled the supply house for stage

[16] Jones, p. 571.

servants of the era. Sebastian, Mrs. Rowson's Spanish slave, quips frequently, yearns constantly for wine, and finally escapes with the rest of the slaves. On his way to freedom, Sebastian decides that he deserves a woman, and "saves" a disguised, comic Jewish moneylender.

The foreign servants in domestic melodrama by Americans, as in the pirate melodrama, did not necessarily show qualities readily recognizable as native to the servant's homeland. Blanco, the comic Swiss servant in Thomas P. Lathy's domestic melodrama, *Reparation* (1800), utters nothing but Anglicisms: "Damme, if ever before that it was good at a tilting match." He, along with Sebastian, loves his bottle. Walter Lee's *La Fayette* (1824), written to celebrate LaFayette's triumphal return to America, takes place in Olmutz, Austria, where the French patriot had been held prisoner. The young host at the local inn, Spicket, has been tricked into marrying an old termagant of a wife. Neither the wife, nor Spicket, nor the young maidservant, Sweetlips, act at all like Austrians. The only attempt to set off any of the three from the usual occurs when Lee depicts Sweetlips as a country lass.

Spicket: Hew, who have we here – a dapper wench, by Jove.
Sweetlips: Sarvant, sir, sarvant.
Spic.: Well, my pretty one.
Sweet.: Mayhap you will tell me, sir, if this here house be the "Fly Inn?"
Spic.: Yes, this is the Fly Inn.
Sweet.: May be as how you'll tell me where to find the landlord.
Spic.: I am the landlord.
Sweet.: He! he! he! vy folks did tell me that the landlord of the Fly Inn was –
Spic.: A fine, handsome, young fellow – hey?
Sweet.: Oh, lord no, sir, they did tell me he way a great, old, fat, cross fellow, which you an't, I am sure.

The general run of servants first fulfilled the requirements of supplying comic or farcical action. On rare occasions did they differ markedly from play to play, no matter what nationalities the authors had intended.

Yet where the author knew well the characteristic speech and manners of a nationality whose exaggerated qualities he rendered comic in a drama, the foreigner can not be gathered under the category mentioned in the preceding paragraph. J. Robinson, a member of the Old American Company on its sojourn in the West Indies, returned to the United States and wrote *The Yorker's Stratagem* (1792). Robinson acted the part of the comic West Indian Negro, Banana, whose mother wants him to marry the wealthy Louisa. Banana, on the other hand, yearns for the little colored Priscilla. Robinson attempted, with a fair degree of success, to capture certain comic elements of the West Indian Negro of that era. One must imagine the antics Robinson performed in blackened face and outrageous costume as he explained why he (Banana) arrived late at the ceremony.

Banana: My mumma want fo' ride grande, gallop away prookety, prookety, prook; me know me da foole, and me want fo' walk toffy, toffy; you sabby, toffy catch quickly; me mumma want me for marry wid de fine lady, I want fo' go lib wid my own love Prissey.

Judith Murray manages to endow with a remarkably accurate accent her comic New York Dutch innkeeper in *The Traveller Returned* (1796). Vansittart, the Dutchman, lives in eternal apprehension that his wife's cupidity will get the two of them arraigned for theft. When Mrs. Vansittart unfolds to him her plan for stealing a trunk belonging to a guest, Vansittart reveals his fears in an amusing manner, "O mercy on us! mercy on us! I to think there pe creat tangers ant creat difficulties." Judith Murray comically characterizes her innkeeper through his apprehensive nature and strong accent. Vansittart, of course, is foreign to the same extent as the comic Irish in plays of the same period.

James Workman created, as one of the comic elements in *Liberty in Louisiana* (1804), Sawny McGregor. Sawny and his Irish cohort Phelim O'Flinn, form a team of con men *sans pareil*. They travel down the Mississippi, one town ahead of the law, to enter New Orleans just before the first American governor arrives.

Sawny: The de'il take ye, Mr. Phelim O'Flinn. Where can he hae pack'd himsel? I hae luk'd up and down for ye; ... What a curs'd fule this maister O'Flinn is! Ay, gude troth, and a wee bit of a knave. For a' that he has a pleasant guidly disposition – he'll fight brawley, but he hates the laws, and acts as if there was nae sic a thing as property. He's a devilish gude companion, though. Mony a hungry weam should we baith hae had, gin Phelim were as delicate about taking other people's property as Sawny McGregor is – I'd fast till I was famished afore I wad nock a goose or a bublie-jock on the heed, and put in into my poke, as Phelim does – for I'm vary honest; though I dinna ken ony sin in taking share on't, when roasted, to satisfy the cravings o' nature.

As popular as were the pirate plays during America's continued difficulties with the Algierian and Tripolitan corsairs, playwrights were continually on the search for a new method to serve up an old topic. James Ellison managed to invent a fairly unique Moorish Jew, Ishmael, to lend comic interest to *The American Captive* (1812). The characterization is not founded on any attempt at verisimilitude – as were Banana, Vansittart, and Sawny – but although obviously derivative, serves to show how an author can create amusement by intensifying the cupidity of a stereotype. Ishmael is such a miser that he forces Abdommilek, his servant, to wait until butchers and other vendors throw away tainted food so it may be picked up without expense. When Ishmael counts his treasure, he pauses to apostrophize a sequin.

Ishmael: Vat a comely form! The vorld talks of *peauty*, of *voman's* peauty! Spahaw! compared with this, 'tis all *deformity*! 'tis transient, fleeting, fades upon the sight, but this! not so vith this; ages shall pass avay, and this be still the same. *Time* brings no wrinkles here! smiles ever dwell upon its front; aye, it shall live in endless bloom. . . .

By reverting to a two-century old type, Ellison created a ludicrous miser whose penuriousness finally brings about his comic rebuke; Ishmael ends up stripped of his wealth.

The funny foreigner in early American drama may be separated largely into two varieties: those whose depictions were based upon observation of national types, and stereotypes utilized to enliven the action of a play according to the dictates of form. The most numerous and outstanding members of the first group were the stage Irishmen. At first a stereotype based upon English drama, the son of Erin picked up added characteristics as he stayed, worked, and grew to accept and even fight for the democratic way of life. While the Irish immigrant acquired citizenship, the stage Irish caricature remained loyal to his homeland, and a double strain of characterization thus appeared by the end of the first half century of post-Revolutionary drama. Even the ludicrous Irish, softened under the application of sentimental qualities, became more amusing than ridiculous. The caricatures of British personae tended toward bitter and corrective satire. Commencing with soldiers of the Revolution, the general attitude toward British manners and mores leaned toward the serious, keeping caricatures of British dandies, travellers, and soldiers to a minimum. Yet these three ubiquitous typifications culminated in Captain Pendragon, a Briton rendered so uniquely comic that he transcends the usual caricature. French comic characters resembled the Irish more than the British. Since an American of the early Republic was inclined to look upon foreign customs as definitely odd and particularly undesirable, the exaggerated punctilio, marked accent, and lax mores of the Frenchman he came to know through dramatizations and in person led to decided comic treatment. Although the French were America's first avowed allies, the excesses of the Gallic Revolution and Napoleon's conquests estranged the American Federalists. This encouraged many a caricature of the French emigré – even to the extent of endowing him with outrageously ludicrous antisocial attitudes in need of comic correction.

More than a degree or two of doubt may be raised about discerning a truly unique foreign characterization in the second variety of early American dramatic foreigners. So nearly British were the manners of American society, that when an American attempted to write a comedy of manners for a local setting, the attitudes of the fashionable characters were as much British as American. For that reason, the comic British servants resembled more their immediate predecessors in Sheridan and Goldsmith than they did some real servant noted to accompany British travellers. The ludicrous titled gentleman, often appearing in a corrective comedy where his aberration would call for humorous retribution, may be traced to no particular attitude toward the British, the French, or the Germans – but finds his origins in earlier exaggerations borrowed from British drama. The same holds true for comic servants in melodramas. One of the formal dictates of melodrama decreed that comic servants should appear to relieve the apprehensive atmosphere. In their search for originality, French, British, German, and American playwrights awarded such servants as great a variety of nationalities as their imaginations could furnish. Yet the important characteristics of the servants changed not one jot no matter in which country the action occurred. Such foreigners, in actuality, could hardly be called foreign except by stretching the definition.

V. FROM ROMANTIC FOREIGNER
TO ABORIGINAL ADAM

Since the American dramatic heritage of the late eighteenth and early nineteenth centuries consisted preponderantly of British works, the influence of English drama and its prevalence upon the American stage can hardly be overestimated. As has been pointed out in preceding chapters, a plurality of foreign types in early American drama descend directly or tangentially from similar characters in the British drama. American playwrights used the foreigner for polemic reasons but the characters, especially if European, are traceable to British progenitors. Dramatists in the new Republic were sensitive to the derivative nature of much of the material that found its way before footlights during the early years of American drama.

As early as 1767 Andrew Barton, the pseudonymous author of the comic opera, *The Disappointment,* penned a prologue that recognized at least a geographical difference between English and colonial letters.

> Tho' distant far, from fam'd Britannia's isle
> Where comic-scenes, call cynics forth to smile;
> Our artless muse, hath made her first essay
> T'intrust and please you with a modern play.

Barton's comic opera, although written about a mid-eighteenth century craze for seeking buried treasure on the Hudson, derives its salient characteristics from British predecessors.

The prologue to Tyler's *The Contrast* (1787) indicates a more apparent divergence to be desired between British and American dramatic material: a good indication that much difference did not exist at the time.

> Our Author pictures not the foreign climes,
> The fashions, or the follies of the times;
> But has confin'd the subject of his work
> To the gay scenes – the circles of New-York;
> On native themes his Muse displays her powers,
> If ours the faults, the virtues too are ours.
> Why should our thoughts to distant countries
> roam,
> When each refinement may be found at home?

At nearly the turn of the century, the same condition evidently prevailed; else why the constant lament that only British drama and its American emulators captured most the critical praises? David Everett, in a prologue to *Daranzel* (1798) – a tedious and derivative blank verse tragedy – complains about the preference of foreign to American pieces.

> Your approbation's smiles let genius share;
> From chilling frosts its budding blossoms spare.
> Let not the panders of your taste oppose
> The foreign bramble, to the native rose.

And yet in 1818, the production date of Isaac Harby's *Alberti* – which chronicles the tribulations of Alberti, defender of the late fifteenth-century Florentine "republic" – the American dramatist expresses his dislike of the warm reception American critics accord British works. If anything, the situation has worsened.

The last objection against "ALBERTI" – is the most formidable – *it is an American production!* To this charge (as I do not know how to get over it) I must plead guilty. I have even the hardihood openly to acknowledge, nay, be proud of the accident of birth, which has placed me under the protection of laws that I revere, and in the bosom of a country that I love.

In 1829 the angry protestations against continued judgment of foreign dramatic efforts as better than native ones had not abated. James N. Barker wrote the prologue to Richard P. Smith's *Eighth of January,* claiming, to use Barker's metaphor, one more invention created by American ingenuity, an American play.

> Although my countrymen may view to-night
> No eastern tinsel glittering on the sight,
> And critic fops may sneer, and stand aloof,

> Because the fabric's western web and woof –
> Americans who could be truly free,
> Will never scorn domestic industry –
> Now, while each foreign frippery claims
>   admission,
> Deny their homespun chance of competition.

Americans persisted, it would appear, to prefer the Europe⹁ʳ to the indigenous as far as drama was concerned, from the first recorded theatrical presentations in the colonies to an undetermined date beyond 1830.[1]

From the evidence pointing to a continued reliance upon British importation for much American dramatic fare – Odell, Pollock, and James list ever increasing numbers of British plays right past the Revolution, the War of 1812, and 1830 – a conclusion may be drawn which states that a goodly portion of the playwriting produced highly derivative, if not downright imitative drama. Comedies of manners were set in Britain, melodrama occurred in dark forests or in isolated mountain castles, comic opera could have a locale of anywhere from Bath to Peiping, *drame* happened in Europe, and tragedy rarely transpired in the United States (Dunlap's *André* (1798), and Barker's *Superstition* (1808), being exceptions). American playwrights saw which way the public weather-cock pointed, and accordingly – if they were people such as

[1] While to commence an argument concerning the reasons for such emphatic and long-lived preference for British drama lies beyond the province of this book, a contemporary comment on the situation – a statement not liberally coated with a patina of hyper-patriotism – might illuminate the subject from another angle. Mordecai M. Noah, in the preface to *She Would be a Solider* (1819), claims that the fault might lie at home. "These prejudices against native productions, however they may be deplored as impugning native genius, are nevertheless very natural. An American audience, I have no doubt, would be highly pleased with an American play, if the performance afforded as much gratification as an English one; they pay their money to be pleased, and if we cannot afford pleasure, we have no prescriptive right to ask for approbation. . . . We will succeed in time, as well as the English, because we have the same language and equal intellect; but there must be system and discipline in writing plays – a knowledge of stage effect, – of sound cadences, fitness of time and place, interest of spot, spirit of delineation, nature, poetry, and a hundred *et ceteras*, which are required, to constitute a good dramatic poet, who cannot, while in this country and occupied in other pursuits, spring up over night like asparagus, or be watered and put in the sun like a geranium in a flower pot."

William Dunlap, who sustained himself on his theatrical endeavors for some years – wrote for rather than against the prevailing tastes of the times. Managers of acting companies and theatres did not wish to see their houses dark for want of attendance, hence were strongly biased towards plays they thought would fill all the seats. The cycle backed over itself, and much of the material seen on American stages between the Revolution and 1830 was either of foreign import or purport. (The 1812 production of Barker's *Marmion,* according to a letter from Wood the manager, quoted by Odell, vol. 2, p. 383, ran well until the author's true identity was released. Once the public learned an American had written it, the play no longer drew.)

Now that the plays which were expressive of specific attitudes toward foreigners have been discussed in previous chapters, plays whose authors intended a definite outlook toward foreign customs, mores, politics, or people, there remains that bulk of dramatic material aimed primarily at emulating already fashionable foreign drama. These plays, a few of which have appeared in other chapters because they contained specific types of foreigners, do not convey any message or moral which bears upon the nationality of the characters.

The plays to be discussed in this chapter break into three general categories: those with action intended to occur contemporaneously, those written by John Howard Payne while abroad, and those removed in time and place for reasons romantic or sentimental. The mannered comedies and farces and the melodramas of the first category have antecedents in British drama so well known and numerous that to trace them carefully would require a list of interminable length. Suffice it to say that the farces and comedies of manners descend directly from the works of Congreve, Goldsmith, O'Keeffe, the Colmans, Samuel Foote, Colley Cibber, Arthur Murphy, and Sheridan – to name just a few of the more successful playwrights who wrote in the genres.[2]

An early example, one already discussed in part, appeared in 1794. Mrs. Marriott's *The Chimera,* complete with songs, takes place in contemporary England. It follows one of the usual farcical

[2] See Nicoll, vols. II & III; Baugh, pp. 833 ff, 1053 ff.

lines of action, confronting young beauty with a covetous old
roué. In this case, the girl feigns madness to fool aged Lord Aberford. Eventually Aberford, convinced that he has been stabbed to death with a fan, signs his goods over to the girl's true love.
The play does not reflect any antipathy toward British characters,
manners, or mores, even though the ancient Lord does attempts
to prevent the fruition of young love. The play was set in England,
for one reason, because Americans expected their mannered farces
to take place there as a result of a long acquaintance with similar
imported plays. William Milns, who wrote both *All in a Bustle*
and *The Comet* during the late 1790's, also looked to Britain for
his models. In fact *The Comet*, which was produced at the John
Street Theatre in New York on February 1, 1797, had been previously played in London.[3]

Thirty years later, farces set in Britain were still being published. Charles S. Talbot's *Squire Hartley* (1827) demands more
than a passing glance. Talbot, gifted with an ability to write
sprightly dialogue, created a farcical comedy of manners that resembles in conception and action Sheridan's *The Rivals*. There is
much ludicrous in the play: brogue and witticisms of the Irish servants Dermot and Peggy, Squire Hartley's mannerisms when disguised as Jemmy Gawky, the haughty impersonation of Sir Edward McDermot undertaken by Dermot, and the weak antics of
Sir Edmund Faintly the faint fop (he giggles constantly, repeating
ever, "I shall expire"). But Talbot does not viciously ridicule or
condemn any one type or nationality. The play dramatizes the
difficulties young Squire Hartley experiences in attempting to slip
Emily Allcure away from her father's overly-zealous protection.
At the same time Hartley steadfastly refuses to permit Susan, his
sister, to have a thing to do with the worthy Captain Vernon.
Each of the two acts builds to a climax through an attempt by the
disguised young Hartley to whisk away Emily. The play ends upon
a comic wedding, with Emily intended to marry the faint Sir Edmund, but running away with Hartley. Each of the couples, Vernon
and Susan, Dermot and Peggy, Hartley and Emily, weds happily

as the farce spins to its close. The types in the play – the quack, the aged fop, the Yorkshire countryman, and the Irish baronet – are held up as objects of amusement. Yet there occurs no direct or implied comparison between these caricatures, each with a comic aberration, and a more normative character who might live in America or resemble an American in manner or morals. Talbot took a comic conception and worked it into a partly farcical comedy of manners.[4]

Commencing in the waning years of the eighteenth century and continuing past 1830, melodrama brought the most varied, yet similar, numbers of foreigners to the American stage. Among a myriad of less important sources, the work of August von Kotzebue and Gilbert de Pixérecourt supplied American adapters with a considerable number of domestic and adventure melodramas. William Dunlap, Charles Smith, and Richard P. Smith, to name three, adapted both French and German melodramas to the requirements of the American theatre. English playwrights, among whom appear the more prolific melodramatists Thomas Holcroft and Edward Fitzball, had their work pirated and produced on the stages of the United States. A perusal of any history of a theatre in early nineteenth century America furnishes lengthy lists of melodramas whose action happened anywhere on the globe.[5] Since melodramas all utilize essentially the same elements – a villain who initiates a threat to hero and heroine, a number of incidents rendering the danger to the innocents more acute, and a finish bringing poetic justice – authors sought variety in the kinds of danger that could be arranged, in different settings, and in the nationalities of the characters. Melodramas were set in impenetrable European forests, in dark pirate prisons, on the high seas, in India, Araby, and China. Wherever the author's invention might take his formula, there

---

[4] Other examples of comedies of manners are John Minshull's *He Stoops to Conquer* (1804), Joseph Hutton's *School for Prodigals* (1809), James N. Barker's *How to Try a Lover* (1817), all representative of the type where action occurred in other lands with no attempts to compare foreign and American manners.

[5] See Quinn, pp. 74-112 for Dunlap's works; James, Odell, and Clapp, for melodramas on the stages of Philadelphia, New York, and Boston in the nineteenth century.

would the action transpire. A sole example will suffice as model for the rest of the genre.

In the Bowery Theatre on February 22, 1828, William Dunlap's *Thirty Years, or the Gambler's Fate* first met an American audience. The play was translated from the French *Trente Ans, ou la Vie d'un Joueur* by Prosper Goubaux and Victor Ducange. The action occurs in three "days" or acts. On the first day in Paris, 1790, George St. Germain marries the tender and loving Amelia. George gambles and loses, forced to wager his money through the evil influence of Warner. The gambling leads to a robbery, in which George is implicated. Rodolph, George's friend, attempts to extricate him, and the first act closes upon the initial step in the ruination of a gambler. Fifteen years later, on the second day, George has achieved destitution. Divested of all his money, he turns to his wife for her dowry. Warner plots George's final downfall, only to have his plans partially foiled when the police arrive to arrest George. In the progress of the action, George shoots his benefactor and good friend, Rodolph, mistaking him for Amelia's supposed lover. George and Amelia flee. The third day takes place in 1820 at a Bavarian inn near Munich. George, impoverished and broken, has wandered abroad ever since that fateful day in 1805. He begs food at the inn, ominously deserted in the deep and silent forest. A fairly well-to-do traveller arrives and asks directions for the next stage of his journey. George undertakes to guide him, and once out of sight of the inn, stabs the man for his money. Warner happens by, coincidentally followed by Amelia and Albert, George's now grown son. Warner wounds Albert in an attempt to steal from him. The inn catches on fire. George saves his son from the flames, then kills Warner and commits suicide.

Of an importance approaching that of the moral lesson, which stands out even from this attenuated synopsis of the action, the amount of terror that could be aroused in the audience through the use of spectacle, foreign settings, and evil actions also may be noted in *The Gambler's Fate*. Especially in the final act does the strangeness of an unusual scene perform a function germane to the arousal of apprehension and terror. The deepness of the night, the quiet and portentious inn, and the remoteness of a Bavarian forest near Munich all prepare the audience for dark and despicable deeds. Dunlap, although he did not write the play, chose it for translation because it would supply enough unusual qualities to differ superficially from other melodramas. The foreign locations supplied a part of the difference, and awakened interest in an American audience of 1828.

The plays of John Howard Payne add substantially to the number of dramas that treat the foreigner solely as a facet of interest. Payne spent most of his creative life in Europe. As Quinn puts it: "Payne's position in our dramatic history is a peculiar one. His most significant work was done abroad and his direct inspiration was foreign. Yet his theatrical training was received in America, and his general attitude, like Irving's, remained materially unchanged by his long residence in Europe. His themes were universal rather than parochial." [6]

Commencing with the standard melodrama, *Julia, or the Wanderer* (1806), Payne's dramatic output extended over thirty years and consisted of more than sixty plays. He wrote for a British audience, and his plays met with American success. Payne translated French melodramas, combined sources to evolve tragedy, adapted comedies of manners, wrote comic opera, reworked French ballet-pantomime (one of these theatrical entertainments supplied the source for *Clari, or the Maid of Milan* (1823), for which Payne wrote the perenially favorite air "Home Sweet Home"), and reworked French domestic tragedy. The foreigners depicted in his plays – foreign to an American audience – do not reflect specific attitudes such as those which found the Irish ludicrous, the French immoral, and the British affected. Payne wrote for a public that demanded entertainment above all else, and the plays he adapted or translated contain such a variety of characters foreign both to British and American audiences that to hold Payne accountable for a specific attitude, as it was possible to do with Barker, Noah, Dunlap, Tyler, or Munford, would be impossible. Along with other American plays of the nineteenth century, those by Payne indicate the existence of an attitude which viewed the foreigner as one of many ingredients a playwright could mani-

[6] Quinn, p. 186.

pulate in order to fascinate his audience. That same notion, applied
from the viewpoint of the playgoing public, found the foreigner
to be interesting *sui generis.*

In order to clarify the last point in the preceding paragraph,
two comparisons shall be undertaken. In 1822, Mordecai M. Noah
and Payne each wrote a play capitalizing upon the general interest
in the Grecian revolt for their effectiveness. Noah's play, *The
Grecian Captive,* was produced at the Park Theatre, June 17,
1822; Payne's *Ali Pacha* was first played at Covent Garden, October 19, 1822, then had a New York enactment on May 8, 1823.
Quinn, referring to Noah's play, states, correctly that "the characters from Ali Pacha down are as much like Americans as they
are like Grecians or Turks".[7] While Noah places his action in
Athens during the Grecian fight for freedom, the characters that
populate his drama could well have fought through an American
Revolutionary play. Ali Pacha is a foe to Greek liberty, and as
such gains a large measure of opprobrium. He covets Zelia, beloved
of the young Greek Ypsilanti. The Greeks, led by Zelia's father,
win a battle at Rhodes. Ali tells Zelia that only by marrying him
can she save her captured father. Amidst much patriotic and idealistic bombast, the melodrama moves to its end, when the Janis-
saries kill their leader for permitting his passion for Zelia to make
him free her father. Whenever Greek meets Greek, no matter what
the incidental occupation of the moment, Noah halts his action to
interpolate commentary on liberty. Noah's characters, to rephrase
Quinn, do not have any distinctly Greek or Turkish qualities. The
play appeals as much to patriotism as it does to an interest in far
off places. Noah used his play as an excuse to repeat nationalistic
material similar to that so popular in the twenty years following
the Revolution.

Payne's two-act romantic melodrama also owes its inception to
the Grecian struggle immortalized for Britain by Byron's participation and death. In comparison to Noah's work, it does not have as
many liverty-loving zealots in its cast. The main interest lies in the
love story between Helena, the sister of the Greek patriot Zenocles,
and Selim, the adeopted son of the tyrant Ali Pacha. Zenocles ap-

[7] Quinn, p. 153.

pears but briefly in the two acts, and the lack of his presence indicates the unimportance of politics to the love story. In Noah, on the other hand, love and patriotism strove for supremacy in young Ypsilanti; each finally achieving an equal measure of victory. Payne's Selim discovers his true nationality to be Greek in time to sanctify his love for Helena. Although Payne's characters do resemble, at least in their reactions to the problems they confront, the usual melodramatic types – Selim and Helena are more acted upon that acting, and must be saved rather than actually saving themselves – they indicate that their author was more interested in portraying unusual events and places than finding a new method to refurbish the glories of revolution and liberty. The production of both plays in America signifies that the theatregoing public did interest itself in foreign parts and people. Noah capitalized on that interest to repeat a refrain familiar to Americans, while Payne followed the practices of the period by applying the format of romantic melodrama to a contemporarily popular circumstance. The American waved his flag, the expatriate composed a romance.

The second comparison involves one of Payne's best plays. *Charles the Second*, first produced at Covent Garden, May 27, 1824, which Payne adapted from Alexandre Duval's *La Jeunesse de Henry V* (1806) (in its turn, adapted from Sebastien Mercier's *Charles II, roi d'Angleterre*, 1789).[8] The play is a comedy of manners, sprightly in language and rapid of action. It enjoyed a long and profitable popularity, being played as late as 1830. The plot concerns the manner in which the now reformed but hitherto rakish Duke of Rochester, under the command of Lady Clara, whom he hopes to marry if successful, cures the King of his nighttime habit of venturing out on the town in a disguise. Rochester convinces the King that he has learned the whereabouts of a delectable little bar-maid, and the two plan to visit the tavern, impersonating a pair of sailors. A retired sea captain, a dispenser of maxims and ditties as well as of ale, owns the tavern. His niece Mary, the soubrette of the play, has fallen in love with Rochester's page, Edward, who enters the tavern disguised as a music teacher

---

[8] Quinn, p. 180.

shortly after Rochester and Charles arrive. He recognizes the two sailors at once, but his fears are laid when Rochester takes him into confidence. After much carousing, singing, and tippling, during which Captain Copp reveals his low opinion of profligate monarchs, Rochester manages to steal the King's purse. He then departs with Edward to leave Charles alone with the wrathful tavern keeper and his bill. Copp locks the destitute and chagrined King in a room and goes for the watch. Edward and Mary reenter, and after tantalizing the King with the possibility of reprieve, let him escape out the window. Copp rushes in with a shotgun and fires both barrels after the fleeing monarch.

In the third act, Lady Clara has awaited Charles, whom she apprehends slipping back into the palace. An amusing speech about night work on matters of state ensues, after which Copp arrives to return the King's pocket watch, left at the tavern as surety and forgotten by Charles in his flight. Copp assumed that the sailor who refused to pay his reckoning had stolen it from the King. Of course Copp and Mary recognize their ruler, and the play ends with Edward and Mary betrothed, Charles repentent and reformed, and Rochester in possession of a positive commitment from Lady Clara. At no time does Payne indulge in that eminently American pasttime, moralizing. The play contains no comment about the evils of a profligate nobility or monarchy save Copp's speech to the drunken and disguised Charles, and that moves along well because of the irony in the situation. The reformation grows from the incidents in the plot, and is not foisted upon either the audience or the King to the accompaniment of a polemic on morals. Sympathy for Copp, the common man, occurs not because of an embodiment of all the virtues which flower in simple and humble souls, but because his homey homily and salty ditties make him interesting and human. The same sort of a judgment applies to Rochester and Charles. At neither is any opprobrium levelled, for their carousing does no harm to anything but the reputation of the Throne. That Charles perceives in the end, and he changes his ways.

In comparison, Maria Pinckney's *The Orphans* (1818) may be termed a characteristically American, sentimentally pedagogical, comedy of morals. Mentioned previously in Chapter Two as one among a number of plays which expressed disapproval of foreign mores, the piece condemns the type of environment which nurtures an unsentimental lack of compassion for the destitute. Americans, before the final gun of the Revolution had been fired, intermingled British sentimentalism with Swiss-French bucolic romanticism. Richardson and Rousseau left their impress writ large upon the first fifty years of American morality, to the extent that society affected the virtues of philanthropy, sensitivity to misfortune, and a lachrimose reaction to even the hint of undeserved degradation. Maria Pinckney felt the prickings of righteousness when she reflected on the relative fortunes of orphans in the United States in contrast to those unlucky enough to be reared abroad.

So Pinckney, determined to enlighten Americans about their own benevolence, created Lady Flinty, the shrewish, illiterate, spendthrift harridan who does her sisters-in-law and step-daughter out of their rightful inheritance. Lord Spendall Flinty has the misfortune, first, of being married to Lady Flinty, and second, of quietly acquiescing to all her wishes. Eventually Lady Flinty manages to have the girls turned out of the drafty but rainproof castle into the windy world. A benevolent farmer takes them in, with whom they live until succored by Freeman, Lord Flinty's right-thinking, republican brother. Each marries the young man of her choice.

Incidental to the main story, a scene transpires in a tavern where British sailors and Freeman converse concerning the battles on Lake Erie. They describe the gallantry and ability of the doughty Yankees, and wish them the best of fortune. Even the tendentiously immoral Lord Edward reforms because of his acquiescence to the arguments of Freeman and Frederick, the good and only temporarily poor son of a miser, and marries one of the sisters after having attempted to seduce her. Generally, the nobility are unkind, unsentimental, insensitive, and immoral; the mechanics, laborers, and pro-American commoners all have hearts of oak. The lower classes are naturally good, the upper classes naturally bad.

Pinckney takes a situation that could have been productive of comedy similar to that embodied in *Charles the Second* and turns it into a sermon on the evils of the British class system and morality. Payne, on the other hand, could well have written a comedy of morals, causing the King to act immorally, which would have brought about much more embarrassment than that merely sufficient for reformation. But Payne chose not to, while Pinckney sought to compare mores. The difference bespeaks a divergence in attitudes: in the one play foreigners serve in the capacity of agents in a moral lesson, and in the other the characters (while not foreign to the British of 1824, nevertheless one hundred and fifty years removed from them) move under the aegis of comedy. Payne utilized the interest that would be engendered by the personages themselves, while Pinckney placed didacticism before characterization.

So, while Payne suffers the stigma of expatriatism he nonetheless typifies the dramatists who saw the foreigner as an object of interest rather than a means for preaching a message. Throughout his thirty years as adapter and dramatist, Payne wrote successfully in every genre currently popular. In 1819 he combined five sources to create *Brutus, or the Fall of Tarquin,* which opened at Drury Lane on September 3, 1818, with Edmund Kean in the title role. Popular on the stage for seventy years, it served as the histrionic vehicle for the important actors of several decades. Junius Brutus Booth, Henry Wallack, Edwin Forrest, John McCullough, and Edwin Booth all appeared in it at one time or another.[9]

The Fall of Algiers (1825) represents a successful attempt at comic opera. Again an interest in the possibilities offered by foreign settings evinces itself. In the field of comic afterpieces and operatic farce, *The Lancers* (1827) and *Peter Smink* (1822) both achieved some recognition. The situation in *Peter Smink*, when Bayard gets trapped at a mill behind the German lines, probably served as the source for an almost identical scene in Richard P. Smith's *The Eighth of January* (1829), where Jackson gets caught by the British, but escapes because he signs an armistice in time. *Richelieu* (1826), adapted from Alexandre Duval's *La Jeunesse de Duc de Richelieu* (1796), represents Payne's efforts in domestic

---

[9] Quinn, pp. 170-171.

tragedy. He attempted another play of this type, *The Italian Bride* (ca. 1830), which appears only in manuscript. After he returned to America he adapted its scene to Baltimore, but the play was never produced.[10]

The attitude toward foreigners that has formed the substance of this chapter gained more adherents among dramatists and the public after tempers had cooled following the War of 1812. No burning foreign issues cropped up after Napolean's final defeat in 1815. The Missouri Compromise and its attendant problems, along with the panic of 1819, the Monroe Doctrine in 1823, and the disputations over tariffs, all served to thicken the sea wall which Americans were in the process of erecting against foreign pressures. The romantic influence, omnipresent in British drama and especially effective in American playwriting, surged to new heights. The history of early American drama could well be qualified with the adjective romantic, so prevalent and influential were the forces of romanticism upon authors in the new Republic.[11] And with the ever-growing popularity of British pieces in the American theatre, local authors at all concerned about having their work acted attempted to write to the public taste. The types of romantic plays are many. But those by American authors which glow with the purer hues of romanticism are the tragedies, the pirate and slave melodramas, Indian plays, and the romances of sentimental, melodramatic, or tragic pretensions.

Of the pirate plays which remained perenially popular as both afterpieces and main offerings throughout the entire early period of American drama, the first was Susanna H. Rowson's *Slaves in Algiers* (1794). The authoress intended it to show how Americans battled for freedom no matter where on the globe they might find themselves enslaved by the trammels of tyranny.[12] The spirit of liberty combines with the attraction of unusual events in strange surroundings. By 1818 the occurrences along the Barbary Coast

---

[10] Preface to *America's Lost Plays*, vol. V, eds. Codman Hislop and W. R. Richardson (Princeton, 1940).

[11] See Quinn and especially Moody for the manifestations of romanticism in early American drama.

[12] See Chapter I, p. 34.

had interested many a playwright. Maria Pinckney, among those intrigued by the dramatic possibilities of Algierian enslavement of American citizens, wrote *Young Carolinians, or Americans in Algiers* (1818). The ideas which motivate the Americans and Algierians have roots deep in the loam of romanticism. Antipathetic characters act in response to the urgings of uncontrollable passion, while sympathy goes out to the Algierians and Americans whose notions more nearly approximate those of Christianity and sentimental romanticism.

Richard P. Smith wrote *The Bombardment of Algiers* in 1829, adhering to the standard melodramatic format in his adaptation from the French original, *Le Bombardement d'Alger*, by Frédéric du Petit-Mère.[13] The play contains a Dey who eventually reforms, although, several times during the course of the action he threatens the hero, Chevalier Choiseuil, and the heroine, Valentine. A comic cafe owner and a friendly, noble Mohammedan by the name of Barbuctar complete the list of main characters. Their characteristics resemble those of similar melodramatically romantic sterotypes to be found in any number of plays prior to and succeeding *The Bombardment of Algiers*. The major qualities of character depend upon sensitivity to the plight of captured Christians. The French Chevalier, of course, evinces all the noble and gallant sentiments required by romanticism: he suffers in tormented silence the loss of his wife, he once acted magnanimously toward a captured Mohammedan, the ethics by which he guides his life respect honor, country, religion, and marriage – in that order and with no incompatibility or conflict among them. Those Algierians who try to help the captured Christians receive audience favor, those who restrain the captives or who would break the high code of romantic honor, of course turn into the villains. The Dey attempts to force Valentine to become his wife, although he knows she is Choiseuil's long-missing spouse. Foreign policy counts for naught in Smith's Barbary Coast pirate melodrama. Foreign alliances and disaffections loomed less important to the placement of audience sympathy in American drama as the nineteenth century aged.

---

13 Quinn, p. 218

Another indication that, as the Revolution faded farther in to the haze of history, politics and drama intermingled with less frequency, appears in the types of romantic tragedies written. As early as 1765 romantic, imitative, yet original blank verse and historical tragedy had been attempted. Thomas Godfrey's *The Prince of Parthia* (1765), two years after its publication, became the first play written by a native of the colonies to be placed upon a professional stage. As Quinn states "The tragedy is based upon real human emotion. The passions of love, jealousy, hatred, and revenge, the sentiments of loyalty, pity, and terror are fundamental."[14] After the Revolutionary War had fed fires of patriotism previously banked down in the minds of authors, tragedy occurring in historic times took on the cast of chauvinism. Plays such as Peter Markoe's *The Patriot Chief* (1784) sought past parallels for the recently successful American rebellion. But as the era wore on, tragic patriotism faded from popularity and playwrights turned again to the strain of tragedy whose originators had lived during the reigns of Elizabeth, James, the two Charles, and William and Mary.

In 1822 appeared the anonymous *Alfred the Great*. The author chose to dramatize the period when the Saxons and the Danes were warring. But rather than take advantage of the possibility for a patriotic parallel evident in Alfred's fight against foreign invasion and oppression, the playwright caused a conflict between pagan evil and Christian beneficence. Priests guide Alfred, while the Danes consult an old witch for favorable prognostications. Alfred, at first defeated and in hiding, eventually manages to regroup his forces, steal into the enemy encampment disguised as a minstrel to learn of their strategy and encourage his captured wife, then return to his army and lead it to victory. Symbolically, a noble Dane embraces Christianity in the closing moments of the tragedy.

Two years after *Alfred the Great* had been published, James N. Barker's tragedy, *Superstition*, received popular plaudits at the Chestnut Street Theatre in Philadelphia. Taking place during the witch-hunting period of colonial history, the tragedy involves

---

[14] Quinn, p. 22.

Charles, a young Briton recently arrived with his mother in the new land, and Mary, the daughter of Ravenswood, religious bigot. During the course of the play, the Pilgrims are attacked by Indians, saved by an Unknown (Charles' father, who had fled the charge of regicide after the Restoration), and start a witch trial. Ravenswood, driven by his religious zeal, his dislike of the strangers in his Puritan village, and his fear that Charles and Mary will wed, prosecutes the young British immigrant and his mother at the witch trial. Just as succor arrives, Charles is executed and Mary dies of a broken heart.

Barker, the ardent Democrat, the man who had rewritten *Marmion* to censure the British, wrought a tragedy in which honor and courage conspire to condemn a young man whose every previous good action seems to turn against him during the trial. Charles, like the British Sir Reginald and George Edgerton who arrive too late to save him, receives no blame because of his nationality. Fate, spurred by bigotry and xenophobia in the guise of Ravenswood's religious rectitude, changes each of Charles' acts of magnanimity into the manifestations of the forces of darkness working through his body. No partisan politics operate in *Superstition*.

Succeeding Barker's play by six years, James H. Kennicott's *Irma, or the Prediction* (1830), uses the Revolution as a backdrop for a villain-instigated romantic tragedy. Remington, in love with Irma sixteen years prior to the war, predicts when she marries someone else, that she will spill her own blood in the years to come. When the Revolution flares up, Remington joins the British. He kills Irma's husband while escaping from capture, and drives her insanely to murder her daughter. While no foreigners appear in *Irma*, the tragedy shows the use to which romantics put a war usually reserved for promulgating patriotic messages.

In 1766, Major Robert Rogers capitalized upon European interest in the American savage and wrote *Ponteach*, depicting the Indian as nobly suffering indignities at the hands of the colonists. James N. Barker followed the same inclination in 1808 with the comic opera *The Indian Princess*, the first Indian play to be performed in America.[15] Never a man to miss an opportunity to

[15] Quinn, p. 139.

"Americanize" American drama, Barker dipped into colonial history to find a native topic. The preface to *The Indian Princess* expresses Barker's dislike of the adamant critical bias which decried all American drama. Almost twenty years later, George Washington Parke Custis' *The Indian Prophecy* (1827) ushered in the vogue for Indian drama that gripped the playgoing public for thirty years. Even though Indian plays were written partly to further chauvinistic patriotism, they nevertheless did not depend upon nationality for identifying degrees of sympathetic or antipathetic characterization; with the exception that the savages, by definition, were noble protagonists.

The first Forrest Prize play, *Metamora*, by John Augustus Stone, was initially produced at the Park Theatre, New York, on December 15, 1829. Stone wrote the Indian play in response to Edwin Forrest's advertisement that he would award a five hundred dollar prize and half the proceeds of the third night for the " 'best tragedy, in five acts, of which the hero or principal character, shall be an aboriginal of this country' ".[16] With the famous American star in the title role, Stone's play had such a resounding and instantaneous success that Forrest retained it in his repertory throughout his career. While the antagonists in the play are British, they do not represent any attempt by Stone to censure England. The inherently noble Metamora embodies the romantic characteristics of familial love, courage, and a stoic acceptance of death as he fights against the depradations of the settlers, and dies rather than surrender at the close of the play. A second story line concerning mistakenly identified orphans and misled love operates among the settlers. In the end the villains lie dead while the young lovers unite, with all the prospects of fortune possible from belated knowledge of gentle birth and endowment of riches. The villainy in the play results from attempts by Lord Fitzarnold to betray Metamora (for which the Indian kills the viscount) and to force his will upon the young heroine. Stone portrays him as a profligate British nobleman, but those characteristics do not really dictate his actions as completely as does his general opposition to virtue and

---

[16] Richard Moody, *Edwin Forrest* (New York, 1960), p. 88.

native nobility delineate him as the villain. The public fancy succumbed to the Indian drama, and within short years the records of the stages in major cities of the North American continent show the remarkable and sustained popularity of the type.

Two other Indian dramas prior to 1830 have crossed the stream of time to the present: Nathaniel Deering's *Carabasset* (1830), played at the Portland Theatre, February 16, 1831, and George W. P. Custis' *Pocahontas,* produced at Philadelphia's Walnut Street Theatre, January 16, 1830. Deering chose to dramatize an incident in the history of New England, when the British wiped out a settlement of the Norridgewok Indians. Deering's Indians, like Stone's, speak in highly figurative language from which later depictors of the Red Man drew their inspiration. The savages respond nobly to the necessities of battle, refusing to kill women and children, fighting courageously until the surviving chief leaps from a cliff to his death. The foreigners in this piece do not react to motives other than those demanded by the necessities of romantic villainy. Ravillac, out to wreak revenge on the British, kills Carabasset's wife and child and violates the sanctity of a church to murder a French priest in a successful attempt to arouse the British and Indians against one another.

In Custis' play Indians perpetrate the evil, for the British settlers under Smith treat the natives with equity. Matacoran, who plans to kidnap Pocahontas and blame it on the British, has his plans foiled by Rolfe. Matacoran then convinces Powhatan that the British intend do rob him of his kingdom. A group of braves captures Smith, but the play adheres to legend, and Pocahontas rescues the English leader. Matacoran's perfidy halted, the Indians and British swear friendship as Rolfe and Pocahontas plight their troth. The divergence among the characterizations of foreigners in these early Indian plays shows that the antipathetic agents did not function at the center of interest. The noble savage, first inhabitant of the American paradise, stood at the focal point of the plot. No matter that the villains were French, British, clerics, or other Indians, they existed to prompt the protagonist into utterances and actions which proclaimed his native and primeval love of liberty, good morals, and excellent ethics.

It may be argued that the gothic romances such as Dunlap's *Fountainville Abbey* (1794), the romantic tales such as Joseph Hutton's *The Wounded Hussar* (1809), which is a musical after-piece telling of noble peasants and ignoble nobility, and the bucolic pieces such as the anonymous *Shepherdess of the Alps* (1815), complete with a Baucis and Philemon, indicate that the foreign characterizations responded heartily to romanticism much earlier than during the decade following the War of 1812. Certainly, whenever the inclinations of a playwright sent him to lands across the sea, to sources redolent with honorable yet thwarted love, and to the tomes of history for the noble passions of a bygone era – all these requisites of romanticism – the characterizations could be considered romantically tinctured. Yet at the same moment that the pressure of British drama from Shakespeare to Colman caused many an American playwright to emulate the successful work of his transalantic cousins, other American authors wrote plays in which foreigners appeared without the softening garb of romantic motivation.

When the frequency of derogatory caricatures and characterizations dropped off and the ranks of the romantic foreigners swelled proportionately, one may chart the upward inclination of an attitude which viewed foreign agents and settings as interesting because of their charming differences from the local and familiar; an attitude dependent, in part, upon the waxing popularity of American romanticism inherited from Europe. All history and all lands became the province of the romantic dramatists – whether comic, tragic, or melodramatic. The agents which populated the plays of romanticially biased authors were formulated more in accordance with the exigencies of genre than in conformity to some national stereotype or polemically immoral caricature.

Americans gradually lost their compulsion for comparison, since the United States had won three wars, had warned all foreign powers to stay off of the Western continents, and had erected tariffs to protect their manufactures, agriculture, and self-esteem. Outbursts of patriotic sentiment when Payne returned to his native land clothed in success, and fierce loyalty to the American star, Edwin Forrest, were indications of the firm, new patriotism that sprang from American self-confidence. The drama presaged this movement as it turned from consideration of and comparison with foreign customs, politics, and ethics, to a treatment of the romantic and primeval originators of America's doughty spirit of liberty and courage, the free American savages. The romanticism which moved away from familiar settings to colorful lands and distant events prepared the way for Indian drama to further the notion of an American paradise where liberty, equality, and democracy flourished in a natural state.

VI. CONCLUSIONS

The foregoing chapters have presented topically a body of material that serves as the basis for a series of conclusions about the formation, duration, variegation, and termination of a number of attitudes early Americans possessed concerning foreigners. The enunciation of an attitude toward an extra-national people implied to a majority of those early Americans a basic contrast between dissimilar facets of what were hoped to be divergent cultures. Their act of contrasting produced two attitudes, one relating to the group or person doing the comparing, and the other to that which was being compared. Much of the matter which comprised the attitudes toward foreigners held by the first two generations of Americans, therefore, reveals the ways in which those generations thought about themselves, their achievements, their ethics, their politics, their culture. The flux of attitudes expressed in drama and covering a seventy year period prior to 1830 presents difficulties if one attempts to study it either topically or chronologically. To follow a strictly topical method in drawing conclusions means that the temporal connection of historical events would be slighted; to rely on chronology alone as the guide would result in a series of occurrences strung out along a line, each isolated from others by the interpolation of irrelated yet sequential incidents. In this chapter the method shall be to assemble the topics treated in the first five, arrange the important attitudes causally, and treat the issue chronologically. Some breaks in temporal sequence can not be avoided, but the movement of the mass will proceed according to the progress of time.

In order to chart a trend, several playwrights will have had to treat material in a manner that permits conclusive evidence of a pervasive attitude to be observed. Much of the material, as is true when any imaginative literature becomes subject to analysis, depends upon the peculiar outlook of an individual playwright. To pronounce the unique product of a single mind indicative of a trend in the cultural attitude of a certain element of the population would be foolhardy. The toll taken by time on the dramatic products of an earlier era also tends to prevent the examination of many plays which might point up the existence of a pronounced attitude. So in some cases, that which may seem to be an injudicious employment of a single example for a major conclusion occurs because plays fall into the classification of ephemera retained or lost by the whimsy of individuals; and all too often those most topical and most interesting to the person in search of an attitude disappear but for a record of the title. Hence when a sole play particularly presages, concurs with, or reflects an attitude toward foreigners, it can be utilized to represent a trend only if evidence of that trend may be noted elsewhere.

Another problem presents itself in the dramatic depiction of stereotyped foreigners. When does a stereotyped caricature long existent in drama cease being a stereotype and start being a representation of an attitude toward inhabitants of a foreign country? Or does it at all? Or does the presence of one playwright's characterizations created to combat a stereotype serve notice of a different attitude? These riddles may be answered only in the specific examples, although they can be posed as general questions. The evidence of an intent on the part of a playwright to create a caricature differing from its predecessors would indicate that the author meant to set down his ideas on that type of character. But unless other similar deviations from the usual caricature appear, no trend may be charted.

Before the period of the Revolution no definite views concerning foreigners arose in the drama. In the first place, not much playwriting went on in the colonies. Prior to Godfrey's *Prince of Parthia*, produced in 1767 after the author had died, Governor Hunter's *Androboros* (1714), the anonymous *Paxton Boys* (1763), and a number of commencement exercises from the colleges of

Philadelphia and New Jersey supply the total of extant work in dramatic form written by indigenous colonists. And the dramas now known represent only the group of colonists whose progenitors had lived in England. Also inhabiting the eastern seaboard of North America were emigrants of other nationalities. The Dutch in New York, the Swedes in Delaware, the Germans in Pennsylvania, the Huguenots in New York, Massachusetts, and South Carolina, and the Scotch and Irish in western Pennsylvania, Virginia, and the Carolinas all deserve some sort of recognition as having an influence on who would be called foreign. The definition of a foreigner, even after the Revolution had forced a choice upon colonists of all nationalities, did not entail merely the views of the English stock; but among the Scotch Jacobites and the dispossessed Irish a readiness to deny any allegiance to Great Britain would oppose a pre-Revolutionary trend among all British colonists to express loyalty to insular Britain.

The colonists actually viewed each other as foreigners, since, in varying degrees, each colony thought of itself as a unique religious, political, cultural, and economic entity. Indeed, the differences far outweighed the similarities prior to the Seven Years War – or the French and Indian War, depending upon whether Briton or colonist supplied the name. Historians point to the wars of King William, Queen Anne, and King George as affecting a measure of unity among English-speaking colonies. Yet it was not until the French and Indian War had depleted the treasury and forced the Crown to ask colonies previously little taxed for finances, that colonists already somewhat united in their reaction against the French and Indians turned on the government that once protected them and demanded a remission of restrictions. The need for the colonists to unite against a common enemy, the French, worked to the disadvantage of the British Crown when the already somewhat unified colonies reacted against increased taxes. Thus arose, among the majority of the colonial population, a tendency to separate local from British interests.

The first indication of an idea of unity to appear in a dramatic piece occurred in the commencement exercises of the early 1760's, expressing the feelings of the colonists about such abstractions as freedom and natural liberty. Yet soon the tone changed, for with the Stamp Tax, the Quartering Act, and the Intolerable Measures the colonists argued vehemently that the British Throne usurped the same liberty and freedom it had recently helped to perpetuate. In the 1770's, colonial tolerance for what were considered Parliamentary injustices supplied Mercy Warren cause to satirize the British governors and military in *The Adulateur* (1773). In both this piece and *The Group* (1775), which was written prior to the outbreak of actual hostilities and in order to solidify Revolutionary sentiments, the authoress clearly defines the position of "this country" versus the Crown. Those who, in her drama, oppose the cause of less taxation and fewer restrictions become traitors. The colonists Mrs. Warren defines with the word "patriots". Once the British had been nominated the usurpers of colonial freedom of governance and trade by a plurality of the English-speaking colonists – the largest nationality – it was but a short step to elect the English antipathetic contingent foreign upon the outbreak of the war.

The foreigner in American drama, then, was born of strife. He did not evolve gradually from a variety of national conceptions, to establish quietly an existence apart from some evanescent notions of local attributes, customs, mores, or interests. On the other hand, he also did not spring fully delineated from the pen of the first polemicist to call the British "Enemies of the Revolution". The origins of the foreigner lie in the differing pre-Revolutionary factions which argued the pros and cons of Crown colonial policy. An eminent patriot-to-be such as Robert Munford could, as late as 1770, write a play which upheld the conception of representative government under the Crown. So when Hugh Brackenridge, John Leacock, and other but anonymous patriot-playwrights vilified the British as ignoble, infamous, degenerate, immoral, tyrannous, and ungallant enemies, they did so in response to the violent passions which tore through the rebelling colonies, dissociating friend from friend, disrupting families, and forcing each inhabitant of America to declare himself either Tory or Whig. The British in the patriotic and polemic drama possess no redeeming characteristics other than a remorse belatedly experienced once a

crucial battle has been lost or a significantly immoral act con-
doned.

In brief, the idea was to make the British as evil and the Americans as noble as possible within the confines of the dramatic
form. To that end the Revolutionary dramatists in favor of schism
not only resorted to seriously conceived propaganda in dramatic
form, but turned to outright satire. The British blockaded in Boston served as butts for coarse patriotic humor in *The Blockheads*
(1776), many puns and situations depending upon the Red Coats'
starved condition. Eager to define the differences between patriot
and enemy, Whig playwrights opposed atrocity with kindliness,
scurrility with magnanimity, immorality with morality, cowardice
with bravery, bribery with frankness, and trammels with freedom.
In this period of conflict appeared the idea that the American
inclination to freedom and democracy issued from the soil of the
North American continent. In Brackenridge's *Battle of Bunkers-
Hill* (1776), Howe informs the bemused Burgoyne of the inherent
hardiness and valor possessed by the inhabitants of American
woods and valleys. Loath to attribute anything to inherited British
ideas of freehold and government, the American apologist turned
to Rousseau and Locke for ideas that would operate well in de-
fining that primitive state of virtue and valor immanent in the
defenders of freedom.

The drama of the Revolutionary period supplies evidence to support the contention that a large number of colonists favored the
Loyalists. Even were it not for the figures that tell the historian of
one hundred thousand Tory emigrants embarking from America,
the existence of Loyalist drama and strong pre- and post-war arguments against the British show that the rebels had more than a
token opposition to overcome among their own countrymen. It is
obvious, of course, that had the outcome of the Revolution been
otherwise, the establishment and endurance of the positive anti-
foreign element in American drama would have been deferred
indefinitely. In 1774 appeared two short dialogues, both objecting
to the patriots' formulation of the Committees of Correspondence
and the First Continental Congress on the grounds that they
preached sedition and treason, and that they were really instru-

ments that worked against rather than for the colonists' best interests. During the Revolutionary War, Tory pamphleteers and
playwrights used the presses of Boston, Philadelphia, and particularly New York in the battle of the pen against the rebels.

Even the Tories recognized a difference between American and
British interests, although they firmly believed that rebellion was
not the best way to settle grievances. Loyalists such as Jonathan
Sewall attempted to point out the ways in which the Whigs had
misguided themselves, referring to the long history of amicability
between Crown and colonies as reason for the rebels to stop the
war. In accord with the bitterness of feeling toward the Whigs,
Tories, in plays such as *The Battle of Brooklyn* (1776), employed
pejorative terminology identical to that used by the Whigs, with
the difference that the epithets "traitor" and "enemy to the
country" applied to the rebels. As far as the Loyalists were concerned, the British were far from foreigners, and the war was civil
rather than revolutionary. All Revolutionary dramatic propaganda shows that the English colonists, no matter of what political
conviction, had come to think of America as their country. Americans, in actuality, were on the verge of achieving for themselves
an identity apart from that of their mother country. In fact, so
adhesive were the ties binding Loyalists to America that late in the
war, prior to the British evacuation of New York, a play pleading
for a reestablishment of close Anglo-American relationships was
printed in that British stronghold. The only mention of the French
in drama of the Revolution appear in that play. The author characterizes the French – foreign to him – as two-faced and grasping,
desiring an alliance solely to extend their influence over the
United States. It mattered not at all that Tory or Whig had differing conceptions of the Briton as friend or enemy; the Revolution
precipitated the establishment of American notions about people
of European countries in particular, ideas that helped in the formulation of a national identity.

The Revolution separated colonies from mother country; post-
Revolutionary dramatists set out to sever the American identity
from its origins. The bitterness created by wartime passions carried
over into the early national period, characteristically represented

by a strong and durable strain of anti-British sentiment in the drama. Whatever customs, manners, or mores early Americans imbued with the spirit of chauvinism decried, became representative of British culture. Determined to separate the new from the old socially and ethically as well as politically, post-war dramatists scored American Anglophiles, American political ideas, American society, and American mores that seemed even remotely attached to anything English. The anonymous playlet *Sans Souci* (1785), in the manner of Mercy Warren's work, takes to task the elements of Boston society that still practiced English customs fashionable prior to the Revolution. Two years later, Tyler's *The Contrast* accomplished precisely what its title indicates by setting apart definitively the elements of decadent European society (represented by the Anglicized fop) with the more ideal system the true sons of Columbia were attempting to perfect. The anti-foreign elements brought to light in *The Contrast* were employed by later dramatists for reasons other than those for which Tyler had intended them. Tyler primarily meant to contrast the "natural" American institutions to the overcivilized, *ipso facto* decadent foreign cultures. In order to accomplish his aims, Tyler endowed the fop with the antipathetic qualities of affectation in speech and manner, an immoral outlook, and an effete delight in the fripperies of fashionable dress. Tyler took the precepts of British sentimentalism, combined with them the attributes of patriotism, Rousseauistic primitivism, and the dislike of a fashionable and therefore classed aristocratic society, and arrived at a statement of the natural and ideal American culture.

Those Americans who were caught up in the enthusiasm for the new and natural polity looked to Europe for nothing but ideas to oppose. Wishing to divorce themselves entirely from their cultural origins, literate and intelligent Americans found in the contrasts between the effete, decadent, classed, monarchical systems and America's naturally good democracy, springing from an association with the primeval land, sufficient reason to deny any mutual provenance for their Republic and Britain's oligarchy. The products of European classed society – represented in *The Contrast* by the American fop who absorbed too many British ideas – had been over-civilized to an extent that no longer allowed them to accept or practice the simple, sentimental virtues and life. European civilization was thought of as being in a state of senescence, with the result that its culture had become outmoded. American democracy of government, economics, society, and culture, on the other hand, was growing through that Lockean impressionable infancy which, according to Rousseau, marked the virtuous and simple primordial society that had roots in a rural mode of life. Therefore, when the insensible urban depravity of the Anglicized Dimple loses to the moral and patriotic, unspoiled sentimentality of the American Manly, the democratic system receives vindication.

Attitudes which found in any foreigner the grounds for a comparison between local and alien ideas underwent a change about the time of the French Revolution. Represented by Dunlap's reference to French "bag and tails" in *Darby's Return* (1789), and by the antipathetic French fop in Low's *Politician Outwitted* (1789), a strong current of domestic political unrest over foreign alliances ran through the country. Americans sympathetic to the French doubled their attempts to decry the British, while Federalists saw nothing but rampaging anarchy in the upheaval of French political order and monarchy. The division between American Federalists and Jacobin-Democrats became more pronounced as the final decade in the eighteenth century unfolded and the Reign of Terror, the *Directoire*, and the Empire were initiated. Where British had previously been condemned because they represented the decadence of foreign institutions, they now were rendered antipathetic because of their opposition to the French rebellion against the evil of an aristocracy. On the other hand, the Federalists, who espoused the conception of an aristocracy of native worth and ability, thought that the French *citoyens* sinned against the natural order of events in precipitating the hasty and indiscriminate slaughter by guillotine. Yet the characteristics utilized to delineate either antipathetic French or British agents drew their substance from those first systematized by Tyler. Quite the contrary occurred, though, when a dramatist wished to depict a foreigner sympathetically. Then the character would admit openly his democratic principles, his nationality dependent upon the playwright's political persuasion.

The Frenchman in Federalist drama by such playwrights as Low, Dunlap, Minshull, and Murdoch differed from his predecessor in British drama in so far as American and English attitudes toward government were dissimilar. The stereotype of the Frenchman as an overly punctilious aristocrat, an affected barber, or a socially pretentious servant, which could be found in any number of eighteenth century English plays, also appeared in American drama. But the British employed the caricature for reasons of social ridicule, while the Americans, since they had a pronounced interest in politics, used the caricature to embody their idea of what happened to a person when he lived overly long in a mainly urban classed society. The two characterizations differed in didactic intent. American dramatists tended to view foreigners until approximately the turn of the century, as means to present an argument concerning comparative politics, mores, manners, or customs. This general tendency in relation to the politics of separate authors, spoke for the attitudes viable in post-Revolutionary America; attitudes representative of the concerns which crossed the minds of inhabitants of the new Republic.

Another trend in post-Revolutionary drama was concerned with the notion that immorality could occur only in alien lands, perpetrated by foreigners. Closely linked to the hypothesis that considered America man's best political, cultural, and moral hope – a latter-day paradise whose populace absorbed virtue and morality from the very atmosphere – this theory sought out examples of strange mores that would offset the simple and Christian morality of the United States. Thus David Humphreys adapted a French play as *The Widow of Malabar* (1790), revelatory of the immorality inherent in the Brahman practice of suttee. Throughout the entire period of American drama treated in the preceding chapters, playwrights turned time and again to other lands for the location of their corrective drama. So prevalent was the practice, so current and popular the notion that America could harbor no disreputable customs, manners, or mores, that some playwrights spoke out against it, stating that they harbored no favoritism and therefore set their corrective drama in America. Yet as late as 1827, William Gilmore Simms placed a temperance dialogue in Italy, responding to the same motivation that sent other authors before him to foreign settings for plays which preached morality.

Playwrights also turned to the history of other lands for the source material for drama which attempted to compare the American Revolution to countless previous battles against tyranny. This trend endured well into the nineteenth century. But, as exemplified by Frances Wright's attempt to recreate Swiss history in *Altorf* (1819), and Woodworth's return to Revolutionary topics in the 1820's, it acquired a more romantic than didactic basis. The people who could accept the natural benefits of a democratic system could also work a magical metamorphosis upon those foreigners who left their own lands and travelled through the new Republic. If the travellers were astute enough to judge fairly the American system, they then foreswore their effete and decadent foreign customs which had contrasted so unfavorably with those in the paradise they were visiting. After the first decade in the new century, foreign and American dandies, although still characterized by affectation, immoral proclivities, and overly-fashionable dress, could become sympathetic characters if they would accept natural and simple American manners and mores. Thus an attitude arose that considered the already primordially beneficial attributes of democratic politics, mores, and customs as combative elements which could do battle against the printed comments of travellers unsympathetic toward the culture and society of the United States.

The catalytic ability of the American system to accelerate a change for the better among those who would openly accept its institutions also functioned in application to certain groups of immigrants. The efficacy of this attitude may be ascertained by noting the differences between the British and American stage caricatures of the Irish. One can not state that the Irish, because of their preeminence as ludicrous figures in early American drama, were generally considered to be irresponsible, fun-loving, light-headed, ludicrous, and bellicose. These qualities had been borrowed from British drama. Yet within a few years after the Revolution, Dunlap had used O'Keeffe's Darby to propound patriotic sentiments, and by 1801 John Minshull had placed two amusing but not ludicrous Irish farm laborers in a comic opera. Minshull's characters announce that they have fully accepted the simple and virtuous – if not yet abstemious – way of life. A willingness to work, and a readiness to recognize the excellence of new over old ethics motivates the sympathy felt toward the two laborers. While there persisted into the nineteenth century a tendency to apply American virtues to Irish characters, the caricature which depended upon British progenitors for its distinguishing characteristics continued a lively existence right past the close of the early period in American drama: in 1828 Dunlap utilized the type.

A weak, isolated, but perceptible attitude which evolved from the observation of actual immigrants appeared in 1820 with a complete "Americanized" sentimentalization of the Irish refugee. Almira Selden, writing little moralities for her schoolchildren, perceived a parallel between the plight of the Irish fighting against British domination and the situation of the Americans during their own Revolutionary War. It is, however, impossible to find a dominant attitude represented in the utter "Americanization" of the Irish in 1820, and in their appearance as protagonists of a few later comedies and romanticized historical dramas. Yet so powerful was the enduring conception Americans held of their own democracy as the ultimate in beneficent government, that the pressure of an attitude could mold and change, in a few instances, the accepted Irish stereotype into a more sympathetic character.

Another attitude held by a few Americans deserves mention not because of its widespread popularity among dramatists, but because of its maturity and sensibility, almost out of place in an age and country where partisan extremes in ideology and politics were more accepted than questioned. Robert Munford, William Dunlap, and Mary Carr Clarke attempted to question the very morality of war and its violent aftermath at three widely separated dates in the early history of American drama. Shortly after the Revolutionary War, Munford wrote *The Patriots,* a play which probed the motives that make men assume the mantle of patriot in pursuit of personal aggrandizement. Munford spoke out against the persecution of innocents and the abuse of power that would permit the mere mention of the word "Tory" in connection with a man's name to act as reason to confiscate his property and condemn him to prison. In 1798 Dunlap wrote *André*, a tragedy. In it he stated that no matter for what cause war is fought, it inevitably kills those who least deserve to die. Dunlap utilized events still vivid in the minds of his audience to underline his humanitarian message concerning the dilemma caused when friendship and duty come into conflict. Mary Clarke chose the War of 1812 as her battle-ground. She wrote *The Fair Americans* (1815) to contend that allegiance to an enemy faction during time of war does not automatically obliterate honor, courage, and morality. Mrs. Clarke's attitude, like that of her two male predecessors, objected to the substitution of political partisanship for moral judgment when assessing one's fellow man.

While attitudes mentioned to this point persisted with varying intensities into the nineteenth century, a change in the way certain Americans visualized the foreigner began to make itself palpable about the time of Jefferson's election. The domestic political conflict between Democrat and Federalist, the local manifestation of the battle that had gone on in the drama between foreign aristocrat and native democrat, resolved itself in an anti-aristocratic victory. One needs only turn to Nichols' *Jefferson and Liberty* (1801) to understand that when Adams and the Federalists relinquished control of the government, many Americans thought that true democracy had finally arrived. Federalists and British aristocrats were equated – and not without some justification, for many Federalists thought that an aristocracy based upon native ability rather than primogeniture would eventually prevail in the United States.

But once the Federalist threat to democracy subsided, Americans apparently ceased to align their domestic political affiliations in strict accordance with their foreign sympathies. This occurred in part because both British and French infractions of American maritime commercial freedom disabused many Americans of their previous ideas concerning the benefits of a closer union with either of the two European powers. In addition, sufficient time had passed to permit a quieting of violent wartime animosities. Complaint concerning the American acceptance of British drama, fashion, and culture began to appear with more frequency in the prologues, prefaces, and epilogues to American plays. Such evidence points to a gradual return to an acceptance of European taste as arbiter in matters appertaining unto society and culture. Rather than a wary acceptance of the advances of "Europe's knowledge, / By sharp experience bought", that Dunlap desired, Americans openly began to welcome uncritically British fashion, custom, and literature. This did not transpire on the stroke of midnight, December 31, 1800, or at the moment Jefferson lifted his hand from the Bible, but occurred gradually. No actual beginnings can be assigned the commencement of American interest in foreign custom and people for non-constrasting reasons. The trend becomes apparent around 1800, intensifies during the period prior to the War of 1812, and then reappears in possession of a different set of characteristics.

Prior to the advent of melodrama and the frequent complaints about American preference for British literature and drama, the foreigner had been frequently characterized as sympathetic or antipathetic in the measure that he exhibited or denied characteristics recognizable as those that would be held or condemned by Americans in a similar situation. Thus Barbary pirates, European fashion plates, or Brahman priests served primarily didactic ends when they appeared in post-Revolutionary drama. But when the romantic proclivities already inherent in drama that turns to foreign settings in an attempt to engender interest intensified through the increasing popularity of melodrama, didacticism relinquished its preeminence to romanticism and to a curiosity about the foreigner for his peculiar qualities. By the second decade of the nineteenth century, the numbers of melodramas, romantic tragedies, comedies of manners, and comic operas which contained foreigners who did not represent portions of an argument opposing American to foreign systems, had multiplied to where the attitude they exemplified may be deemed characteristic of an influential segment of the literate and cultured populace.

By the time the War of 1812 had been fought to a stalemate – with a consequent, but brief, return to popularity of patriotic pieces – even previously polemic subjects had acquired a romantic patina. Although the eminently Democratic and patriotic dramatists Mordecai Noah and Samuel Woodworth still wrote nationalistic plays both prior to and following the War of 1812, they found it necessary to subjugate the anti-American characteristics of British villains to romantic motivations for antipathy. Foreign mores were still contrasted to their ideal American counterparts, but the comparison took place secondarily to the problems confronted in adapting agent to action. Even when plays satirized the British in retaliation for travelogues which found fault with various American institutions and customs, the depictions had lost the bitterness present in post-Revolutionary drama.

In brief, Americans had begun to judge the foreigner in relation to values other than those asserted by a young and revolutionary country attempting to differentiate its own ideology from those of other and more powerful nations. By the time Americans realized that three wars had been brought to satisfactory conclusions, they found their impregnability affirmed by the Monroe Doctrine and its influence in the courts and parliaments of European nations. Dramatic interest in the romantic elements of foreign countries and characters did not deny the presence and prevalence of a patriotic attitude which remained sensitive to American differences. It did, however, indicate that Americans had settled into a self-confidence still ready to answer all foreign criticism, but which responded to censure without the somewhat puerile antagonism apparent in late eighteenth century Republican drama. The American of the 1820's boisterously proclaimed his unique qualities, only he did so with full consciousness that his future growth and improvement was assured.

Prior to the Jacksonian revolution, American drama had carried the seeds of a change in attitude through its gradual relinquishment of a didactic interest in foreigners. By the year of Jackson's inauguration and the transcendence of the frontier political elements, Indian plays, representing the first indigenous American drama to acquire great popularity, carried to maturity the conception of America as a paradise where even its aboriginal inhabitants – not to mention its later white citizens – had enjoyed the natural and primitive liberty, democracy, and equality acquired from the primeval freedom of a land unsullied by decadent civilizations. In fact, so strong was the pull of the frontier, that by 1829 the eastern city dweller, in Brice's *Country Clown,* took over the place and qualities of the previously antipathetic foreigner. In Jackson democracy found a new lease, in the West Americans found a waiting continent, and in the drama Indian nobility and liberty signified the shift in American attitudes away from an emphatic interest in foreign matters to an enduring consideration of native issues.

APPENDIX

The appendix contains a list of plays utilized in determining early American attitudes toward foreigners. Not all the plays contain foreigners, but all do express a point of view concerning the United States in relation to foreign culture. The appendix gives author (if known), place and date of publication, and place and date of the first production (if the play was produced). Abbreviations for the following theatres have been used:

Bowery: Bowery Theatre, New York.
Broadway: Broadway Theatre, New York.
Chestnut: Chestnut Street Theatre, Philadelphia.
C. G.: Covent Garden Theatre, London.
D. L.: Drury Lane Theatre, London.
Federal: Federal Street Theatre, Boston.
Haymarket: Haymarket Theatre, Boston.
John St.: John Street Theatre, New York.
Park: Park Theatre, New York.
Southwark: Southwark Theatre, Philadelphia.
Walnut: Walnut Street Theatre, Philadelphia.

Adams, Charles L., *Favelle; or, The Fatal Duel* (Boston, 1809).
Alfred the Great (New York, 1822).
Americana; or, A New Tale of the Genii (Baltimore, 1802). (City Theatre, Charleston, Feb. 9, 1798.)
Barker, James N., *The Indian Princess; or, La Belle Sauvage* (Philadelphia, 1808). (Chestnut, April 6, 1808.)
——, *Marmion; or, The Battle of Flodden Field* (New York, 1812, 1816). (Park, April 13, 1812.)
——, *Tears and Smiles* (Philadelphia, 1808). (Chestnut, March 4, 1807.)
——, *Superstition* (Philadelphia, 1826). (Chestnut, March 12, 1824.)
The Battle of Brooklyn (New York, 1776).

Beach, Lazarus, *Jonathan Postfree; or, The Honest Yankee* (New York, 1807).

Beete, John, *The Man of the Times; or, A Scarcity of Cash* (Charleston, 1797). (Church Street Theatre, Charleston, April 24, 1797.)

The Better Sort; or, The Girl of Spirit (Boston, 1789).

The Blockheads; or, The Affrighted Officers (Boston, 1776).

The Blockheads; or, Fortunate Contractor (New York, 1782).

Brackenridge, Hugh H., *The Battle of Bunkers-Hill* (Philadelphia, 1776).

——, *The Death of General Montgomery, in Storming the City of Quebec* (Norwich, 1777).

Breck, Charles, *The Fox Chase* (New York, 1808). (Chestnut, April 9, 1806.)

——, *The Trust* (New York, 1808).

Brice, James F., *A Country Clown; or, Dandyism Improved* (Annapolis, 1829).

Burk, John D., *Bunker Hill; or, The Death of General Warren* (New York, 1797). (Haymarket, Feb. 17, 1798.)

——, *Female Patriotism; or, The Death of Joan d'Arc* (New York, 1798). (Park, April 13, 1798.)

Clarke, Mary C., *The Fair Americans* (Philadelphia, 1815).

——, *The Benevolent Lawyers; or, Villainy Detected* (Philadelphia, 1823).

Cockings, George, *The Conquest of Canada; or, The Siege of Quebec* (London, 1766; Philadelphia, 1772). (Southwark, Feb. 16, 1773.)

Columbia and Britannia. By "A Citizen of the United States" (New London, 1787).

Coombe, Thomas, *An Exercise, Containing a Dialogue and Two Odes* (Philadelphia, 1767).

Custis, George W. P., *The Indian Prophecy* (Georgetown, D.C., 1828). (Chestnut, July 4, 1827.)

——, *Pocahontas; or, The Settlers of Virginia* (Philadelphia, 1830). (Walnut, Jan 16, 1830.)

Debates at the Robin-Hood Society in the City of New York. On Monday Night, 19th July, 1774 (New York, [1774?]).

Deering, Nathaniel, *Carabasset* (Portland, 1830). (Portland Theatre, Feb. 16, 1831.)

A Dialogue between a Southern Delegate and His Spouse. By Mary V.V. (pseud.) (New York, 1774).

The Disappointment; or, The Force of Credulity. By Andrew Barton (pseud.) (New York, 1767; Philadelphia, 1796).

The Double Conspiracy; or, Treason Discovered but not Punished (Hartford, 1783).

Duché, Jacob, *An Exercise, Containing a Dialogue and Ode on the*

Accession of His Present Gracious Majesty George III (Philadelphia, 1762).

Dunlap, William, *André* (New York, 1798). (Park, March 30, 1798.)

——, *The Archers; or, Mountaineers of Switzerland* (New York, 1796). (John St., April 18, 1796.)

——, *Darby's Return* (New York, 1789). (John St., Nov. 24, 1789.)

——, *The Father; or, American Shandy-ism* (New York, 1789). (John St., Sep. 7, 1789.)

——, *The Father of an Only Child* (New York, 1807).

——, *The Glory of Columbia – Her Yeomanry* (New York, 1817). (Park, July 4, 1803.)

——, *A Trip to Niagara; or, Travellers in America* (New York, 1830). (Bowery, Nov. 28, 1828.)

——, *Yankee Chronology; or, Huzza for the Constitution* (New York, 1812). (Park, Sep. 12, 1812.)

[Elliott, Samuel or James?]. *Fayette in Prison; or, Misfortunes of the Great* (Worcester, 1802).

Ellison, James, *The American Captive; or, The Siege of Tripoli* (Boston, 1812). (Boston Theatre, Dec. 11, 1811.)

Evans, Nathaniel, *An Exercise Containing a Dialogue and an Ode on Occasion of the Peace* (Philadelphia, 1763, 1772).

Everett, David, *Daranzel; or, The Persian Patriot* (Boston, 1800). (Haymarket, April 16, 1798.)

——, *Slaves in Barbary*. In *The Columbian Orator*, 1810.

Finn, Henry J., *Montgomery; or, The Falls of Montmorency* (Boston, 1825). (Boston Theatre, Feb. 21, 1825.)

The French Revolution: Including a Story, Founded in Fact, of Leontine and Matilda (New Bedford, 1793). (Dartmouth College, 1790.)

Freneau, Philip, *Poem, on the Rising Glory of America; Being an Exercise delivered at the Public Commencement at Nassau-Hall, September 25, 1771* (Philadelphia, 1772).

Grice, C. E., *The Battle of New Orleans; or, Glory, Love, and Loyalty* (New York, 1816). (Park, July 4, 1816.)

Hall, Everard, *Nolens Volens; or, The Biter Bit* (Newbern, N.C., 1809).

Harby, Isaac, *Alberti* (Charleston, 1819). (Charleston Theatre, April, 1819.)

Hawkins, Micah, *The Saw-Mill; or, A Yankee Trick* (New York, 1824). (Chatham Garden Theatre, New York, Nov. 29, 1824.)

Heaven on Earth; or, The New Lights of Harmony. By Peter Puffem (pseud.) (Philadelphia, 1825).

Henry, John, *A School for Soldiers; or, The Deserter* (Kingston, Jamaica, 1783). (John St., April 24, 1788.)

Hitchcock, Edward, *Emancipation of Europe; or, The Downfall of Bonaparte* (Greenfield, Mass., 1815).

Hopkinson, Thomas, *A Dialogue and Ode, Sacred to the Memory of His Late Gracious Majesty, George II. Performed at the Public Commencement in the College of Philadelphia, May 23, 1761* (Philadelphia, n.d.).

Humphreys, David, *The Widow of Malabar; or, The Tyranny of Custom* (New York, 1790). (Southwark, May 7, 1790.)

——, *The Yankey in England* (N.p., n.d. [1815?]).

Hutton, Joseph, *Fashionable Follies* (Philadelphia, 1815).

——, *The Orphan of Prague* (Philadelphia, 1808).

——, *The School for Prodigals* (Philadelphia, 1809). (Chestnut, Feb. 20, 1809.)

——, *The Wounded Hussar; or, Rightful Heir* (Philadelphia, 1809). (Chestnut, March 29, 1809.)

[Ioor, William], *The Battle of the Eutaw Springs* (Charleston, 1807). Charleston Theatre, Jan. 10, 1807.)

Ioor, William, *Independence; or, Which do You Like Best, the Peer or the Farmer?* (Charleston, 1805). (Charleston Theatre, March 30, 1805.)

Judah, Samuel B. H., *A Tale of Lexington* (New York, 1823). (Park, July 4, 1822.)

Kennicott, James H., *Irma; or, The Prediction* (New York, 1830). (American Theatre, New Orleans, April 6, 1830.)

Lathy, Thomas P., *Reparation; or, The School for Libertines* (Boston, 1800).

[Leacock, John?], *The Fall of British Tyranny; or, American Liberty Triumphant* (Philadelphia, 1776).

Lee, Walter, *La Fayette; or, The Fortress of Olmutz* (Philadelphia, 1824). (Park, Feb. 23, 1824.)

[Low, Samuel?], *The Politician Outwitted* (New York, 1789).

Markoe, Peter, *The Patriot Chief* (Philadelphia, 1784).

Marriott, Mrs., *The Chimera; or, Effusions of Fancy* (New York, 1795). (Southwark, Nov. 17, 1794.)

Mary of Scotland; or, The Heir of Avenel (New York, 1821). (Anthony Street Theatre, New York, May, 1821.)

McHenry, James, *The Usurper* (Philadelphia, 1829). (Chestnut, Dec. 26, 1827.)

The Military Glory of Great Britain (Philadelphia, 1762).

Milns, William, *All in a Bustle; or, The New House* (New York, 1798). (Park, Jan. 29, 1798.)

——, *The Comet; or, He Would be an Astronomer* (Baltimore, 1817). (John St., Feb. 1, 1797.)

Minshull, John, *He Stoops to Conquer; or, The Virgin Wife Trium-phant* (New York, 1804).

——, *The Merry Dames; or, The Humourist's Triumph over the Poet in Petticoats, and the Gallant Exploits of the Knight of the Comb* (New York, 1805). (Bedlow Street Theatre, New York, July 22, 1805.)

——, *Rural Felicity: with the Humour of Patrick, and the Marriage of Shelty* (New York, 1801). (Bedlow Street Theatre, New York, Jan. 15, 1805.)

The Motley Assembly (Boston, 1779).

Munford, Robert, *The Candidates; or, The Humours of a Virginia Election.* In *A Collection of Plays and Poems* (Petersburg, Va., 1798).

——, *The Patriots.* In *A Collection of Plays and Poems* (Petersburg, Va., 1798).

Murdoch, John, *The Beau Metamorphized; or, The Generous Maid* (Philadelphia, 1800).

——, *The Politicians; or, A State of Things* (Philadelphia, 1798).

Murray, Judith S., *The Traveller Returned.* In *The Gleaner* (Boston, 1798). (Federal, March 9, 1796.)

——, *Virtue Triumphant.* In *The Gleaner* (Boston, 1798). (Federal, March 2, 1795.)

Nichols, J. Horatio, *Jefferson and Liberty; or, Celebration of the Fourth of March* ([Boston], 1801).

Noah, Mordecai M., *Marion; or, The Hero of Lake George* (New York, 1822). (Park, Nov. 25, 1821.)

——, *The Grecian Captive; or, The Fall of Athens* (New York, 1822). (Park, June 17, 1822.)

——, *She Would be a Soldier; or, The Plains of Chippewa* (New York, 1819). (Park, June 21, 1819.)

Paulding, James K., *The Bucktails; or, Americans in England.* In *American Comedies* (Philadelphia, 1847).

Payne, John H., *Ali Pacha; or, The Signet Ring* (New York, 1823). (C.G., Oct. 19, 1822; Park, May 8, 1823.)

——, *Brutus; or, The Fall of Tarquin* (New York, 1819). (D.L., Dec. 3, 1818; Park, March 15, 1819.)

——, *Charles the Second; or, The Merry Monarch* (London, 1824). (C.G., May 27, 1824; Park, Oct. 25, 1824.)

——, *The Fall of Algiers* (London, [1825]). (D.L., Jan. 19, 1825; Philadelphia, 1826.)

——, *The Italian Bride.* Ms. dated ca. 1830; reproduced in *America's Lost Plays* (Princeton, 1940).

——, *Julia; or The Wanderer* (New York, 1806). (Park, Feb. 7, 1806.)

——, *The Lancers* (London, n.d.). (D.L., Dec. 19, 1827; Bowery, March 4, 1828.)

——, *Peter Smink; or, The Armistice* (London, n.d.). (Royal Surrey Theatre, London, July 8, 1822; Park, Oct. 14, 1826.)

——, *Richelieu; A Domestic Tragedy* (New York, 1826). (C.G., Feb. 11, 1826; Chestnut, 1829.)

Pepper, George, *Kathleen O'Neill; or, A Picture of Feudal Times in Ireland* (Philadelphia, 1832). (LaFayette Theatre, New York, March 10, 1827.)

Pinckney, Maria, *The Young Carolinians. The Orphans.* In *Essays Religious, Moral, Dramatic, and Poetical* (Charleston, 1818).

Pogson, Sarah, *The Female Enthusiast* (Charleston, 1807).

Robinson, J., *The Yorker's Stratagem; or, Banana's Wedding* (New York, 1792). (John St., April, 1792.)

Rogers, Robert, *Ponteach; or, The Savages of America* (London, 1766).

Rowson, Susanna H., *Slaves in Algiers; or, A Struggle for Freedom* (Philadelphia, 1794). (Chestnut, Dec. 22, 1794.)

Sans Souci; alias, Free and Easy (Boston, 1785).

Sawyer, Lemuel., *The Wreck of Honor* (New York, 1824).

Selden, Almira, *The Irish Exiles in America.* In *Effusions of the Heart* (Bennington, Vt., 1820).

Sewall, Jonathan, *The Americans Roused in a Cure for the Spleen; or, Amusement for a Winter's Evening* (America, N.Y., 1775).

Shepherdess of the Alps (New York, 1815).

Simms, William G., *A Dramatic Dialogue.* In *Lyrical and Other Poems* (Charleston, 1827).

Smith, Elihu H., *Edwin and Angelina; or, The Banditti* (New York, 1797). (John St., Dec. 19, 1796.)

Smith, Jonathan S., *The Siege of Algiers; or, The Downfall of Hadgi-Ali-Bashaw* (Philadelphia, 1823).

Smith, Richard P., *The Bombardment of Algiers.* Ms. dated 1829, reproduced in *America's Lost Plays* (Princeton, 1940).

——, *The Eight of January* (Philadelphia, 1829). (Chestnut, Jan. 8, 1829.)

[Smith, William], *An Exercise, Containing a Dialogue and an Ode* (Philadelphia, 1766, 1775).

Stearns, Charles, *Bernard of Berlin. The Gamester. The Female Gamester.* In *Dramatic Dialogues for the Use of Schools* (Leominster, Mass., 1798).

Stone, John A., *Metamora; or, The Last of the Wampanoags.* In *America's Lost Plays* (Princeton, 1940). (Park, Dec. 15, 1829.)

Talbot, Charles S., *Paddy's Trip to America; or, The Husband with*

Three Wives (New York, 1822). (Washington Hall, New York, 1821 or 1822.)

——, *Squire Hartley* (Albany, 1827). (York, Upper Canada, March, 1825.)

Taylor, Vermilye, *The Banker; or, Things as They Have Been* (New York, 1819).

——, *False Appearances* (New York, 1819).

The Trial of Atticus, Before Justice Beau, for a Rape (Boston, 1771).

Tyler, Royall, *The Contrast* (Philadelphia, 1790). (John St., April 16, 1787.)

The Village Wedding (Boston, n.d. [179-?]).

Warren, Mercy O., *The Adulateur* (Boston, 1773).

——, *The Group* (New York, 1775).

Watterson, George, *The Child of Feeling* (Georgetown, 1809).

White, John B., *Modern Honor* (Charleston, 1812). (Charleston Theatre, March 6, 1812.)

White, William C., *The Clergyman's Daughter* (Boston, 1810). (Federal, Jan. 1, 1810.)

Woodworth, Samuel, *The Forest Rose; or, American Farmers* (New York, 1825). (Chatham Theatre, New York, Oct. 7, 1825.)

——, *King's Bridge Cottage* (New York, 1826). Richmond Hill Theatre, Feb. 22, 1833.)

——, *La Fayette; or, The Castle of Olmutz* (New York, 1824). (Park, Feb. 23, 1824.)

——, *The Widow's Son; or, Which is the Traitor?* (New York, 1825). (Park, Nov. 25, 1825.)

Workman, James, *Liberty in Louisiana* (Charleston, 1804). (Charleston Theatre, April 4, 1804.)

Wright, Frances, *Altorf* (Philadelphia, 1819). (Park, Feb. 19, 1819.)

BIBLIOGRAPHY

Bailey, Thomas A., *The American Pageant* (Boston, 1956).

Beard, Charles A., and Mary R., *The Rise of American Civilization* (New York, 1930).

Carpenter, Frederic I., *American Literature and the Dream* (New York, 1955).

Clapp, William W., *A Record of the Boston Stage* (Boston, 1853).

Duggan, George C., *The Stage Irishman: A History of the Irish Play and Stage Characters from the Earliest Times* (London, 1937).

Dunlap, William, *A History of the American Theatre* (New York, 1832).

Encyclopedia of American History, ed. Richard B. Morris (New York, 1953).

Fish, Carl R., *The Rise of the Common Man*, in *A History of American Life*, ed. Arthur M. Schlesinger and Dixon R. Fox (New York, 1950).

Glenn, Stanley L., "Ludicrous Characterization in American Comedy from the Beginning until the Civil War", unpubl. disser. Stanford University, 1955.

Hill, Frank P., *Bibliography of American Plays* (Stanford University, 1934).

Irving, Washington, *Letters of Jonathan Oldstyle*, ed. Stanley T. Williams (New York, 1941).

James, Reese D., *Old Drury of Philadelphia. A History of the Philadelphia Stage, 1800-1835* (Philadelphia, 1932).

Jones, Howard M., *America and French Culture, 1750-1848* (Chapel Hill, 1927).

Knight, Grant C., *American Literature and Culture* (New York, 1932).

Lerner, Max, *America as a Civilization* (New York, 1957).

Lewis, R. W. B., *The American Adam* (Chicago, 1955).

A Literary History of England, ed. Albert C. Baugh (New York, 1948).

Literary History of the United States, 2 vols., ed. Robert E. Spiller, Willard Thorp, Henry S. Canby (New York, 1948).

Lynn, Kenneth S., *The Dream of Success* (Boston, 1955).

Mathews, Charles, *The London Mathews; Containing an Account of This Celebrated Comedian's Trip to America* (London, n.d. [ca. 1824]).

Matthiesen, F. O., *American Renaissance* (New York, 1941).

Mesick, Jane L., *The English Traveller in America, 1785-1835* (New York, 1922).

Moody, Richard, *America Takes the Stage; Romanticism in American Drama and Theatre, 1750-1900* (Bloomington, 1955).

———, *Edwin Forrest; First Star of the American Stage* (New York, 1960).

Nicoll, Allardyce, *A History of English Drama, 1660-1900*. 4th ed., 6 vols. (Cambridge, 1961).

Odell, James C., *Annals of the New York Stage,* 13 vols. (New York, 1927-1942).

Parrington, Vernon L., *Main Currents in American Thought* (New York, 1930).

Paulding, James K., *The Bulls and the Jonathans; Comprising John Bull and Brother Jonathan, and John Bull in America,* ed. William I. Paulding (New York, 1867).

Pollock, Thomas C., *The Philadelphia Theatre in the Eighteenth Century* (Philadelphia, 1933).

Reed, Perley I., *The Realistic Presentation of American Characters in Native American Plays Prior to Eighteen-Seventy* (Columbus, O., 1918).

Schevill, Ferdinand, *A History of Europe* (New York, 1949).

Schlesinger, Arthur M., Jr., *The Age of Jackson* (Boston, 1945).

Seilhamer, George C., *The History of the American Theatre,* 3 vols. (Philadelphia, 1888-1891).

Smith, Henry N., *Virgin Land* (Cambridge, Mass., 1950).

Spiller, Robert E., *The Cycle of American Literature* (New York, 1955).

Tyler, Moses C., *A History of American Literature* (Ithaca, 1949).

INDEX

Adams, Charles L., 57
Adams, John, 27; satirized, 71
Adams, Samuel, 26, 27
The Adulateur, 61, 26-28, 181
Alberti, 52, 158
Alfred the Great, 172
Ali Pacha, 165-166
Alien and Sedition Acts, 33, 46
All in a Bustle, 131-132, 161
Altorf, 47, 52-53, 187
American Adam, 38-39, 48
The American Captive, 154
American Company, 23, 45
American Paradise, 39, 73, 92-93, 97, 177
André, 36, 90-95, 159, 189
Androboros, 19, 179
The Archers, 47-48, 53

Ye Bare and Ye Cubbe, 19
Barker, James N., 51-52, 67, 133, 148, 158-159, 160, 172-173
Barry, Spanger, 123
Barton, Andrew (pseud.), 157
The Battle of Brooklyn, 79-81, 183
The Battle of Bunkers-Hill, 38-41, 182.
The Battle of the Eutaw Springs, 69, 70, 128
The Battle of New Orleans, 99, 128
The Beau Metamorphized, 69, 101, 135, 136-137, 142
Beete, John, 119, 136
The Benevolent Lawyers, 111, 131
Bernard of Berlin, 57
The Better Sort, 68, 100-101, 142

Bird, Robert M., 111
The Blockade, 41, 137
The Blockheads, 32, 81-82, 142
The Blockheads, or the Affrighted Officers, 41-42, 43, 137, 182
Boker, George H., 111
Le Bombardement d'Alger, 171
The Bombardment of Algiers, 171
Booth, Edwin, 169
Booth, Junius B., 169
Boston Massacre, 25, 27
Brackenridge, Hugh, 30, 37, 38-42, 181, 182
Breck, Charles, 57, 103
Brice, James F., 192
Brougham, John, 111
Brutus, or the Fall of Tarquin, 169
The Bucktails, 59, 69, 138, 142
Bunker Hill, 50, 51
Burgoyne, General John, dramatized, 38-40, 41; author, 41
Burk, John D., 48, 50

The Candidates, 18
Captain O'Blunder, or the Brave Irishman, 116
Carabasset, 175
Census of 1790, 15
Charles II, roi d'Angleterre, 166
Charles the Second, 166-167, 168
The Child of Feeling, 59
The Chimera, 135, 141-142, 160-161
Clari, or the Maid of Milan, 164
Clarke, Mary C., 84, 95-96, 111, 122, 129, 131, 188, 189

The Clergyman's Daughter, 57, 58

Clinton, General Henry, dramatized, 40, 70

Cockings, George, 22, 75

College of New Jersey, 16, 25

College of Philadelphia, 17, 23

Colman, George, 145

The Comet, 141, 142, 161

The Committee or the Faithful Irishman, 115

The Conquest of Canada, 22-23, 75-77

The Contrast, 31, 61-66, 71, 184

Corday, Charlotte, characterized, 53

A Country Clown, 194

Cumberland, Richard, 116

A Cure for the Spleen, 30, 79

Custis, George W. P., 104, 150, 174, 175

Daranzel, 51, 158

Darley's Return, 107-109, 123-125, 185

The Death of General Montgomery, 36, 42

The Debates at the Robin-Hood Society, 77

Deering, Nathaniel, 175

Dialogue and Ode, Sacred to the Memory ... of George II, 16

A Dialogue between a Southern Delegate and His Spouse, 29-30, 78

The Disappointment, 157

Dobb, Francis, 111

The Double Conspiracy, 43

Douglas, David, 23, 24

A Dramatic Dialogue, 57

Ducange, Victor, 163

Dunlap, William, 13, 19, 35-36, 44, 47, 53, 54, 68, 71, 84, 86, 95, 101, 107-109, 126, 127, 129, 146, 149, 159-160, 161, 176, 185, 188, 189

Duval, Alexandre, 166, 169

The Eighth of January, 99, 129, 158-159, 169

Elliott, Samuel, 46, 97

Ellison, James, 154

The Emancipation of Europe, 53, 54

The Englishman Returned from Paris, 144

European Traveller's in America, 100-102

Evans, Nathaniel, 17, 75

Everett, David, 51, 57, 158

Exercise ... on Occasion of the Peace, 17

Exercise ... on the Accession ... of George III, 17

The Fair Americans, 95-96, 122, 129, 189

The Fall of Algiers, 169

Farquhar, George, 115

Fashionable Follies, 149

The Father, 68

The Father of an Only Child, 88-90

The Father, or American Shandyism, 35, 54, 86-88

Favelle, or the Fatal Duel, 57

Fayette in Prison, 46, 97

The Female Enthusiast, 53

The Female Gamester, 57

Female Patriotism, 48-50, 52

Finn, Henry J., 69, 105, 129

First Continental Congress, 23, 29-30, 78

Fitzball, Edward, 162

Foote, Samuel, 144

The Forest Rose, 67, 68

Forrest, Edwin, 169, 174

Fountainville Abbey, 176

The Fox Chase, 57, 103, 104

Franklin, Benjamin, 27

French and Indian War, 16, 21-22

The French Revolution, 33-34, 36, 44-45, 53

Freneau, Philip, 25-26

Gage, General Thomas, dramatized, 40

The Gamester, 57

Gardiner, General, dramatized, 38, 40

Garrick, David, 68, 144

George II, 16, 17

George III, 17

The Glory of Columbia, 126-127, 129

Godfrey, Thomas, 172

The Grecian Captive, 165

Grice, S. E., 99, 128

The Group, 23, 28-29, 38, 181

Hallam, Lewis, 23

Hamilton, Alexander, satirized, 71

Hancock, John, 27

Harby, Isaac, 52, 158

Haymarket Theatre, Boston, 50-51, 146-147

He Stoops to Conquer, 132

Heaven on Earth, 149-150

Henry, John, 82-83, 123

Henry, Patrick, 26

Hitchcock, Edward, 53

Holcroft, Thomas, 162

Hopkinson, Thomas, 16, 17

House of Burgesses, 18

Howard, Richard, 115

Howe, General William, dramatized, 38-40

Humphreys, David, 55-56, 186

Hutton, Joseph, 122, 136, 138, 141, 149, 176

The Indian Princess, 133, 173-174

The Indian Prophecy, 150, 174

The Irish Chief, 111

The Irish Exiles in America, 109-110

Irish servant, comic, 117-121

Irma, or the Prediction, 173

Irving, Washington, 67

The Italian Bride, 170

Jackson, Andrew, 11, 191, 192

The Jealous Wife, 145

Jefferson and Liberty, 71, 189

Jefferson, Thomas, 11, 67

La Jeunesse de Duc de Richelieu, 169

La Jeunesse de Henry V, 166

Joan of Arc, dramatized, 48-50

John Bull, prototype, 31

Johnstone, Jack (Irish), 123

Jonathan, stage character, 31, 33

Jonathan Postfree, 66

Julia, or the Wanderer, 133, 164

Kathleen O'Neill, 111

Kean, Edmund, 169

Kennicott, James H., 173

Kotzebue, August von, 162

La Fayette, 106-107, 152

La Fayette, Marquis de, dramatized, 46, 96-97, 106, 152

The Lancers, 169

Lathy, Thomas P., 152

Leacock, John, 30, 36, 37, 181

Lee, Walter, 152

Liberty in Louisiana, 36, 46, 132, 153, 154

Life's Vagaries, 145

The London Company, 23-24

Love à la Mode, 116, 117

Low, Samuel, 67, 143, 146, 150, 185

Macklin, Charles, 116

The Man of the Times, 119, 136

Marat, Jean P., dramatized, 53

Markoe, Peter, 32, 47, 172

Marmion, 51-52, 160, 173

Marriott, Mrs., 135, 141, 160

Mc Cullough, John, 169

Mc Henry, James, 111

Mc Lean's Journal, 125

Mercier, Sebastien, 166

The Merry Dames, 147-148

Metamora, 174

The Military Glory of Great Britain, 16

Milns, William, 131, 161

Minshull, John, 71, 125, 132, 147, 148

Miss in Her Teens, 68, 100

The Missouri Compromise, 170

Modern Honor, 60

The Monroe Doctrine, 11, 170

Montgomery, 69, 70-71, 105, 129

Montgomery, General, dramatized, 42

Moody, John, 115, 123

The Motley Assembly, 43

Munford, Robert, 18, 84-85, 181, 188

Murdoch, John, 45-46, 69, 97, 101, 135, 136

Murray Judith S., 103, 118, 153

Napoleon, dramatized, 54, 170

Nichols, Horatio N.

Noah, Mordecai M., 138, 149, 159, 165, 191

O'Keeffe, John, 108, 116, 125, 145

On the Rising Glory of America, 25-26

The Orphans, 58-59, 167-168

Paddy's Trip to America, 69, 110, 130, 131

Patrick in Prussia, 108, 116

The Patriot Chief, 32-33, 47, 172

The Patriots, 85-86, 188

Paulding, James K., 59, 69, 138

The Paxton Boys, 19, 179

Payne, John H., 133, 160, 164-170

Pepper, George, 111

Peter Smink, 169

Petit-Mère, Frederic du, 171

Pinckney, Maria, 58-59, 106, 167, 171

Pixérecourt, Gilbert de, 162

Pocahontas, 104, 175

Pogson, Sarah, 53

The Politicians, or a State of Things, 45, 97

The Politician Outwitted, 66, 67, 143-144, 151, 185

Ponteach, 19, 173

The Poor Soldier, 108, 116, 125

Powell, Charles, 51

The Prince of Parthia, 172, 179

Putnam, General, dramatized, 40

Quartering Acts, 25

Reparation, 152

Revolutionary War, American, 10, 12, 15, 37-45, 69, 70, 71, 72, 74-75, 150

Richelieu, 169

The Rivals, 116, 161

Robinson, J., 45, 153

Rogers, Robert, 19-20, 173

Rowson, Susanna H., 34, 36, 151, 170

Rural Felicity, 71, 125

St. Patrick for Ireland, 111

Sans Souci, alias Free and Easy, 60, 71, 184

Sawyer, Lemuel, 57

The School for Prodigals, 122, 136, 138, 141-142

A School for Soldiers, 82-84

Selden, Almira, 109, 188

Sewall, Jonathan, 31, 79, 183

Shadwell, Charles, 115

She Would be a Soldier, 138-141, 159

Shepherdess of the Alps, 176

Sheridan, Richard B., 116, 161

Sheridan, Thomas, 116

Shirley, James, 111

The Siege of Algiers, 53, 54

Simms, William G., 57, 58, 187

Sir John Oldcastle, 115

Slaves in Algiers, 34-35, 36, 151, 152, 170

Slaves in Barbary, 57

Smith, Charles, 162

Smith, Jonathan S., 53

Smith, Richard P., 99, 111, 129, 131, 158, 162, 169, 171

Smith, William, 23-24, 29, 75

The Sprightly Widow, 71

Squire Hartley, 131, 161

Stamp Act Congress, 17, 24

Stamp Acts, 25

Stearns, Charles, 57

Stone, John A., 174

Superstition, 159, 172-173

Talbot, Charles S., 69, 70, 110, 130, 131, 161

A Tale of Lexington, 70
Tears and Smiles, 66, 67, 148
Tell, William, dramatized, 47
Temptation, 111
Thirty Years, or the Gambler's Fate, 163-164
Townshend Acts, 25
The Traveller Returned, 118, 153
Trente Ans, ou la vie d'un joueur, 163
Trial of Atticus, 24-25
A Trip to Niagara, 101-102, 127, 142
The Triumphs of Love, 105
Trollope, Frances, 12, 68
The Twin Rivals, 115
Tyler, Royall, 31, 61, 67, 146, 157, 184

The Usurper, 111

Virtue Triumphant, 103
Wallack, Henry, 169
Wallack, John, 127
War of 1812, 11, 71, 72, 170, 176
Warren, Joseph, 26; dramatized, 40
Warren, Mercy Otis, 26-28, 30, 38, 43, 146, 181

Washington, George, dramatized, 16, 17, 84, 90-95, 124, 137, 150
Watterson, George, 59
Weld, Isaac, 68
The West Indian, 116
White, John B., 59, 60
White, William C., 57
The Widow of Malabar, 55-57, 186
The Widow's Son, 70
A Wife at a Venture, 131
Wignell, Thomas, 108-109, 123
Wolfe, General James, dramatized, 76
Woodworth, Samuel, 68, 69, 106, 191
Workman, James, 36, 46, 132, 153
The Wounded Hussar, 176
The Wreck of Honor, 57-58
Wright, Frances, 47, 52-53, 56, 187

XYZ Affair, 51, 97

Yankee Chronology, 71
"Yankee Doodle", 31
The Yankey in England, 66
The Yorker's Stratagem, 45, 153
The Young Carolinians, or Americans in Algiers, 106